Youth On Religion

Globalisation has led to increasing cultural and religious diversity in cities around the world. What are the implications for young people growing up in these settings? How do they develop their religious identities, and what roles do families, friends and peers, teachers, religious leaders and wider cultural influences play in the process? Furthermore, how do members of similar and different cultural and faith backgrounds get on together, and what can young people tell us about reducing conflict and promoting social solidarity amid diversity?

Youth On Religion outlines the findings from a unique large-scale project investigating the meaning of religion to young people in three multi-faith locations. Drawing on survey data from over 10,000 young people with a range of faith positions, as well as a series of fascinating interviews, discussion groups and diary reports involving 160 adolescents, this book examines myriad aspects of their daily lives. It provides the most comprehensive account yet of the role of religion for young people growing up in contemporary, multicultural urban contexts.

Youth On Religion is a rigorous and engaging account of developing religiosity in a changing society. It presents young people's own perspectives on their attitudes and experiences and how they negotiate their identities. The book will be an instructive and valuable resource for psychologists, sociologists, criminologists, educationalists and anthropologists, as well as youth workers, social workers and anyone working with young people today. It will also provide essential understanding for policy makers tackling issues of multiculturalism in advanced societies.

Nicola Madge is Professor of Child Psychology in the Centre for Child and Youth Research at Brunel University, London. She is the author of a wide range of publications on children and young people's issues that include religion, ethnicity, disability, disadvantage and self-harm. She is the Principal Investigator for the Youth On Religion study on which this book is based.

Peter J. Hemming is a lecturer at Cardiff University's School of Social Sciences, where he teaches sociology of education and childhood studies. Peter's research interests include children and young people, schools, power and identity, faith-based education, citizenship studies and sociology of religion. He is also a former primary school teacher.

Kevin Stenson is Honorary Professor of Criminology at the University of Kent and Visiting Professor at the London School of Economics and London Metropolitan University. His research interests include crime, policing, community safety, ethnicity, culture and religion.

With contributions from:

Professor Nick Allum
Department of Sociology,
University of Essex

Dr Melania Calestani
Faculty of Medicine,
University of Southampton

Professor Anthony Goodman
Department of Health and Social Sciences,
Middlesex University

Dr Katherine King
School of Tourism,
Bournemouth University

Dr Sarah Kingston
Faculty of Health and Social Sciences,
Leeds Metropolitan University

Professor Colin Webster
Faculty of Health and Social Sciences,
Leeds Metropolitan University

Youth On Religion

The development, negotiation and
impact of faith and non-faith identity

**Nicola Madge, Peter J. Hemming
and Kevin Stenson**

**with Nick Allum, Melania Calestani,
Anthony Goodman, Katherine King,
Sarah Kingston and Colin Webster**

Foreword by Grace Davie

Routledge
Taylor & Francis Group

LONDON AND NEW YORK

First published 2014
by Routledge
27 Church Road, Hove, East Sussex BN3 2FA

and by Routledge
711 Third Avenue, New York, NY 10017

Routledge is an imprint of the Taylor & Francis Group, an informa business

British Library Cataloguing in Publication Data
A catalogue record for this book is available from the British
Library

Library of Congress Cataloging in Publication Data
A catalog record for this book has been requested

ISBN: 978-0-415-69669-2 (hbk)
ISBN: 978-0-415-69670-8 (pbk)
ISBN: 978-1-315-85106-8 (ebk)

Typeset in Times
by Swales & Willis Ltd, Exeter, Devon, UK

Printed and bound in the United States of America by Publishers Graphics,
LLC on sustainably sourced paper.

Contents

Figures

Tables

Foreword

Grace Davie
University of Exeter

I was delighted when Nicola Madge invited me to write the Foreword to this book – for two reasons: it reports on a project that takes religion seriously and it supplies abundant empirical evidence about the views of young people on this increasingly important topic. In so doing the authors counter a persistent tendency which assumes that younger generations have little or no interest in religion. There is, it follows, no need to take their views into account. This is not the case. The respondents in this enquiry emerge as articulate and thoughtful: policy makers as well as social scientists would do well to listen, and listen carefully, to what they say. Indeed as these authors make clear (Chapter 3) these young people are, in a sense, social scientists in their own right: their perceptions are sharp and their comments interesting. They recognise that religion remains an important factor in the global order taken as a whole, and in the country and communities of which they are part.

So what do they say? The following comments are necessarily selective but they have been chosen to capture the complexities of the issues involved and the directness with which these respondents speak. Take, for example, the assumptions that are commonly made about religious affiliation: White people are expected to be Christian and Asians are thought to be Muslim. This is not the case:

> 'I'm from Ethiopia and people think I look like a Muslim, but I'm not a Muslim. People on the street tell me "Salaam aleikum" but I tell them that I'm Christian, because for me it is important.' (PRINCE: male, Christian Ethiopian Orthodox, religion very important)

> 'Sometimes they just assume that I am Muslim because I am brown and it's just the easiest thing to assume.' (SHARON: female, Sikh, religion important in some ways but not others)

'Because like there's a Tamil community, so they think I'm Tamil first of all – because they don't really know what Sinhalese is because Tamils are a majority. But I have never really had someone say I was Christian. They either ask me if I am Hindu, and because all my friends are Muslim, they assume I am Muslim as well . . . When I tell them I am Buddhist they will be like in shock.' (NELI: female, Buddhist, religion quite important)

Or take the following, very forthright comments about the media:

'I think the media just hates religion, they don't have anything good to say about religion at all.' (GORDON: male, Christian, religion quite important)

'I don't think people without religion are really portrayed that much, and it's always people on the extreme side. Like there's never any articles about just your average, everyday Muslim, or Christian or something like that.' (JOANNA: female, no religion, religion not very important)

'I don't think we get portrayed that much in the media and stuff. I think it's more Islam and stuff. I don't really see Sikhism in the media that much to be honest.' (SIMRAN: female, Sikh, religion quite important)

'They're not going to be interested in something they already know. Yeah, the Catholic Church believes this. Oh, we already knew that.' (CHUCK: male, Christian, religion important in some ways but not others)

Religious education in schools is rather different. Teachers are by no means the most significant influences on the beliefs of these young people, but over three-quarters of the sample indicate that RE lessons constitute a principal source of information about religion in an increasingly diverse society. First-hand experience is, however, crucial:

'I think Religious Education is only useful if there's people in the class of the religion so they're able to give first hand insight into it. If there's just a teacher teaching what a book says about it, because that might not always be right, there might be lots of different variants on a religion.' (STUART: male, no religion, importance of religion not specified)

And for this reason visits and experiential learning are also important:

> 'I remember when I went, my first trip was to a church and I was like wow, this is big. And like the whole stained glass window thing. And we came back and we had to write it up and research it all. And we kind of found out what it means and what it's for. But like, for me, I'd never been so to know about other religions is good.' (KIKI: female, Sikh, religion very important)

These examples catch the eye, but in no way should they be seen as 'typical'. Indeed to regard them as such would undermine two crucially important findings from this study: that the young people who make up the sample are very varied, and that they make their own choices about religion. Individual agency is central as the respondents work out their answers to difficult questions. That said 'patterns' (the essence of social science) emerge in the form of different 'types' of religious commitment or understanding. There are four of these: strict adherents, flexible adherents, pragmatists and bystanders. Locality is also significant – understandably in that religious choices are worked out differently in different places (in this case Bradford, Hillingdon and Newham), which are themselves subject to very specific pressures in a constantly changing society. It is easy enough for a social scientist like myself to conclude that, at one and the same time, Britain is becoming both more secular and more religiously diverse; it is much more challenging to discover what this means for a range of individuals with very varied religious backgrounds who are obliged to co-exist in different parts of urban Britain.

The implications are considerable: for individuals, families, friendship groups, the school system, neighbourhoods and the country as a whole. For all these reasons, it is important to listen carefully to the voices of a generation, who are on the threshold of their adult lives and who will emerge as decision-makers in the next decade. Careful readers of this meticulously researched book will be rewarded for their pains. Not only will they emerge better informed, they will be better equipped to deal sensitively with the consequences of religious diversity. Above all they will – I think – be impressed by the sheer reasonableness of these young people who are clearly aware of their differences, both cultural and religious, but who are looking for ways to build an effective and harmonious society. Good for them.

Acknowledgements

Research requires nurturing, support, encouragement and endeavour. The Youth On Religion study grew and matured due to a great deal of assistance on all these fronts. So many people played a part in the process, and we would like to begin by offering our sincere thanks to all those who have not been specifically mentioned by name below.

The birth of the project followed a large grant from the AHRC/ESRC Religion & Society programme (AH/GO14086/1). We acknowledge the receipt of this grant with gratitude and record our appreciation of the considerable support received throughout the project from Professor Linda Woodhead, Director of the programme, Dr Rebecca Catto, Research Associate, and Peta Ainsworth, the programme administrator. Being part of a wider programme provided excellent opportunities to mix with other researchers working in related areas and to benefit from an exciting interplay of ideas.

The project itself was conducted in the three locations of the London Boroughs of Hillingdon and Newham, and Bradford in Yorkshire. We would especially like to thank all the young people who gave their time and enthusiasm to provide the information on which this book is based, as well as their schools and teachers who made the space within busy timetables for us to carry out the study. We hope that all of you will recognise our interpretation of the central messages emerging from the research. Many other people in the study areas helped to facilitate the research and among these we extend our thanks to Eric Blaire, Claire Clinton, Fiona Gibbs, Sue Goodman, the Reverend Quintin Peppiatt, Jani Rashid, Duncan Struthers and Stephen Timms MP.

We would like to acknowledge other colleagues who played a significant part in the study. Dr Christy Barry was a tireless administrator to the project throughout its life and kept us all cheerful and organised despite our geographical distance. We were also lucky to have Dr Abby Day and Dr Philip Lewis as consultants to the project, and we benefited greatly from their advice. In addition, we would like to register our appreciation of Jenny Leslie for her help with data analysis. Finally, we would like to thank Professor Grace Davie for writing the foreword to this book and adding the final flourish.

1   Background and context

Background

Rapidly increasing numbers of young people are growing up in multi-faith locations in Britain. Some come from long-established British families, some belong to British families with much shorter histories in Britain, and others have arrived from different geographical and social settings in their own lifetimes. All these young people have experienced change in their lives, either through the transformations of the neighbourhoods they have grown up in, or through migration from one milieu to another during the trajectories of their early years. Whether or not they are religious themselves, all are likely to have been affected in some way or another by the religious beliefs and practices of those in their localities. The purpose of this book is to respond to calls from Grace Davie and others (Davie, 2007a; Barker, 2010a) to put the study of religion back at the heart of enquiry and to provide empirical evidence to inform theoretical debates about religious belief and expression in multi-faith Britain. It reports on an investigation of the meaning of religion in the lives of young people from a range of faith positions in three selected religiously diverse locations, and interrogates their religious identities and how these have been developed and negotiated. Through a detailed look at their subjective lives, and the contexts in which these are lived, it provides a contemporary and interdisciplinary perspective on the vexed questions of 'who are we?' and 'how do we all get on?' in these unprecedented times.

This chapter sets the scene for the context of the Youth On Religion (YOR) study and the interpretation of the findings. Drawing on lessons from the grand themes of social science as well as more contemporary enquiry, it outlines how globalisation and population change have affected the character of many urban areas in the UK over recent years. It describes how religion has assumed a pre-eminent position in the process, albeit alongside accounts of increasing secularisation and shifts in the modes of religious expression. Recourse to the theorising of Durkheim, and other classic and more recent scholars on the impact of great demographic and other structural changes, gives rise to the hypothesis of prevailing liberal values amongst both those influenced by the human rights agenda and those whose families have, over recent generations, experienced the move from traditional rural communities to British urbanity. The individual identities of young people within this broad setting reflect first, their biological, physical and cognitive development, second, cultural values and prevailing discourses, and third the local economic, spatial and other contexts in which young people are making the journey to adulthood (Gunter, 2010; MacDonald et al., 2010).

Based on the Durkheimian thesis as well as interpretive perspectives, it seems likely that these young people will both espouse liberal values about individual rights and assert their own control over their personal lives. It is also anticipated that they will present differing aspects of identity according to context and their role within it. Behaviours and attitudes in all these respects are linked to the way they lead their lives and get on with one another. Concepts of multiculturalism and social cohesion, and their relevance to young people growing up in diverse communities, are also pertinent.

Establishing a focus

The world today is very unlike that of even 50 years ago. Immigration has been the most visible outcome of globalisation and, as Scheffer (2011) describes, cities around the world have become almost unrecognisable over the past generation or two. In Britain, changing populations have led to the establishment of many highly diverse urban areas set within the broader context of a much more traditional Britain, and transformed the meaning of what it is to be English or British. Recent data from the 2011 Census for England and Wales indicate that, overall, the white population has declined from 91 to 86% over the past decade, and that 3.8 million, or half the total of 7.5 million, of those born outside the UK arrived during the past ten years. The most sizeable groups of the foreign-born population are, in order of magnitude, from India, Poland, Pakistan and Ireland. In addition, the mixed ethnicity population now numbers over 1 million. This population influx has been accompanied by movement out of city areas by White British members of the population: there was a fall of 600,000 from this group within London in the period between the 2001 and 2011 Censuses (Goodhart, 2013). These patterns of change mean certain localities are becoming increasingly multi-ethnic, and often religious, accentuated by the larger than average families of many of those with strong religious beliefs (Kaufmann, 2010). Newham (one of the current research areas) has been particularly affected in these ways and shown a marked increase in religiosity among its population: it has also become the first location where White British citizens are now in the minority.

The issue of religion in this context is complex and changing. In Britain, for example, there have been significant shifts in the relationship between the Church of England and the nation state over many years. There has been continuing erosion of the monopoly position of Anglican Christianity (Guest et al., 2012), driven in part by the growth of the welfare state following World War II, rising faith in the market and the media since the 1970s, and the effects of globalisation and mass migration (Woodhead, 2012). These great changes have created opportunities for new forms of religious faith involving both the long-standing indigenous and newer sections of the population.

One outcome is a much greater emphasis on religion in public discourse over recent years. This has largely overtaken, or at least complemented, earlier emphases on the racial differences within our society or the significance of ethnicity and its cultural implications (Snow, 2007; Malik, 2010). As a vivid illustration, Mondal (2008) reports a young person who suggests that Muslims are now at the top of the agenda for the British National Party, representing the political far right. This replaces the focus on Black people a decade ago. In many ways, and as these and other commentators have pointed out, a shift to the examination of religious differences and their impact on the operation of society reflects the greater visibility of religion both nationally and locally. This is fuelled both by high awareness of extremist and terrorist actions carried out in the name of religion, and by the very evident increase in mosques, temples and other places of worship in many of our communities (Peach and Gale, 2003).

At the same time, however, there has been copious discussion of the secularisation thesis proposed by Max Weber (1948). In brief, this posits that the rise of new forms of rationality, embodied in science and technology, challenge more traditional forms including religious belief systems. A long-term process of disenchantment underpins a move to a more prosaic view of everyday reality. Religion does not necessarily disappear during this process, but changes in character and style. It is argued that pluralities of faith in modern societies also contribute to a decline in religion, in part because the rational thinker might wonder, if different religions are in evidence, whether any single faith position is in fact tenable. These ideas have been much debated as the meanings we attribute to 'secular' and 'religious' have changed over time and become more complex (Martin with Catto, 2012). However, apparent signs of a trend towards secularisation have received superficial support from recent Census 2011 data which note a decrease in the self-reported population of Christians from 72 to 59%, accompanied by a 10% increase to 14 million in those reporting 'no religion'. Observed patterns of decline in public religion have been interpreted in different ways. These include suggestions that religion is dead (Brown, 2009), in part because religious beliefs are less sustainable once religious practice ceases. Other recent commentators have pointed to the increased incidence of 'believing without belonging' (Davie, 1994), where churchgoing is seen as a matter of personal choice and not a formal requirement of religious belief, fuzzy religiosity (Voas and Day, 2009) in which people are neither Christian nor non-Christian, or 'vicarious religion' (Davie, 2007b) where some people let others do religion for them and turn to the faith only in moments of need. In these ways there has been a notable shift from obligation to consumption when it comes to religion (Davie, 2005).

These positions imply that religion is not dead or dying but is in a process of transformation (Hervieu-Léger, 2000; Davie, 2007a), or that traditional religion is being superseded by alternative spiritualities (Heelas et al., 2005; Barker, 2010b; Vernon, 2011). They are supportive of Emile Durkheim's claim that religion remains necessary in modern society even if it changes in form (Durkheim, 1912). Furthermore, communitarians, who have debated with liberal secularists for generations, argue that religion remains resilient because it lies at the heart of community life and identity: it meets essential human needs and can adapt to the new conditions of urban life (McIntyre, 1981; Taylor, 2007). They see the roots of morality, religion and law not in rational systems of thought or in grand designs of policy makers, but from the bottom up, in everyday collective life. The focus is on the connections, developed over generations, between the blood ties of kinship, and ethnic and religious networks, with strong attachments to places. Hence communitarians may be tolerant of minority ethnic and religious subcultures because of the role they play in maintaining moral codes and passing them onto the next generation (Etzioni, 1993).

Much of the discussion of secularisation is based on an apparent decline in Christianity. This must nonetheless be seen in the context of increased numbers in the population from Muslim, Hindu, Sikh, Buddhist and 'other' faith positions, groups which are likely to be religiously fervent and have higher fertility rates than White indigenous groups (Kaufmann et al., 2012). Within Christianity, the rising importance of evangelism and denominations such as Pentecostalism (Martin, 2002) as well as increased numbers of Catholics from Eastern European countries (Bates, 2006) should also be taken into account. These latter groups are not generally considered in relation to the secularisation thesis and important questions remain about their levels of religiosity in Britain in both present and future generations. A key issue is whether minority cultures will remain able to reproduce their religiosity and fulfil the imperative of cultural transmission (Parsons, 1951) or whether they will 'secularise' alongside everyone else. What is the role of so-called Westernisation in this process? Levey and Modood (2009) report that it had been anticipated that religiosity would decline in diverse Western democracies because of combined effects of Westernisation, consumerism and broader patterns of secularisation, but that this seems not to have happened. Contributory to recent observations is likely to be the gathering evidence that some members of younger generation Muslims are attributing more importance to their religion than their parents (Lewis, 2007; Mondal, 2008). In Valentine and Sporton's (2009) study, young refugees and asylum seekers from Somalia found a Muslim identity less problematic than one linked to being British, Black or Somali. It seemed that being Muslim was the identity that provided them with the most continuity and most easily transcended context.

This is but one issue among many about the negotiation of religious identity in contemporary Britain. Before turning to theoretical discussion of and empirical evidence on a range of relevant questions, it is important to define religion for the purposes of this book. Countless texts have been written on its meaning both in general and in particular, but there is resonance in Jackson's (1997) claim that religion, like culture, is neither simple nor static, but rather complex and in a permanent state of change. As the focus of the YOR study is the subjective accounts of young research participants, the meaning of religion for the present purposes is not regarded as a unitary definable concept but rather whatever young people mean by it. The approach is thus to allow subjects to give their self-chosen labels to their faith positions, and to report on whatever they deem to be significant in responding to questions on religion. Moreover, religion is regarded in terms of distinct aspects that may or may not co-exist, so that people may give themselves a religious label, say they believe in God or a higher power, feel they belong to a religious community locally and globally, go to a place of worship on a regular basis, and pray in private (Hemming and Madge, 2011). More likely, however, they may do some but not all of these things. The essence of this book is to listen to a wide variety of individual perspectives on the role of religion in everyday life and to try to make sense of them.

Religion in a context of change

Through her call for heightened attention to theoretical and empirical enquiry on the meaning of religion in the modern world, Davie (2007a) legitimates a return to the writings and concerns of the classic scholars to inform contemporary analysis. Religion was seen as playing a central role in the industrialisation and transformations of Europe a century ago, and it is likely that many parallels can be drawn between the situations then and now.

The early founders of social science in late 19th century Europe, including Emile Durkheim, Max Weber, Ferdinand Tonnies and Georg Simmel, were trying to understand the dramatic changes wrought by urbanisation and industrialisation. People were leaving rural agricultural village life where, generally, the divisions and technologies of labour were simpler, and people lived their lives within small social circles in which most shared values and were known to each other; they moved to cities where multiple religions and other belief systems jostled with each other and anonymity was possible (Simmel, 1903). Writing at this time of widespread movement from the countryside to the towns, Durkheim (1893) witnessed the dissolution of traditional communities alongside the development of more complex societies, and became concerned with how social order and social cohesion were maintained under these changing circumstances. He observed strong links between the economic and social structure of society on the one hand, and religious adherence and expression on the other, and believed that religion was fundamental in binding people together and promoting community well-being. In recent parlance, religion played a major role in providing the 'glue' of social solidarity or community cohesion. Key mechanisms were common core values and moral categories such as the difference between right and wrong, a distinction between the sacred and the profane, and shared rituals and traditions. Durkheim believed that religion played such an important function in society that it would never disappear even though its form and sacred symbols might change. Allegiance to a god was not an essential requisite and, ultimately, religion might take on a civic form.

Durkheim wrote in the tradition of French secular republicanism following the French Revolution of 1789 and was much influenced by his predecessor Auguste Comte, who coined the term *sociologie* or the science of society. Comte had founded a secular, civic religion termed positivism, complete with temples and rituals. The worship of God was replaced with the celebration of the collective organisation of society and intellectual endeavour, and professors celebrating the fruits of science and philosophy substituted for religious doctrine and priests (Pickering, 1993; Davies, 1997). In more recent times, examples of civic, quasi-religions meeting Durkheimian criteria might include the changing form of Marxism-Leninism after the Russian revolution of 1917 when it moved from being a theory of change for revolutionaries to functioning as a belief system that provided the core moral and explanatory basis for Soviet rule (Marcuse, 1958). These conceptions of a secular society differ from Dawkins' (2006) view that does not regard shared rituals and symbols as important and posits that the functions of religion can be provided by science and technology.

Despite the great differences between Durkheim's Europe and present conditions there are parallels in terms of the scale and rapidity of social change and movement of people from rural village communities in poor countries, dominated by fairly homogeneous belief systems and cultural codes, to the shifting cultural mosaic of large Western cities (Scheffer, 2011). An important aspect of Durkheim's theorising on social change that particularly resonates today is his distinction between mechanical and organic solidarity within society. In its mechanical form, typically found in traditional communities, solidarity depends on a collective conscience that provides a common core of values and moral rules and allows little scope for individuality. Many of these traditional rural communities were, however, largely oral in character until the relatively recent development of mass literacy, and culture was transmitted through actions and word of mouth (Ong, 1982). Religious belief and practice in these contexts is embedded within tribal/ethnic beliefs, rituals and other practices rather than based narrowly on holy texts such as the Qur'an or Bible, and inevitably shows some flexibility over time and space. In these conditions it can be difficult to differentiate between religion, as we may understand it in advanced societies, and the everyday cultural life of a society.

In its organic form, by contrast, found particularly in socially diverse areas of modern cities, solidarity does not depend in the same way on homogeneity of belief, rituals and intolerance of those who do not conform to norms, but is maintained by both a collective conscience and economic interdependence. The change to organic solidarity, and the development of a new collective moral order to bring together diverse subcultures and individuals and enable them to live in harmony, is long in gestation and can take generations. This gestation may be accompanied by what Durkheim termed anomie, or an absence of order, and social conflict (Durkheim, 1893). Although Durkheim was writing about a different time in history, and a different location, his theorising gives rise to hypotheses about current societal processes. Societies characterised by organic solidarity permit people to assume different roles in society, become more dissimilar, and show weakened identity with the group, and the question arises as to whether young people growing up in modern multi-faith areas of Britain demonstrate these patterns. Do they show signs of strong identification with their origins, whether these are from within or outside the UK, are they committed to diversity, or are they responsive to both priorities? This is a key question for the present research.

The values of solidarity, which permit a degree of moral and cultural diversity, include a focus on a positive form of individualism that flowered during the 18th century European Enlightenment, henceforth here termed liberal individualism (Durkheim, 1893; Douglas, 1967). The roots of individualism lay in the loosening ties between church and state in Europe from the 17th century onwards, the struggle to limit the powers of central, sovereign governments, and the attendant new, sacred value placed on the fulfilment of the individual, and the rights of religious and other minorities (Hunter, 1998). This liberal individualism is a core feature of liberal ideology. It differs markedly from egoism in being more altruistic, and emphasises the rights and personal fulfilment of individuals provided they also consider the rights and needs of others and set limits on their own desires and ambitions. On this point, Durkheim (1953) was trying to provide a sociological basis for Immanuel Kant's (1788) moral philosophy in that a social and moral order must be based on shared moral imperatives and the principle that others are seen as ends in themselves and not simply means to achieve personal goals.

Liberalism interacts with nationalism and other ideologies and has taken a range of different forms historically with the rise of various democratic, nation and welfare states since the early 20th century (Stenson, 2012). These range from the French state's commitment to rationalism and *laïcité*, officially enshrined in a law of 1905 formally separating church and state, and recently echoed by the French law forbidding the use of religious clothing or insignia, such as the Muslim veil, in public institutions (Saunders, 2009), to the position of countries such as the UK and the Netherlands that have been more accepting of the rights of faith and ethnic groups to self-expression within the framework of a shared state (Scheffer, 2011). This latter version of liberalism is more favourably disposed to communitarian arguments (McIntyre, 1981; Taylor, 2007). National variations in the institutional and cultural relations between religion and the state should not be underestimated with, in more strongly secularised states, religion being seen as the province of the private sphere of life. Nevertheless, recent commentators emphasise, in practice, a rich variety at every social level in how those relations operate. There is no necessary evolution towards secularisation, the borders between public and private spheres are often fluid with, in the case of the United Kingdom, a state religion, religious influences and rituals still playing a significant role in the life of state institutions (Berger 1999; Martin, 2010; Hemming, 2011).

Others have contributed to debates about the shifting contexts within which identities and beliefs are forged and changed (Giddens, 1991; Beck, 1992; Castells, 2000). These authors argue that major changes witnessed in communities and big cities in recent years have impacted on identities through changed experiences and expectations. Globalisation has led to a new modernity in which there is less reliance on culture and tradition, and old mores have disappeared. The outcome is that individuals have become more self-reliant, absorbing the modern language of liberal individualism with its emphasis on human rights, human agency, equality and respect. Bauman (2000) has described current times as a period of 'liquid modernity' where traditional forms of solidarity are fragile and people are less embedded in local networks, including religious congregations and belief systems, than in the past. According to this thesis, and in a complex world where there is access to multiple sources of information and moral reference points, young people do not describe themselves as simply following tradition, or submitting to the authority of family and community elders and religious leaders. Rather, their emphasis is on choice and negotiation. Nonetheless, the specifics of globalisation as outlined by Beck, Giddens and others vary with place and grouping, and in the extent to which young people become disembedded from local family and neighbourly relations and from traditional cultural values and mores (Savage and Savage, 2010).

These discussions are relevant to the circumstances of young people living in culturally diverse settings within contemporary Britain. First, it does seem likely that the circumstances of families long-established in Western society can be contrasted with those of certain minority religious groups, such as perhaps Muslims and Sikhs, who may have migrated from small rural communities in India and Pakistan to large diverse cities in Britain. Lewis (2007) documents some of the cultural challenges faced by many people in Muslim communities, including shifts from belonging to a majority religion in a rural setting to being part of a minority group in an urbanity, a lack of knowledge about the Western historical and cultural context, and intergenerational struggles for reform of Islamic institutions. Whereas beliefs and practices may have bound the generations together in the homeland, with religion and its cultural traditions a common way of life, the move to a pluralistic culture involves complex transformations. Young people become faced with many more options, influences and pressures than their parents and grandparents ever had, and may experience conflict and confusion. They may also have to cope with older people in their communities feeling anxious and trying to shore up the collective boundaries of their faith and culture, of which religion was but a part, perhaps trying to pressure them to conform to what they see as traditional religious and moral expectations.

The pertinent questions amidst change become how far young people who have moved through cultures remain embedded in the traditions of their families, how far they adopt the values of their peer culture, and to what extent they effect a compromise. It may be that their families creatively refashion elements of the mechanically solidaristic community patterns they brought with them from their old countries, clustered around churches and other places of worship, as found within other migrant communities in the earlier decades of the 20th century, such as in Chicago and other American cities (Thomas and Znaniecki, 1918). Furthermore, what are the reactions of young people from established British families to diversity, and how far do they assimilate and accommodate these societal changes? What role do all these young people play in cultural change and in helping to forge a mosaic of links between their more immediate identities and community networks and loyalties and those of the wider culture (Suttles, 1972; Scheffer, 2011)?

The development of religious identity

The main focus so far has been on large-scale, cultural, demographic and institutional change and attempts to theorise their significance. While useful in identifying general patterns, these accounts leave gaps in the story by failing to explain individual differences in reactions to surroundings. The missing link relates to how individual identity, and specifically religious identity, develops in diverse and changing settings and the factors influencing variation.

The study of identity represents a large-scale industry with contributions from psychological, sociological, geographical, philosophical and other perspectives. It focuses on personal identity as a unique sense of self as well as social identity that relates to membership of social groups (Bradley, 1996), and describes both who one is and who one is not (Said, 1978). Almost all accounts emphasise that people have multiple rather than unitary identities (Wetherell, 2009) with the salience of particular aspects varying according to context and setting (Valentine and Sporton, 2009). Whatever the perspective, most positions regard identities as evolving in response to experience (Turner, 1991; Gergen, 1999), including that of living in a global society (Bourn, 2008). Narrative accounts attempt to describe this developing sense of the self as life experiences are integrated within a pre-existing identity framework (Somers, 1994; Crossley, 2000; Wetherell, 2009) and are useful in charting religious journeys. The study of identity is also extended to the analysis of populations. In the UK, theory and research have gone beyond the world of the academy and been incorporated within central government agendas. These now recognise the need to make sense of new plural identities and their underpinnings in the age of digital technology and social media, and to incorporate this knowledge into policies impacting on younger citizens (Foresight Future Identities, 2013).

Amidst these many accounts, the position of the interpretive social scientists is particularly pertinent to discussion of the negotiations young people undertake in developing a personal sense of religious identity in multi-faith areas: structural patterns come into being, and are reproduced and modified, only through the action and interaction of individuals and groups (Berger and Luckmann, 1966; Lindesmith et al., 1999). The enduring theories of symbolic interactionists, and more broadly what can be termed the interpretive school of social science, have significant roots in George Herbert Mead's (1934) theory of the social self. His components of the social self are the 'I' (the forward looking aspect of mind that is open to new experience), the 'me' (which crystallises the images of oneself reflected by significant others around us) and the 'generalised other' (the internalised standards of behaviour required in one's milieu), stressing how common experiences gain meaning only through contact with significant others. The unfolding, fluid relations between selves and others are mediated by the exchange of symbols that can range from linguistic symbols to codes of dress, and from consumer goods to ritual behaviours. In other words, children and young people are very much active participants in the process of their own socialisation and the transmission of roles and values within their daily settings.

Influenced by the legacy of the Chicago School of Sociology between the 1920s and 1940s, the theorists following Mead sought to understand the process and outcome of massive population movement from Europe to American cities, and stressed the crucial involvement of other people and influences in developing and sustaining views both of the self and others (Sampson, 2012). They were concerned with the meanings people give to their everyday experiences and posit that categories of thought and knowledge emerge only from acting in the world and through contact with significant others (Rock, 1979). Their theories are also rooted in Weber's (1949) Verstehen sociology, emphasising the need to understand actions from the actor's perspective, and have more recently been integrated with structural explanations that oppose essentialist or determinist explanations of identity (Giddens, 1984).

Erving Goffman played a key role in providing a theoretical bridge between the study of larger social structures and the minutiae of social interaction. Influenced by Durkheim, he argued that social order and solidarity are created and reproduced, and conflict largely avoided, through rituals and subtle negotiations undertaken in the multitude of daily interactional situations and encounters (Goffman, 1959). For example, Goffman (1963) examined the various ways in which people cope with the stigmatisation of their identities and behaviours. Adaptations may range from concealment and passing for 'normal', and forming supportive subcultures with those similarly labelled, to open celebration of stigmatised identities and challenging dominant norms and labels. These interpretive methodological tools are used throughout this book to illuminate how young people exercise agency in the ways they negotiate the challenges and circumstances of their lives. Four aspects of interpretive theorising are singled out as having particular relevance for the exploration of their views and behaviours, and their negotiation of religious identity, within multi-faith communities. These are accounts of socialisation, patterns of interpersonal contact, multiple realities, and impression management that are now considered in turn.

Berger and Luckmann (1966) discuss the process of socialisation from the symbolic interactionist position, drawing an important distinction between primary and secondary stages. According to their thesis, primary socialisation occurs in the early years and involves the transmission of knowledge about the world from significant others, usually parents. Children do not usually fully understand this knowledge at first, and the transmitted world 'confronts them as a given reality that, like nature, is opaque in places at least': in this sense, the parent's subjectivity becomes the child's objectivity. Secondary socialisation, which follows primary socialisation, can involve the integration of new forms of knowledge into existing perceptions, and a change in understanding as the young person comes to realise that the parental world is not the only one. Unlike primary socialisation, secondary socialisation does not necessarily result from identification with significant others and may be a consequence of new forms of knowledge imparted by, for example, friends, teachers or other role models. Secondary socialisation is, however, not as deeply rooted as primary socialisation and may be more easily overturned.

According to this account, any theory of socialisation must necessarily explain how the newborn develops into a self-reflective and active participant in the interactive process. As Lindesmith et al. (1999) outline in some detail, many psychological theories contribute to an explanation of growing understanding on the part of the child. To give but a few brief examples, children's social selves develop through the interactions defining their early attachments (Bowlby, 1969), and from contacts with peers and others through the childhood years (Sullivan, 1953; Vygotsky, 1962). As part of this process, objective knowledge becomes replaced with subjective knowledge as appropriate levels of cognitive development are reached (Piaget, 1936) and the comprehension of abstract and moral issues achieved (Kohlberg, 1976). The development of language is critical throughout in enabling children and young people to be able to appreciate and ponder both their own and other people's perspectives on the world, as is the development of emotion (Lindesmith et al., 1999). Coping with divergent social worlds, and having strategies in place to deal with these, is also crucial.

Religious identity has been studied within this tradition, considerably influenced by the central ideas of Piaget, Kohlberg and others and their notion of developmental stages (Hyde, 1990), and suggesting that stages of religious development are largely in line with cognitive change. Goldman (1964) in the UK, for example, directly linked intellectual development to an understanding of religion by examining children's competencies in understanding stories from the Bible. He proposed a stage model whereby 'intuitive thought' was predominant at 5 to 7 years, when many story details were misunderstood or seen as irrelevant. The subsequent development of 'concrete operational thought' between about 8 and 10 years was associated with a focus on particular details in religious stories and pictures, and was followed by a third stage of 'formal operational thought' when religion was seen in hypothetical and abstract ways. Elkind (1964) investigated American children's religious identity and also proposed three stages. In the first stage (5 to 7 years), children had only a nominal conception of religious identity: they were able to give themselves a religious label but had little understanding of its meaning. By the second stage (7 to 9 years), they had a concrete perception of religious identity, linking this to particular activities and behaviours. A more abstract understanding of religious identity was achieved by the third stage (10 to 14 years), when the young person demonstrated an ability to reflect on the non-observable aspects of religion, such as belief. These underlying theories of change have been criticised on both conceptual and methodological grounds, and because they fail adequately to acknowledge that development is socially, culturally and historically specific (James et al., 1998). They are important, nonetheless, in highlighting how religious understanding develops with age, even if different cultural settings help to shape the developmental process.

Berger and Luckmann (1966) indeed claim that socialisation is never complete, a point echoed by Goffman (1959) who writes about a cycle of disbelief-to-belief (or vice versa) in which behaviours enacted largely by rote come to attain a rationale of their own (or those that already have a rationale become overtaken by another). Other writers emphasise the importance of status passages, for example from adolescence to adulthood, or significant 'turning points' (Glaser and Strauss, 1971), concepts of moral careers (Goffman, 1961) that relate to links and commitments to other individuals, and identity transformations (Lindesmith et al., 1999) that can mean a recasting of identity in the light of new experience. These concepts have relevance to the present study. It might be anticipated that concordance in religious views between children and their parents are strongest in the early years but diverge and change as young people become older and in contact with a wider range of social groups and faith positions, gain new forms of knowledge either directly or vicariously, and become more fully engaged in debate on the topic of religiosity.

Patterns of contacts over the period of growing up, in terms of both who young people are in contact with and the nature of contact experiences, are crucial for secondary socialisation. Glaser and Strauss (1964) describe the concept of 'awareness context' whereby partners in interaction are knowledgeable about both the other person's identity and how the other person views them. An important question is whether young people in multi-faith locations have knowledge of this kind, and the process by which it is gained. As Stone (1984) points out, relationships can be interpersonal or structural, determined by fact of kith or kin or constructed for institutional reasons such as between peers within a classroom setting. The extent of shared knowledge in these different settings is of empirical interest in the present study, together with the extent to which peers and others are seen as friends or act as reference groups (Shibutani, 1955; Merton, 1957). The 'typificatory schemes' (Berger and Luckmann, 1966) with which young people classify each other and according to which they negotiate their interactions are also of interest. Do young people regard each other in terms of their religion or ethnicity or are other attributes, such as hobbies and interests, more significant? According to the symbolic interactionist account, contacts are also important for subjective reality by providing the means for conversation. Social contact with the like-minded revitalises knowledge, including religious belief, while discussion with disbelievers can be effective in dissuading the recent convert from a new belief system. The role of discussion of religion between those from similar and dissimilar faith positions is accordingly an additional focus for the present study.

Attitudes and experiences do not, however, develop in a vacuum but are subject to variation in setting. Valentine and Sporton (2009: 737) discuss, for instance, how intersections of lines of difference, such as age and gender, reveal 'multiple, shifting and sometimes contradictory ways that individuals both identify and disidentify with other groups'. These intersections have received considerable attention in the theoretical and empirical literature for their relationship with religious identity (Hemming and Madge, 2011) and some attention is paid to the influence of variables such as age, gender, ethnicity and class in later chapters. Context makes a further difference (Hemming and Madge, 2011) with family, peer groups, school, the Internet and virtual reality, the scientific community and the local neighbourhood among the important settings in question. The significance of these contexts for religious identity in multi-faith locations is explored in later chapters where it is shown how young people can face conflicting messages and values according to their faith position, their peers and the Western culture they are exposed to. In this sense they may be presented with multiple realities. Berger and Luckmann (1966: 108) point out how confrontations between societies with very different histories can challenge existing views of reality and pose a threat as an alternative symbolic universe 'demonstrates empirically that one's own universe is less than inevitable'.

As young people are likely to experience multiple realities or discordance between their subjective and objective worlds, or because they may wish for some reason to conceal their 'true' identity, they may regularly or occasionally engage in impression management. Following in the tradition of Mead, Goffman (1959) developed a 'dramaturgical approach' to human interaction whereby he posited that people are much like actors in that the roles they play depend on the theatre they are performing in and the parts they are portraying and improvising. In other words, and in relation to the current study, a young person might dress and behave in different ways when in different settings with either family or friends. The multi-faith cosmopolitan research areas provide numerous opportunities to encounter different audiences and cultures, and take on different roles: they permit people to act 'front stage' in certain settings but 'back stage' when feeling more private and away from scrutiny. An appropriate 'identity kit', comprising props such as dress, language and behaviour needed to construct the image of self it is wished to display, may also be adopted for each role. This dramaturgical model must, however, be used with caution. There is a danger that the self becomes viewed as a scheming strategist, a fixed personality donning masks to achieve advantage at will (Gregson and Rose, 2000). This is not the assumption adopted in this study where selves are regarded as creative agents. They emerge and are transformed only within interactional performances and the social relationships within which they are embedded. Moreover, the degrees of self-consciousness exhibited in performances can vary from the habitual to the highly self-conscious (Garfinkel, 1984; Bicknell, 2003).

The work of Simmel (1903), who was a key influence on Goffman, is also important in this context. Interested in the evolving form of self in the context of industrialisation and change, he focused much of his theorising on family journeys from demographically simple to more complex worlds, and specifically moves from traditional rural settings to modernised cities. Like Goffman, he explored the presentation of multiple selves in multiple settings (such as in the family, at school and in the community) and was particularly interested in the concept and ingredients of secrecy. As people become more individualised and less tied to neighbourhoods and pre-existing social groupings, so it becomes easier for them to adopt an identity of choice. Often these identities of choice involve forms of secrecy that would never have been possible in simpler settings. It might be argued that such self-display strategies are more likely in diverse communities than in those that are relatively homogeneous. This provides another point of enquiry for the present study.

Positive individualism and individual agency

It is apparent from the foregoing discussion that an essential element of the interpretive social science perspective is that children and young people are active participants in the process of their own socialisation and the transmission of roles and values within their daily settings. Accounts stemming from this perspective highlight the emergent, unfolding and performative nature of the self, the active, creative role of children and young people in socialisation and social interaction, and the importance of the varying social context of action. The development of identity is an interpretive process in which decisions on action, in the Weberian (1949) sense that in more recent parlance is referred to as agency, take into account the reactions of others (Sullivan, 1953).

The childhood studies paradigm that emerged in the 1970s also highlights this concept of agency and how children, as social actors in their own right, not only take some control over their own lives but also have an impact on the world around them (James and James, 2008). This perspective emerged as critical of foregoing accounts of socialisation, arguing that earlier theorists provided deterministic, universal and culture-bound interpretations of childhood, regarded children as merely adults in the making, and assumed that development was a linear and universal process (James et al., 1998). According to these authors, childhood can be regarded only as a social and cultural construction. This approach is valuable in accentuating the role of agency in child development and providing some valid criticism of earlier accounts, such as for example the uniformity of development, age guidelines for specific behaviours, and the disregard of cultural difference suggested by Piaget. It is also not in opposition to the notion of self-directed action on the part of children as outlined by interpretive social scientists (Ryan, 2012). The symbolic interactionist view of socialisation sees it as a process of interaction between children and adults, hence constructing the child as a social actor with a constitutive and self-reflexive role (Musolf, 1996).

Based on these various accounts, the term agency in this book is used to imply self-expressed personal choice and action, whatever the motive and outcome. It is contrasted with the values of liberal individualism that, as explained above, derive from Durkheimian theory and incorporate altruism and respect for the positions of others. Durkheim, as a professor of education and a trainer of teachers, as well as a staunch Republican espousing values of liberty, equality and fraternity, was strongly of the view that teachers should help children to acquire the necessary skills to enable them to flourish in the new urban world of organic solidarity and liberal individualism (Durkheim, 1961; Hargreaves, 1979; Stenson and Brearley, 1991). He maintained that children absorb dominant beliefs and values uncritically, perhaps by rote, under conditions of mechanical solidarity, but learn the skills of moral reasoning and agency, working out moral positions for themselves, under conditions of organic solidarity.

In Britain the state has to some extent taken on the role of providing young people with the values associated with liberal individualism through the duty of schools since September 2007 (and the Education and Inspections Act 2006), to promote community cohesion. One arm of this has been the introduction of Citizenship lessons into the National Curriculum as a compulsory subject at secondary school level since 2012 (although its future is in question beyond 2014). There are limits to what central governments can achieve in diverse and pluralistic societies (Stoker, 2006), but the implementation of Citizenship education attempts to develop young people's understanding of democracy and justice, rights and responsibilities, and identities, diversity and living together in the UK. The purpose of the curriculum is to encourage independent thinking and to equip young people with the confidence to express personal opinions. Although Ofsted (2006, 2010) reports, supported by findings from an 8-year National Foundation for Educational Research (NFER) study (Keating et al., 2009), have suggested variable but improving standards of implementation, retrospective views on citizenship by members of the NFER cohort at 19 to 20 years after leaving school are enlightening. Perhaps most interesting from the perspective of the current study is that young people said they saw citizenship as being mainly about people's rights, and mentioned 'working together to make things better', 'belonging', 'making sure everyone is treated fairly' and 'people's responsibilities and obeying the law'. Whether these liberal views with an emphasis on equality and respect are universal, and whether they are upheld outside the context of citizenship education, provides another avenue of enquiry for the current investigation.

The multiculturalism debate

From a policy and practice perspective, the findings from the YOR study are of particular interest for their findings on how young people in multi-faith areas get on together and how they live with difference. Globalisation and the accelerating movement of populations into European countries has, particularly since the 1950s, put issues of collective and national identity, and the creation of harmonious communities in the face of hyperdiversity, high on the political agenda. Nonetheless, these debates do not sufficiently take account of the views and concerns of people (especially young people) living in communities who are likely to have their own perceptions and agendas (Goodhart, 2013). The pertinent question here concerns the ways they lead their lives and construct their identities at local levels, and their actions and behaviours that contribute in one way or another to the social cohesion of the communities they inhabit.

Recent decades have witnessed shifting ideologies and approaches to diversity and the creation of harmonious communities. Early UK models put the focus on assimilation, and the assumption that newcomers would acquire the values and behaviours of the indigenous population. This was predicated less by a liberal than a nationalistic perspective that reflected limited experience of diversity and problems of accommodation and assimilation of migrants into an established, albeit multi-faceted, culture. In line with increased liberalism, identity politics, and the civil rights and equality agenda promoted by the new emancipatory social movements since the 1960s, this perspective subsequently gave way to what has been termed a multiculturalism model with a greater emphasis on co-existence in parallel. Responses to the 2001 riots in Oldham, Burnley and Bradford nonetheless challenged this model and led to suggestion that multiculturalism had failed as people were leading separate segregated lives (Parekh, 2000; Cantle, 2001, 2008): these views have attracted more recent critics in the German Chancellor Angela Merkel and the British Prime Minister David Cameron in 2010 and 2011 respectively. The outcome has been another shift in emphasis, in line with the belief that a move from diversity and equality to greater commonality of identities and values is needed. The promotion of Britishness and the introduction of Citizenship tests are among the newer priorities of what has generally been called a social cohesion model. Most recently Cantle (2012) has referred to the notion of interculturalism as a further development in the promotion of social cohesion to actively bring diverse groups together to focus on shared rather than divided interests and needs.

The concepts of multiculturalism and social cohesion, and the debates they give rise to, are complex and beyond the scope of this chapter. Moreover they are dependent on the precise meanings given to these terms by their proposers as well as diverse interpretations of contemporary society (Thomas, 2011). Gilroy's (2006) description of the UK as displaying convivial multiculturalism is, for instance, in distinct contrast to the perceptions of Angela Merkel and David Cameron noted above. Furthermore, Gilroy's (2005) argument that young people are increasingly likely to be divided by interests and lifestyles rather than race or ethnicity is also in sharp contradiction to the view of Trevor Phillips, then Chair of the Commission for Racial Equality, that the nation was 'sleepwalking into segregation'. These controversial notions, and particularly the meaning of integration in practice, are nonetheless of interest in the context of the YOR study. Three issues that arise for further enquiry are whether diverse communities become more cohesive over time, whether outcomes depend on population mix, and whether day-to-day contact between diverse groups is an aid to integration.

There is mixed evidence on the implications of time for community relations in contexts of diversity. Putnam (2000) is well known for his advocacy of bridging capital between groups to aid cohesion, and claims to have demonstrated this reality empirically through a study of rapid large-scale immigration in 40 US cities (Putnam, 2007). Despite a long-term positive impact of immigration, he found shorter-term challenges included mutual distrust and suspicion in highly diverse neighbourhoods, and a diminution in bonding and bridging social capital through, for example, withdrawal of voluntary activity in the community. The present study is not in a position to examine these trends in any detail, but can explore and compare attitudes and experiences in Bradford and the London Boroughs of Hillingdon and Newham that have experienced much more recent population change. Listening to what young people say about their communities, and the things they think could be improved, is also relevant.

The mix of populations within communities may also be important, although evidence is again inconsistent. For example, while there is suggestion from the UK Fourth National Survey of Ethnic Minorities that Muslims integrate less and more slowly than other religious groups (Bisin et al., 2008), other research has shown that more Muslim than non-Muslim Britons (82 and 63% respectively) would, from choice, live in religiously diverse and mixed neighbourhoods (Gallup/The Coexist Foundation, 2009). It also seems that while those from Sikh and Jewish backgrounds tend to be highly concentrated in particular parts of London, Muslims are fairly dispersed and Hindus are somewhere in between (Peach and Gale, 2003). It is further apparent that integration can be an issue *within* as well as *between* religious and cultural groups: for example, Polish Catholics are reported to find it difficult to integrate with British Catholics as while Catholicism is 'universal' for the latter, it is a symbol of national culture for the former (Trzebiatowska, 2010).

Berger and Luckmann (1966) point to the significance of population density as well as population mix for community relations. These authors maintain that minority groups may experience discrimination but acquire plausibility as they become more numerous in the population, are absorbed into the community, and come to be regarded as a legitimate reality in themselves. More generally, the 'ethnic density hypothesis' proposes that the proportion of co-ethnics in a locality is associated with the risk of mental health problems, with a higher minority concentration linked to lower levels of psychiatric symptoms. A recent systematic review of studies examining the empirical evidence for this supposition revealed a complex and not entirely consistent literature with mixed findings from the British studies (Shaw et al., 2012). Although not directly related to integration issues within diverse neighbourhoods, where factors such as poverty and unemployment are likely to intersect with cultural mixing (Sampson, 2012), it is likely that any increase in mental health symptoms is due to exposure to prejudice and lack of social support (Halpern and Nazroo, 2000). Indeed the finding that perceived ethnic density has more influence on health than measured density suggests that effects are not straightforward (Stafford et al., 2009). The present study is set in three different multi-faith locations with disparate characteristics. While not able to address matters of integration in detail, it seeks to gather incidental information on these issues in terms of young people's attitudes and experiences in the community and at school.

Intergenerational change might also be expected to make an impact on inter-group relations. There is considerable research evidence to suggest that in many spheres, including adolescent behaviour, criminality and psychiatric disorder, successive family generations in a 'new' country increasingly come to resemble the indigenous population (Arnett, 1999; D.J. Smith, 2005). This thesis is somewhat contradicted by data from the UK Fourth National Survey of Ethnic Minorities suggesting that Muslims born in the UK and living in the country for at least 30 years report just as strong religious identity as those who have recently arrived (Bisin et al., 2008), even though religiosity holds no necessary implications for inter-group relationships. The extent to which faith positions are likely to change over the next generations in the multi-faith locations under study, among the families long-standing in Britain as well as those with shorter histories in the country, and the implications for community relations, are among the issues explored within the present investigation.

Whatever their position on multiculturalism and social cohesion, most observers seem in agreement that cross-cultural contact should be encouraged in the interests of community harmony (Local Government Association, 2006; Cantle, 2008). This is essentially an expression of Allport's (1954) contact thesis, as well as more recent expositions (Putnam, 2000; Turner et al., 2007), and the notion that mixing of people from different social and cultural backgrounds dispels prejudice and builds tolerance. As Phillips (2005) has put it 'contact won't necessarily make you like someone, but it may stop you fearing them and regarding them as an enemy'. Youth work in Oldham and Rochdale, that is responding to the social cohesion agenda by adopting this principle and bringing young people from different backgrounds together for enjoyable shared activities, shows promising signs of success (Thomas, 2011). Evidence of mixing across religious and cultural divides and its outcomes is yet another area for examination within the present study.

The rest of the book

The following chapters describe the methods and findings of the Youth On Religion (YOR) study. Chapter 2 begins by characterising the research settings in the London Boroughs of Hillingdon and Newham and Bradford in Yorkshire, and continues by outlining the study sample and the methods employed to collect the research data. This chapter also provides some information on approaches to data analysis as well as key variables examined throughout the book.

Chapter 3 reports on young people's perceptions of the portrayal of religion in their communities and in society: they are very aware of the changing religious landscape in both social and geographical terms and the impact of Westernisation on traditional religious practice. It also examines attitudes to religion in general as well as attitudes towards particular faith groups, and concepts of equity in the way different groups are regarded and treated, including by the media.

Chapter 4 moves on to look at the religious journeys made by young people from early childhood to the time of the study, highlighting the patterns and contrasts in these pathways. Chapter 5 explores religious expression in more detail, looking particularly at the labels young people give themselves, the religious communities they belong to, and patterns of public worship and private prayer. This chapter also reiterates the nature of changing times and the impact of Westernisation and modernity on many young people's religious lives. Chapter 6 turns to look at the impact of religion in everyday life in terms of morality and doing what is 'right', what young people wear, what they eat, how they treat other people and the environment, and attitudes towards dating and marriage.

The family, and its significance for religious journeys, provides the focus for Chapter 7. How similar are young people's views on religion to those of their parents, and is there a generation effect on divergence from family religious tradition as families become longer-established in the UK? The circumstances and views of the few young people in the YOR study from mixed faith backgrounds are also examined in this chapter. Chapter 8 moves on to consider young people in relation to their friends and schools. Choosing friends from similar and different backgrounds, relationships between members of different faith groups, views on the benefits of multi-faith and single-faith schools, and attitudes to religious education are among the topics discussed.

Chapter 9 returns to young people's neighbourhoods, and their experiences of both tolerance and conflict within the multi-faith communities within which they reside. It also reports on the suggestions from participants in the YOR survey on how people from different religious backgrounds could be encouraged to get on better. The findings from the study as a whole are brought together in Chapter 10. The development of religious identities, the exercise of personal agency, the operation of liberal individualism, and the future of religion are the main topics under discussion.

2 The Youth On Religion study

The Youth On Religion (YOR) study contributes to an interdisciplinary understanding of the processes involved as young people in multi-faith areas make sense of their lives. Influenced by the classic theorists, it utilises a largely interpretive social science approach to examine how they develop and negotiate their religious identities through their interactions with both those around them and the institutional structures that overshadow them (Denzin, 2009). Data to enable the exploration of these questions were collected through schools and colleges in three British multi-faith locations by means of an online survey, discussion groups, paired interviews and e-Journals. In total, around 10,500 young people mainly between 13 and 18 years participated in the survey, 157 17 and 18-year-olds took part in the groups and interviews, and 36 of these 157 contributed to e-Journals. The quantitative and qualitative findings, their interpretations and implications, are brought together in this book.

This chapter outlines the context of the research, its questions, the settings in which it took place, the process of data collection, characteristics of the sample, data analysis and interpretation of the findings.

The research in context

This new study complements much earlier relevant work, but is distinct in being the first large-scale and detailed study of developing religious identity among young people growing up in multi-faith locations. It builds on findings from other investigations focusing on the so-called Generation Y born in the 1980s and 1990s that suggest how this cohort of young people tends to be less overtly religious than earlier cohorts (Savage et al., 2006). It also adds to the knowledge base developed through important British large-scale studies examining beliefs and attitudes towards religion, often with a predominantly Christian focus (Francis and Kay, 1995; Sahin, 2005;

Francis and Katz, 2007), and from studies in the United States (Barry and Nelson, 2005; Smith and Denton, 2005) and Australia (Mason et al., 2007) that have looked at religiosity more comprehensively although not specifically in multi-faith communities.

While the YOR study undoubtedly has greatest relevance for British multi-faith areas, its findings have applicability to other Western countries. Despite very different patterns of religious belief and practice almost everywhere, particularly between Europe and America (Himmelfarb, 2004), there are still some commonalities including experiences of migration and population change (Scheffer, 2011). A recent European-wide survey of teenagers (Knauth et al., 2008) examined the role of religion in young people's lives, including communications with friends, learning about other religions, and positive and negative experiences of religion, and demonstrated how both similarities and differences emerge between young people in disparate locations. Moreover, conclusions reached by a study on American post-boomers, on the role of agency, modernity and flexibility in religious thought (Flory and Miller, 2010), resonate with the YOR findings. There may be clear distinctions in the role of religion across Europe, but there are also marked differences across the three research sites in the present study. This does not, however, contradict the fact that there are parallels and lessons that can be drawn between locations and nation states.

The research questions

Four broad and overlapping research objectives guide the YOR study. These are:

- First, to enquire about young people's religious identities, in terms of how they describe themselves, their beliefs and values, public and private practices, and their sense of belonging to a religious community, in changing times and multi-faith locations. Of central interest is the importance of religion in their lives and how they express their religiosity.

- Second, to investigate the factors influencing the negotiation of religious identity. The impact of age, gender, socio-economic status, family, friends, geographical location, school, media, religious leaders and world events are among the factors under study. The role of personal agency and choice, tensions arising from modernity, and change over time and family generations, are also in focus.

- Third, to examine how religion affects young people's everyday lives. Of interest is how religion impacts on their sense of purpose and morality, and how it influences what they wear and what they eat. Attitudes and expectations of dating and marriage are also examined.
- Fourth, to determine young people's wider perspectives on the role of religion in their local and national communities. Views on the impact of religion in society, and the implications of multi-faith schools and neighbourhoods for social cohesion and maintaining the social order, are among topics of enquiry.

The research areas

Three multi-faith locations, differing in patterns of population and change, were selected for the YOR study. These are the London Boroughs of Hillingdon and Newham, and Bradford in West Yorkshire. All three sites have been affected by the forces of globalisation and cross- and intra-border migration, and all three have experienced rapid changes in economy and demography. Nonetheless, impact has not been fully consistent but rather shaped by local context. Figures 2.1 to 2.3 illustrate some of the similarities

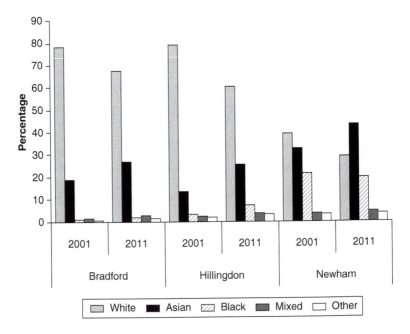

Figure 2.1 Population by ethnic group 2001 and 2011 for the three research areas
Source: Census 2001 and 2011.

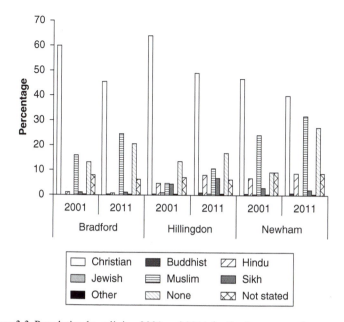

Figure 2.2 Population by religion 2001 and 2011 for the three research areas
Source: Census 2001 and 2011.

and differences within these areas in patterns of ethnicity, religion and place
of birth of the resident population over the past decade. Drawing on 2001
and 2011 Census data, they show how all three have seen: a declining White
population, but an increase in membership from Asian and Mixed Ethnicity
backgrounds; a decline in self-reported Christians but an increase in Muslims and those who say they have no religion; and a decline in the proportion of the local population born in the UK accompanied by an increase in
those born in non-EU countries. One notable difference between localities
is the proportion of White people in the population: this is by far the least
in Newham, representing less than 30% in 2011. Newham also shows the
lowest levels of UK-born members of the population and the highest levels
of those born in non-EU countries. Interestingly, and perhaps surprisingly,
this borough also shows the greatest increase in persons stating they have
no religion. Bradford is, by contrast, the most stable of the three areas. The
decline in UK-born members of the population over the past decade is least
in this location, as is the change in proportions from White and Asian backgrounds. The increase in the Sikh population is the most distinct feature of
Hillingdon compared to the two other locations.

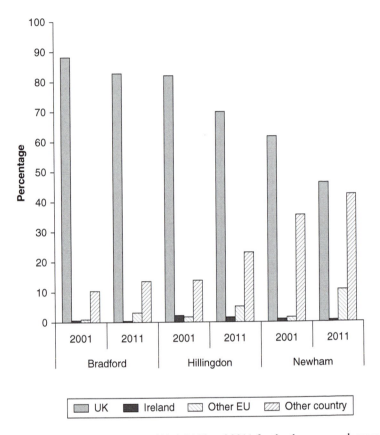

Figure 2.3 Population by place of birth 2001 and 2011 for the three research areas
Source: Census 2001 and 2011.

The following thumbnail sketches of the three research areas provide additional detail on these localities.

London, the global city: Hillingdon and Newham

The local economies of London boroughs are enmeshed in the wider economy and social structure of the great global city of London that, more than elsewhere in the UK, has been subject to recent and dramatic economic change alongside increasing inequality. In particular, manufacturing has receded in importance as services, transport, media and communications have come to the fore (Massey, 2007). Change is linked with considerable population movement both into the capital from around the world (see Figure 2.3) and out of it: while increasingly diverse communities of migrants and longer settled minorities grow in number and proportion within most London boroughs, there has been a significant movement of the indigenous, White and long-settled minority British population, especially young working class families, to outer suburbs and surrounding counties (Watt, 2007, 2008).

These changes are, however, uneven and affect particular boroughs in different ways. Hillingdon, with a population of 243,006 people (2011 Census) on London's western fringe, is now very culturally diverse. There are particular concentrations of Hindu, Sikh and Muslim people originating from the Indian sub-continent and, as shown in Figure 2.1, 39% of the total population is currently from Black and Minority Ethnic backgrounds as opposed to 21% ten years earlier. Based on 2007 Indices of Deprivation, Hillingdon is the 24th most deprived borough in London. Nonetheless, the more densely populated, urban, ethnically diverse wards in the south of the borough are significantly more deprived than the more affluent, White British older population in the semi-rural north on almost all indicators. Most of the south of the borough falls within the top 40% deprived areas in England, with three wards falling among the 20% most deprived category.

In terms of the local economy, the older `Fordist` manufacturing sector, including the once dominant EMI music corporation, that had attracted White working class people from around the British Isles and Ireland since the 1930s, has declined and been replaced by a more varied knowledge-based and service-based local economy. Heathrow Airport and its allied industries, and Stockley Business Park, in the south of the borough, are the main drivers of a vibrant economy with a relatively high rate of employment. 13% of the working age population claim out of work benefits, a rate below the London and national averages. However, the rapid transformation from older to service industries and newer technology-based forms of work has not benefited all families and communities equally. Despite a thriving local economy there remain significant numbers without qualifications or with skills appropriate for the new local labour market (www.hillingdon.gov.uk).

Newham, to the east of London, and with a fast growing, youthful population of 243,891 (2011 Census), is a combination of the old East and West Ham boroughs adjoining the old London docks, and a historic gateway for immigrants on this side of the city. It has the largest proportion of non-White ethnic groups in the UK (71%), particularly Asians and Black Africans, and is now becoming home to substantial numbers of East European migrants. These groups are preponderantly in the first and second generation of settlement, and spread throughout the borough. As elsewhere, there has been a significant outward movement of White British people, especially to Essex (Watt, 2008): visible signs of the departure of the White population include boarded up pubs and deconsecrated churches, once community hubs. The 2007 Indices of Multiple Deprivation rank Newham as the sixth most deprived borough in England and the third in London. All of Newham's wards are ranked within the 40% most deprived in England, and few residents can be described as affluent middle class. Predictably this is related to high levels of limiting and long-term illness and high levels of reported crime (Fussey et al., 2011).

Closure of the London docks by 1980 and the decay of its allied industries initiated a long period of decline and high levels of unemployment in Newham. This led to the start of the exodus of older white family networks to surrounding counties and the entry of new groups, accompanied at times by ethnic tensions, racist violence and activity by far Right political groups during the 1970s and 1980s. Economic decline was partially offset by the state fostered development of the service economy, symbolised by the glittering towers of nearby Canary Wharf, an outpost of the City of London financial services industry, and construction of the 2012 Olympic Park. However, there are well-founded concerns that, despite promises of gains for the local poor populations, these developments have provided limited opportunities for local residents so far (Fussey et al., 2011).

Bradford

Bradford District in the north of England covers a large area of 141 square miles and has a population of 467,665 (2011 Census), with most people living in the more urban areas. A third of the population is from Black and Minority Ethnic backgrounds, many arriving during the 1960s, with a preponderance of Punjabi and Mirpur Kashmiri people originating in Pakistan, as well as some Sylheti Bangladeshis and Black Caribbeans. Bradford is now home to a number of different Muslim communities with their own languages and mosques (Lewis, 2007; Sardar, 2008) that have settled in different parts of the city. Though many families have now been there for three generations, inward migration has continued through, for example, spouses arriving from Pakistan and India. With less ethnic and religious diversity than Hillingdon and Newham, there is a sharper contrast between White British and visible minority populations as well as a degree of ethnic segregation in the school population and residential neighbourhoods (Brill et al., 2011). While by the late 1970s, there were only about seven mosques, often in converted terrace houses (Sardar, 2008; Malik, 2010), this number has since increased considerably. As in Newham, demographic change is reflected in deconsecrated churches and boarded-up pubs, once community centres for working class White people.

Bradford's textile and engineering industries made it one of the wealthiest powerhouses of the English industrial revolution in the 19th century. The immigrant populations came to provide low-cost labour during the twilight phase of these industries, struggling against foreign competition. The collapse of the textile industry led to massive loss of employment between 1960 and 1990 that hit the Muslim population particularly badly (Lewis, 2007). The eclipse of textiles, engineering and allied industries has created a challenging legacy, triggering a range of state financed urban regeneration programmes, and a recent growth in the service sector and telecommunications. Stringent cutbacks since 2010 of central government grants to local authorities and government cuts in regional development funding have, however, contributed to subsequent rising unemployment levels, especially among young people, sharpened inequalities and visible signs of urban decline in poorer areas of both predominantly Asian and White settlement (Brill et al., 2011). Some 9% of wards are in the 20% most deprived in England: this has particularly affected the Black and minority ethnic population as well as areas characterised by White British social housing.

Collecting the research data

The YOR study was designed as a mixed methods study in which a large-scale survey preceded both discussion groups and paired face-to-face interviews with a smaller sample. e-Journal activities were designed for participants in the period between the discussion groups and the paired interviews, both to keep them in touch with the study over the summer period and to provide them with an additional, and more confidential, forum in which to provide views on religion in their everyday lives. Although the qualitative sample was drawn from the same sources as the quantitative sample, the age range of participants in the face-to-face activities was narrower than for those taking part in the survey. It is not known whether or not all those in the groups and interviews took part in the anonymous survey and, if they did, there is no direct data linkage.

The first stage of the study was a survey of pupils in Years 8, 10 and 12 in participating schools and colleges. Following much deliberation (see Madge et al., 2012), it was decided to employ an online questionnaire for the purpose on the grounds that this was the cheaper option involving less administration and no subsequent data entry, formatting for individual needs and responses was facilitated, data collected were fully anonymous, and progress was instantly visible. The main disadvantage of this approach, which may have limited the potential sample size, was that pupils needed access to a computer to complete the questionnaire. In many schools and colleges this restricted opportunities for classes to participate.

An online questionnaire,[1] designed to be undertaken during a single school or college lesson period, was developed and piloted to ensure the suitability of its content, wording, online administration and time to completion. In brief, the topics of the survey included: background information on school, location, age, gender, ethnicity, place of birth and place of birth of parents; feelings of belonging to religious and other groups; influences on perceptions of right and wrong; views on positive and negative aspects of religion; views on differences in religiosity by age and gender; the importance of religion in the participant's life; personal faith position; religious belief and practice; belief in religious and non-religious concepts such as heaven and star signs; friendships and religion; the family and religion; the impact of religious beliefs on everyday behaviour; safety in the community; knowledge and understanding of different religions and beliefs; and suggestions for how young people, schools/colleges and the government can help people from different religions get on well together. As a proxy for socio-educational level, an additional question asked about the number of books in participants' homes. Some of the challenges in developing the questionnaire are addressed elsewhere (Madge and Hemming, 2013).

With full Brunel University Research Ethics Committee support, schools and colleges with appropriately aged pupils in the research areas were approached to ask if they would participate in the study. Madge et al. (2012) provide a detailed account of the complicated and lengthy process of enlisting schools/colleges, often involving a complex 'chain of negotiation' (Valentine, 1999), to conduct the online survey. Schools and colleges generally preferred to administer the survey themselves to allow flexibility: they were accordingly provided with full information packs including lists of Frequently Asked Questions, information sheets for pupils and parents, parental consent letters for any permissions the schools wished to seek, and a voucher to cover printing costs. The online questionnaire was available for an overall period of eight weeks. A number of measures (such as a new daily password to enter the survey, and access to the survey restricted to the school day) were put in place to minimise bias and ensure first, that only those in the identified sample completed the questionnaire and second, that pupils taking part had no prior information on the survey content (unless another pupil had told them what they could remember about it). Daily progress in response rate was monitored online.

A smaller sample of volunteer 17 and 18-year-old pupils was enlisted for face-to-face qualitative data collection through participating schools. Again, and as far as possible, these were drawn from a spread of schools to represent both genders and a range of faith positions. Discussion groups were held first, usually with around six to eight pupil participants and two members of the research team. The content of these discussions was aided by visual prompts and guided by the following themes: religion in the local area/community; positive and negative aspects of religion; and the role of religion in education and society. All discussion groups were digitally recorded with the consent of the participants and fully transcribed.

Participants in group discussions were provided with access to an e-Journal activity that gave them the opportunity, through a secure Internet space, to note thoughts and activities over the summer period before the paired interviews were carried out. The four suggested broad topics for discussion in these e-Journals were: religion and me; religion in my family; religion in my area; religion in society. A further two participants prepared scrapbooks to illustrate their views and experiences of religion.

The interviews, conducted after the e-Journal activity and the summer break, involved self-selected pairs of friends/peers who, with a few exceptions, had taken part in the group discussions. These sessions were usually conducted by a single member of the research team and guided by a semi-structured interview schedule. This was informed by the study research questions but also sought to explore emerging survey findings in more detail. Participants were first asked to describe an important ceremony, festival or ritual they had experienced, saying what happened when, who else was there, whether it was religious or spiritual in some way, and what it meant to them. Further topics of enquiry covered: the personal meaning of their stated faith position; their religious, ethnic and national identity and importance of the different aspects; how they are perceived by others; how their faith position affects their daily life; religion and family; religion and friends; the main influences on their religious beliefs or views about religion; and any thoughts they may have about the future. Again, all discussions were digitally recorded with the consent of participants and fully transcribed.

Later comparison of the information provided by a few study participants in the three contexts of discussion group, interview and e-Journal highlighted how these different settings could markedly influence what young people choose to reveal (King and Hemming, 2012).

The study sample

Participants in the YOR study, who took part on a fully voluntary basis, are considered below in terms of their geographical location, gender, age, faith group and ethnicity.

Research area and school/college

As noted above, participants in the YOR study were selected through the schools and colleges they attended in the three research areas. Numbers of schools and pupils who took part in the online survey and/or the interviews and discussion groups are shown, by research area, in Table 2.1.

Table 2.1 Secondary schools/colleges and pupils* participating in interviews/ discussion groups by research area

	Bradford		Hillingdon		Newham		Total	
	Schools	Pupils	Schools	Pupils	Schools	Pupils	Schools	Pupils
Participation in online survey	10/25	2855	18/21	4160	11/17	3361	39	10,376
Participation in discussion groups and/ or paired interviews	5/25	59	7/21	46	2/3[†]	52	14	157

*Numbers of participants vary across tables due to missing values on particular variables.

†Only three schools/colleges in Newham provided for the age group of these participants.

In addition, 36 young people across the three research areas made at least some e-Journal contribution. Approximately two in five of these were from Bradford, two in five from Hillingdon and one in five from Newham (where two participants additionally prepared scrapbooks to illustrate their perceptions of religion).

Gender

Approximately half the online survey participants were male and half female. There was no significant variation between research areas. There was a predominance of female over male participants in the interviews and discussion groups (101 compared with 56) and e-Journal activities (27 compared with 9), reflecting the greater interest of the former in taking part.

Age

Survey respondents gave their age in years, and responses were recoded into five categories: 12 and under, 13, 14, 15, 16 and over. The distribution by age for the survey sample overall is: 12 years and under (20%); 13 years (26%); 14 years (14%); 15 years (18%); and 16 years and over (20%). All participants in interviews and discussion groups, and e-Journal activities (or scrapbooks), were 17 or 18 years old.

Faith group

Based on the Census 2011 question, participants in the online survey were asked to select one of the following options to describe their faith group: no

Table 2.2 Faith group of participants by data collection method (%)

	Online survey (N = 9966)	Discussion groups/ paired interviews (N = 157)	e-Journals (N = 36)
No religion	20	18	28
Christian	31	22	28
Muslim	35	41	36
Sikh	6	10	6
Hindu	5	3	3
Buddhist	1	0	0
Jewish	1	0	0
Other (including mixed faith and other answer)	3	6	0

Totals in this and subsequent tables may not equal 100 due to rounding.

religion; Christian (including Church of England, Catholic, Protestant and all other Christian denominations); Buddhist; Hindu; Jewish; Muslim; Sikh; or any other religion. An open-ended text box provided an opportunity for comments or any further descriptors to be added. Two classifications were derived from this information, one based on the eight categories listed above, and a second reduced classification including the five categories of no religion, Christian, Muslim, Sikh and other faith. Participants in the interviews, discussion groups and e-Journal activities were asked to describe their faith in their own words, and it is these chosen descriptors that are used in association with verbatim quotations throughout this book. Table 2.2 shows the distribution of the sample across the eight faith position groups, with descriptors for the qualitative sample adapted to best fit these categories.

There is an uneven distribution of participant faith groups by research area, reflecting the composition of the areas and the participating sample. In particular, there is an over-representation of Muslim females in the qualitative sample, largely due to composition of the Bradford sample.

Ethnicity

A measure of ethnicity was captured from the YOR survey with a question based on self-reported identity. The following question was asked: 'How would you describe your ethnicity? Tick more than one box if you need to or use the question after this one to tell us more.' The response alternatives were: White, Asian, Black, British, Irish, Indian, Bangladeshi, Pakistani, Chinese, African, Mixed Ethnicity, Other (please answer the question below).[2] These responses were then recoded to generate a variable with the following broad categories: White, Asian, Black, Mixed Ethnicity, Other. Comparable information was not gathered for participants in interviews,

Table 2.3 Ethnicity by research area: participants in online survey (%)

		Bradford (N = 2742)	Hillingdon (N = 3986)	Newham (N = 3198)	Total (N = 9926)
Ethnicity	White	41	50	16	37
	Asian	47	27	50	40
	Black	2	11	25	13
	Mixed Ethnicity	8	9	7	8
	Other	2	3	2	2

discussion groups and e-Journal activities. Table 2.3 shows online survey participants by research area. Compared with 2011 Census data, there is some under-representation of White members of the sample and some over-representation, particularly in Bradford, of Asian members.

Faith group and ethnicity

There was no straightforward association between ethnicity and faith group in the sample overall although some patterns did emerge (Figure 2.4). The most clear-cut links are for Sikhs who fall mainly within the Asian category, and young people with no religion or who call themselves atheist who tend to be White. Muslims follow a largely consistent pattern and are predominantly Asian although sometimes Black, and the 'other faith' group is quite mixed

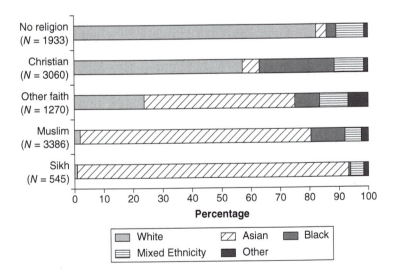

Figure 2.4 The association between ethnicity and faith group

although mainly Asian. The Christian group is the most mixed of all with over half White but including a sizeable minority of Black, Asian or Mixed Ethnicity participants. These patterns reflect the composition of the research areas.

Figures 2.5 and 2.6 further compare profiles of faith group by ethnicity in the three areas for Christians and Muslims. For Christians, the most notable finding is that while the majority are White in both Bradford and Hillingdon, just over half are Black and only 28% White in Newham. For Muslims, the most striking difference between areas is that while most are Asian in both Bradford and Newham, only just over half are Asian in Hillingdon where 30% are Black and 12% are of Mixed Ethnicity. Amongst other faith groups, Buddhists are mainly Asian or White, although numbers are small, and Hindus and Sikhs are almost all Asian.

Books at home

It was not feasible to measure household social class by asking direct questions of young people about parental occupation and education. Nevertheless, a rough indicator of the related concept of cultural capital (Zimdars et al., 2009) was sought by asking respondents: 'How many books are there in your home? If you are not sure, it could help to know that there are

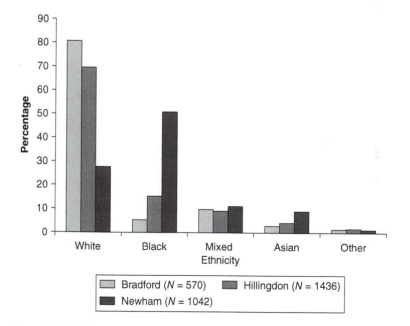

Figure 2.5 Christians by ethnicity by research area: participants in online survey

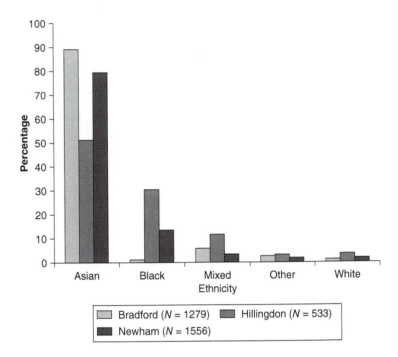

Figure 2.6 Muslims by ethnicity by research area: participants in online survey

usually about 40 books on a shelf measuring 1 metre. Do not include maga-zines.' The response options were: None, 1–10, 11–50, 51–100, 101–250, 251–500, More than 500. The proportions of the overall sample falling into four reduced categories (0–10, 11–50, 51–250 and 251 or more) were 23, 28, 32 and 17% respectively. Newham stood out from the other two research areas in the numbers of books reported: only 11% of participants in this location fell within the top category as compared with 20% in Bradford and Hillingdon.

Data analysis

Although the quantitative and qualitative datasets were, on the whole, ana-lysed separately, they were also examined in parallel and, to some degree, interactively. For example, initial analysis of the survey data influenced lines of enquiry for the interviews and discussion groups, and emerging findings from the qualitative dataset had an impact on subsequent quantita-tive analysis. High levels of concordance between the religious views of young people and their mothers provide an example of the former, while the emergence of a typology of religiosity within the qualitative dataset instigated the exploration of a similar typology within the quantitative dataset. Analysis was thus very much an iterative process of triangulation (Denzin, 2009) between the two disparate but complementary datasets, enhancing and validating the findings.

Survey data

Data were transferred from the online questionnaire database to SPSS 18.02 (SPSS Inc., 2009) software where they were checked, cleaned and labelled. Some modification and addition of variables also took place. First, narrower classifications were derived for variables of age, faith group, ethnicity and books as already described. Second, three new variables were created from existing data: 'generation', 'daily activities' and 'religiosity typology'.

'Generation' linked information on country of birth of participants and their parents and computed a variable, ranging from 0 to 3, indicating the number of family members born in the UK. Although it is recognised that place of birth may be somewhat arbitrary, it was presumed that this variable would have general validity as a measure of the extent to which a young person's family was connected with the UK. For the overall sample, 18, 28, 18 and 35% respectively had 0, 1, 2 and 3 family members born in the UK. Table 2.4 highlights the differences between Christians and Muslims, and between research areas, in these proportions. In brief, Bradford emerged as the most settled location on this measure and Newham the least. Families of Christian participants were, overall, more likely to have a longer connection with the UK than families of Muslim participants. Differences in this respect were weakest in Newham.

Table 2.4 Generations in UK by faith group (Christian and Muslim) by research area (%)

	All three born UK	Two born UK	One born UK	None born UK
Bradford total (N = 2827)	**45**	**25**	**23**	**6**
Christian only (N = 574)	74	12	5	9
Muslim only (N = 1297)	13	41	40	7
Hillingdon total (N = 4126)	**46**	**16**	**20**	**18**
Christian only (N = 1446)	60	17	12	12
Muslim only (N = 544)	5	11	37	48
Newham total (N = 3318)	**13**	**15**	**43**	**29**
Christian only (N = 1062)	18	13	34	35
Muslim only (N = 1578)	3	15	54	28

A 'daily activities' variable capturing the impact of religious beliefs on daily activities was also created based on the four variables of effects of religion on what one eats, what one wears, how one treats others, and how one treats the environment. Each of these variables had five possible responses ranging from 'not affected' to 'affected a lot'. Responses to all four variables were summed and then split into three equal groups representing high, medium and low affect. Newham was again distinct from the two other research areas: 43% of participants were classified as 'affected a lot' in this location as compared with 34% and 18% in Bradford and Hillingdon respectively.

A 'religiosity typology' variable was computed to examine whether qualitative findings suggesting that young people fell into different sub-groups according to their orientations to religion could be supported by the quantitative data. To test this hypothesis, a latent class analysis (LCA)[3] was carried out using the variables of belief in God, importance of religion in daily life, and the 'daily activities' variable mentioned above. The best fitting model produced four classes and the results are shown in Table 2.5. The top row indicates the prior probabilities for each of the four estimated latent classes. The smallest group comprises what have been termed the Strict Adherents, who make up 24% of the sample, while Flexible Adherents, Pragmatists and Bystanders make up 32%, 21% and 23%

Table 2.5 Strict Adherents, Flexible Adherents, Pragmatists and Bystanders in the survey sample

	Strict Adherents (N = 2085)	*Flexible Adherents (N = 2751)*	*Pragmatists (N = 1818)*	*Bystanders (N = 1980)*
Proportion of sample	0.24	0.32	0.21	0.23
Belief in God				
Strong belief	0.99	0.76	0.25	0.01
Weaker belief	0.01	0.24	0.56	0.15
Do not know	0.00	0.01	0.15	0.28
Do not believe	0.00	0.00	0.04	0.56
Importance of religion in daily life				
Important	0.98	0.99	0.15	0.00
Important in some ways but not others	0.02	0.00	0.60	0.00
Not important	0.00	0.00	0.25	1.00
Influence of religious beliefs on daily activities				
High	0.98	0.31	0.11	0.01
Medium	0.02	0.49	0.44	0.13
Low	0.00	0.20	0.45	0.86

respectively. Conditional probabilities make up the rest of the rows and indicate, for example, that Strict Adherents have a probability of 0.99 of expressing strong belief in God, are almost certain ($p = 0.98$) to say that religion is important in their daily lives, and report that their daily activities are affected either quite a bit or a lot by their religious beliefs. Bystanders by contrast have a probability of 0.01 of a strong belief in God, do not find religion important in their daily lives, and have a probability of 0.14 that their daily activities are affected by their religious beliefs. Further explanation and illustration of this typology is provided in Chapter 4.

Two school-level contextual variables were also derived from local authority data showing, first, the percentage of children in each school eligible for free school meals and, second, the degree of ethnic diversity.

The free school meals eligibility variable was introduced as an additional proxy for socioeconomic status, and was computed as a continuous variable that took on the same value for every pupil within each of the survey schools for which information was available.[4] Pupils were then allocated to three groups representing high, mid and low rates of free school meal eligibility. Once again Newham was distinguishable from the other two research areas with 78% of pupils, as contrasted with 40% in Bradford and 13% in Hillingdon, falling within the high eligibility category. Unsurprisingly (see Table 2.6) there was a close correlation[5] between the number of books in the home and free school meal eligibility, suggesting that both variables are likely to be a good proxy for socio-economic status.

A widely used index of diversity, the Normed Herfindahl Index, was computed for each school to derive a measure of ethnic diversity.[6] This took account of the ethnic mix in each school and attributed this status to each individual pupil at any particular school. Young people were classified as attending schools with high, mid or low ethnic diversity. As shown in Figure 2.7, there were marked differences between research areas on this variable: survey participants were most likely to attend ethnically diverse schools or colleges in Newham and least likely to in Bradford.

Table 2.6 Books in the home by free school meals eligibility (%)

		Free school meals		
		Low rate of eligibility (N =3861)	*Mid rate of eligibility (N = 1996)*	*High rate of eligibility (N = 2725)*
Books in the home	0–10	16	29	28
	11–50	24	30	32
	51–250	38	27	29
	251+	22	13	11

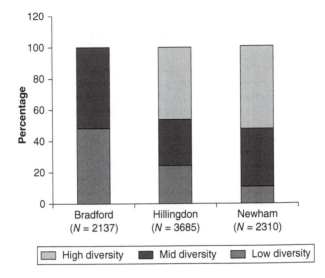

Figure 2.7 Ethnic diversity at school/college by research area

Statistical analysis

Each chapter presents analysis from selected cross-tabulations of core variables along with the chapter-specific outcomes of interest. OLS (ordinary least squares) or logistic regression models were also run where appropriate, to adjust findings for confounders, and to investigate the net effect of key predictors. For this purpose, binary variables were created for all categories of each of the core variables. For area, Hillingdon is taken as the reference category to be compared with the other two. For gender, male is the reference category. 'No religion' is the reference category for faith group and 'White' for ethnicity. The ethnic diversity and free school meal variables were split into three groups, high, medium and low, and used in cross-tabulations, while the continuous versions of these variables were used in the regression analyses. Other continuous predictors used in the modelling are the five-category age variable and number of books in the home.

Qualitative data

All discussion groups and paired interviews were digitally recorded and transcribed and, together with e-Journal entries, imported to NVivo 9 (QSR International Pty Ltd, 2012) software.

Data analysis followed a grounded approach whereby research questions and emerging patterns were explored and elaborated as analysis proceeded (Glaser and Strauss, 1967; Silverman, 2005). The adoption of a multi-stage process of thematic analysis (Braun and Clarke, 2006) facilitated the process. This began with researchers in all three research areas immersing themselves in the transcripts and e-Journal entries to identify significant emerging findings, guided by this qualitative data as well as the research questions and outcomes from the quantitative dataset. These preliminary codes were subsequently discussed by the full research team to achieve consensus on those that arose in any or all of the sites. A definitive list of 30 key thematic codes was then produced taking account both of these consensual themes and YOR research questions. These were: personal feelings, benefits, meanings; accepting religious doctrine; questioning, choosing and exploring; religion as private; inter-relations between believing/belonging/ practising/ affiliation; context and assumptions; life-course patterns; religion/ ethnicity/nationality and mixed identities; culture and religion; constructions of atheism and agnosticism; morals/values and religion; key events and experiences influence belief; belonging to a religious or other community; togetherness/conflict in religious occasions/practices/rituals; family processes and transmission; managing/negotiating religious rules and expectations; religiosity across generations; bodily presentation and experience; gender politics and religion; dating and marriage; discussing and experiencing religion with friends; modern western society; constructions and stereotypes; intra-faith differences, commonalities and interpretations; interfaith contact and understanding; school and education; character of area; personal safety and comfort; local relations between religious groups; and global politics and conflict.

All transcripts were next read through in detail within research areas to identify passages relating to these thematic codes: an inter-rater reliability exercise was conducted to ensure comparability of coding within an acceptable margin. Organising themes were identified within the broader thematic codes and used to summarise the complete dataset. Information was assembled in terms of these themes, noting the predominant direction of findings and listing supporting and dissenting quotations. These quotations are used illustratively rather than analytically throughout this book, mainly identified by pseudonym, gender, self-reported faith group, and level of importance of religion, although a few are presented more anonymously within the main body of the text. The different qualitative sources (interviews, discussion groups and e-Journal activities) are not generally identified.

The findings and their interpretation

The YOR study is a large-scale investigation of the meaning of religion in the lives of young people growing up in multi-faith areas. It is without precedent and is an important contribution to the research literature. It is not, however, without certain limitations. First, the findings reflect the voices of the young people in the study and, using the language of interpretive social scientists, these voices in turn reflect the impressions that they decided, whether consciously or unconsciously, to convey. Nonetheless the consistency in what they said, and the complementarity of the quantitative and qualitative data, provide confidence in the general validity of the findings. Second, there is no claim that research areas, which were selected purposively rather than randomly, or members of the research sample, were representative of communities outside of the school population more generally. An inclusive sampling framework was adopted in which all secondary schools in the research areas were invited to participate, and all pupils of relevant age eligible to take part. In the event, however, non-response (due to either unwillingness to participate or practical feasibility) led to some under-representation of White Christians and an over-representation of Asian Muslims. For the survey, the emergent data are in effect a census of three areas, with incomplete response, and findings are accordingly presented as descriptive of sample characteristics and associations only. Inferential tests, p-values or confidence intervals are not employed as these are only valid, and indeed only make sense, where probability samples are employed. For the qualitative data, those participating in interviews and discussion groups were all young people who decided to remain at school beyond the minimum leaving age and, as such, constitute a particularly educated group. Third, there are limitations to the degree of generalisability possible from the study. Apart from the fact that young people taking part in the study were not fully representative of all members of their age group in the research areas, it is also axiomatic that they are unlikely to share attitudes and experiences with those in less diverse locations in Britain. Fourth, there are limits to the amount of contextual information it was possible to draw on to corroborate the findings. A reliance on theoretical, research and statistical literature in the field is invaluable but no substitute for wider contemporaneous empirical data collection in the setting of the research.

Notes

1 Please contact the first author for further details of this survey instrument.
2 Although these categories reflect race as well as ethnicity, they are derived from measures of ethnicity and are referred to as such throughout this book.
3 LCA can be thought of as conceptually similar to factor analysis, but with the assumption that an unobserved categorical latent variable can be measured by categorical observed variables (McCutcheon, 1987). LCA estimates the parameters of a model where the observed associations between the manifest variables

can be explained by the K-class latent variable, which is to say that the manifest variables are conditionally independent, controlling for the latent variable (McCutcheon, 1987). In other words, LCA identifies a small set of unobserved classes within which respondents are similar to each other and different to respondents in the other classes in terms of their profile of responses to the manifest variables.

4 Around 80% of survey participants attended schools for which information on free school meal eligibility and ethnic density was available.

5 Gamma = −0.22.

6 The precise method for computing the Herfindahl Index was:

$$\text{Ethnic diversity} = 1 - H = \sum_{i=1}^{N} s_i^2$$

where s_i is the proportion of pupils in ethnic group i, and N is the number of ethnic groups represented. This means the value of the index would be 0.0 in a school that contained only white children, but 0.67 in a school with an ethnic split of .33/.33/.34. In other words, the more diverse the ethnic profile of the school, the higher the index.

3   Constructions of religion

Dramatic changes in the religious landscape over recent decades (Woodhead, 2012) in both the UK and elsewhere are unlikely to go unobserved by young people. Perfect (2011) presents British statistics to show, among other things, how there has been a marked overall decline in belief in God over the past 20 years and changing patterns of religious affiliation: proportions of Christians have gone down and other groups, including people saying they have no religion, have become more numerous. Within Christianity there has been change with a decline in Catholic and Anglican churchgoing but an increase in attendance at Pentecostal churches. Population change is also reflected in different religions showing differing levels of active practice, ranging from 80% of Muslims to 32% of Christians. Changing patterns of affiliation and practice have been accompanied by attitudinal shifts, and adults in England and Wales are likely to suggest that religious prejudice is on the increase. Nonetheless, age, disability and ethnic origin are seen as more likely bases for discrimination than are religion and belief.

Young people are, in an informal way, social scientists in their own right. They are engaged in making creative sense of the social situations in which they find themselves, and a starting point to understanding their perspectives on their own identities lies in their perceptions and constructions of these population changes as well as religion in society more broadly. Before looking in more detail at young people's reports on their own lives, this chapter documents their views on the visibility and changing nature of religion in their communities, the role of religion in contemporary society, understandings of specific faith positions, diversity within religious traditions, gender differences, and the portrayal of religion in the media.

The changing face of religion

Globalisation and the marked movement of populations over recent decades have been accompanied by increased religious diversity in locations such as the Youth On Religion (YOR) research areas (particularly the London boroughs), heightened public awareness of changing patterns of religiosity, and tensions between religion on the one hand and modernity on the other. These changes were clearly recognised by almost all young people in interviews and discussion groups, whatever their faith position. They acknowledged that the meaning and impact of religion has changed over recent years and generations, and indeed that it is still changing. In line with prevailing discussions at societal level, they conveyed the distinct impression that they felt religious observance was on the decline and secularity on the rise.

'Not as many people seem to go to church any more, it seems to be like, oh we'll go at Christmas 'cos we need to.' (JOANNA: female, no religion, religion not very important)[1]

'I think it's probably society and the way everything's evolving, and religion's kind of less important.' (BOB H: male, Sikh, religion important in some ways but not others)

Participants from a range of backgrounds had adopted the thesis proposed by Davie (2005) and others to the effect that religion has changed, or transformed, as a result of modernity rather than necessarily declined, and that younger generations practise religion differently from their elders. Some, particularly those for whom religion was quite important, seemed dissatisfied with aspects of organised religion and felt it needed to 'catch up with the times', particularly on moral issues such as contraception and abortion.

'I mean I think that change is real and inevitable. From history and colonisation laws, practices and beliefs have changed in some countries. Change would not have happened without beliefs in certain areas, so with modernisation people change.' (LUCAS: male, Muslim, religion very important)

'It was in the news the other week about how in Bradford now more people go to mosque than church. And I think it shows that not all religions are like decreasing, but I think it shows that as society sort of progresses then obviously religious beliefs change.' (RHIANNA B: female, Roman Catholic, religion important in some ways but not others)

Participants also confirmed many of the observations made by Durkheim (1912) and more recent theorists such as Beck (1992) and Giddens (1991) on population change and its impact. Many pointed out how members of religious minority groups, such as Muslims and Sikhs, were likely to be affected by the stark contrast between past and present cultures. Differences between their roots or homelands and Western society highlighted the distinction between forms of mechanical and organic solidarity, and old patterns of religious observance could be hard to maintain in the newer context. It was not possible to translate practice across continents without some change. This generally led to weakening religious and cultural traditions. As will become a recurring theme in later chapters, they pointed to the Westernisation of religion and talked of 'modern Muslims' and 'liberal Sikhs' who adapted religious expression to fit in with current way-of-life.

> 'You can't live as a minority in England, say if you are a Muslim, and decide that every person around you is a sinner and you can't talk to them because they will contaminate you. You can't live within a British society thinking like that, it's impossible. So that's why I think the younger generation are more open to religious pluralism and peace-making in a sense, which the older generation often do not have.' (KATIE: female, Christian Protestant, religion very important)

Christians and those who reported no religion were particularly likely to imply that declining belief underlay the changing expression of religiosity, and that this was linked with time pressures and materialism on the one hand, and a current-day emphasis on science, technology and education on the other. In this sense they provided some endorsement for Weber's (1948) notion of secularisation. Some felt science and education were compatible with religion, or demonstrated ways in which modern technology, such as the internet, was used by or aided religious practice.

> 'I think it were easier for people to believe in God before there were a big sort of scientific explosion.' (RHIANNA B: female, Roman Catholic, religion important in some ways but not others)

> 'I have downloaded many prayers on my iPod and I think technology has improved much.' (MANISHA: female, Sikh, importance of religion not specified)

Many YOR participants had first-hand experience of transnationalism and migration (Pries, 1999) and took on board the notion that we live in a globalised world where everything is interlinked (Castells, 2004). They demonstrated awareness of the global geo-political context in which religion operated and commented on themes such as terrorism, the war on terror, Al-Qaeda and the Taliban, 9/11, 7/7, the wars in Iraq and Afghanistan, the Israel/Palestine conflict, and recent events in France involving banning of the Islamic headdress in public space. Some reflected on these transnational links.

> 'In the world that we have grown up in . . . we have seen a lot of conflict based on religion. Which is why I think . . . different world faiths are gonna clash all across the Middle East. Even here yesterday there was

the 35 Muslims burning poppies and suddenly you know everyone, all the young people on the Internet, were condemning the other – it's ridiculous. It does cause tensions, we have seen that, you know at the end of the day, terrorist activities, you know 9/11, 7/7.' (DARREN: male, Church of England, religion important in some ways but not others)

These comments concur with Hopkins' (2004) findings from a study of young Muslim men in Scotland who, following the terrorist attacks of 11 September 2001, experienced heightened tensions and discrimination both in the job market and against female relatives wearing Islamic dress in public.

There was suggestion that religion has a different meaning in different generations such as, for example, on understanding of the Qur'an. One young Muslim thought people in his own generation understand much more about what it means than those in his father's generation. He put this down to the greater ease of translation. For him, better understanding of religion could lead to greater attachment than just reading but not knowing what it means. 'Like I know more about my religion than my dad does . . . but my dad will be more faith, he knows the emotional side and faith of it all.' Another Muslim agreed how it used to be a duty to know what you had to do, whereas now it is more about understanding and following your religion because you want to. Another participant, however, felt that older generations are more in tune with religion because they have read more into it and know more about it.

The view that young people do not value religious practice in the same way as older people, and that the intensity of their worship is often less, was also expressed. They may be less likely to go to services that are more geared to older people and boring to younger people. Additionally, older people have more time and practising religion is built into their lives. Young people have so much to do and may prioritise enjoying themselves and doing things with friends over religious practice. They are also more imbued with a sense of personal agency rather than an obligation to follow family tradition, and more likely to choose the parts of the religion they want to follow. But young people might still go along with religion as a kind of insurance policy.

'Also, I think that the new generation is like, it's not like they don't believe in God, but they're not sure if there is an afterlife, like Heaven or Hell. They just want to insure themselves to go to Heaven, so if they say oh I'm Catholic or Muslim or whatever, then they're putting themselves in a religion where they can be going to Heaven or like an afterlife.' (EMMA: female, Catholic, religion important in some ways but not others)

Even if the younger generation seem less religious, it may be that they are just doing it 'in a different way'. 'They still have it inside them, it's more individual', said one participant, older generations do things 'more by the book'. On the other hand, it may be that advances in science had made it harder 'to believe that there could be something higher'.

Positive and negative representations of religion

Religion is often discussed as a generic concept that ignores similarities and differences between faith positions, denominations and individual expression. Durkheim (1912) stressed the significance of religion in this general sense for keeping communities together and maintaining the moral order while, by contrast, Marx and Engels (1846) put forward the notion that religion encourages social division and social inequality.

Positive and negative representations were explored with YOR survey participants who were presented with six statements and asked to indicate how true they are. These statements were divided into the broadly positive and the largely negative. They were that religion: helps people to know right from wrong; teaches people to help others; helps people to feel part of a close community; divides communities; leads to war and conflict; and stops people thinking for themselves.

Figure 3.1 shows the distribution of responses to the three positive attitude statements for the sample overall. Young people's views were on the whole

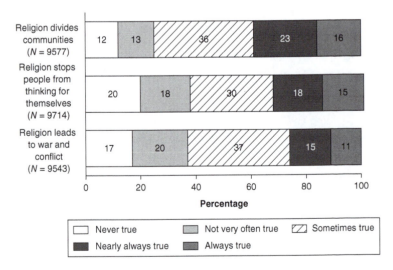

Figure 3.1 Positive attitudes to religion

very positive, with almost three-quarters saying that it is always or nearly always true that religion helps people to know right from wrong, and that religion teaches people to help others. Six in ten said it is always or nearly always true that religion helps people to feel part of a close community.

Despite these positive views of religion, Figure 3.2 shows that young people can also hold quite negative views about religion. Significant minorities of respondents thought it is always or nearly always true that religion divides communities (39%), stops people thinking for themselves (33%) and leads to war and conflict (26%). Nonetheless, opinion on these negative aspects is much more varied than on the more positive aspects of religion. Many more young people think these negative aspects are only 'sometimes true', and between 25 and 40% do not think they are ever or very often true.

Although those with the most positive views might be expected to be least likely to express negative views, this was not in fact the case. The views of young people in the survey are generally more positive than negative about religion, although being positive does not necessarily mean they do not also hold negative attitudes. Muslims hold the most positive views but also, by a small margin, the most negative (Figure 3.3). There is a 'surplus' of positive over negative belief for all religious groups and it is only young people with no religious affiliation who have almost equally balanced views. Further analysis elaborated on these patterns. It also emerged that the more family members born in the UK, the less positive young people are

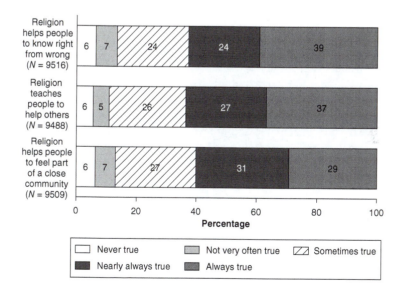

Figure 3.2 Negative attitudes to religion

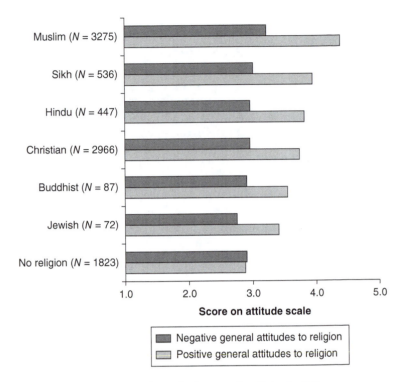

Figure 3.3 Positive and negative attitudes towards religion by faith group

about religion, suggesting that Westernisation may dilute positive attitudes towards religion. Greater ethnic diversity at school was also associated with more negative attitudes alongside positive attitudes, and it seems that encountering peers from a range of religious backgrounds provides opportunities for both favourable and unfavourable experiences. This supports the notion that understanding is based on patterns of interaction (Berger and Luckmann, 1966). Positive attitudes towards religion were more common in Bradford and Newham than in Hillingdon, and point to the possibility of a *locality ethos* that will be explored further throughout this book.

A general ability to see both positive and negative aspects of religion also came through clearly from interviews and group discussions. On the positive side, connections were made between religion and laws, morals, discipline, guidance and being a good person. Most (but not all) these comments were from the more religious young people, confirming the survey finding of some association between personal importance of religion and orientation towards positive representations.

'If you're religious then people tend to think that you've got morals.' (INGRID: female, Christian, religion important in some ways but not others)

'Well I'm not religious but I think the positive of religion is it can make people better people.' (KYLIE: female, no religion, religion not at all important)

As in the survey, young people from a range of faith positions made positive connections between religion and having a sense of identity, having something to belong to, giving hope, and bringing people together by. A few young males linked religion to personal benefits such as safety, comfort, hope and the afterlife, and two made the point that religion was important in bringing people together in the face of possible adversity.

'When it comes to other people having conflict with them then they stay together, don't they? They forget their own differences but they'll join together.' (MIRIAM: female, Islam, religion very important)

Negative aspects of religion were also commonly mentioned. Participants from a range of religious backgrounds mentioned links between religion, tension, conflict and segregation in society, often because different religions have their own ways of doing things and do not always mix together. Many commented on how religion could contribute to war.

'All religions have got some kind of war or conflict in their background because of people doing what they think they're meant to do through God or beliefs.' (JACOB BLACK: male, atheist, religion not very important)

'It's kind of happening around the world, like when you see the incident with the twin towers in America, it's like, it's kind of proof that religion does cause conflict.' (RAJ: female, Sikh, religion important in some ways but not others)

Other popular constructions of religion involved links with extremism and the stereotyping of broad religious groups. Participants with these views tended to be more religious than those who talked about tension, conflict and segregation.

'I know it's only in a few religions, but I think it's when you see things like terrorists attacks . . . and I think it's unfair because the whole religion gets prejudiced against when it is a few people.' (RHIANNA B: female, Roman Catholic, religion important in some ways but not others)

Yet others portrayed religion as something that could be used to control people, was closed to questioning and restrictive, and had the potential to 'over-complicate things'. Non-religious young people, although sometimes Sikhs and Muslims, expressed these views. A few said religion was homophobic and not in line with liberal democratic values of respect for gay people: these were all female, from Christian or non-religious backgrounds, and without high levels of religiosity. It is interesting to note that the admonition of homophobia is part of the liberal individualist ethos that is presented by schools and reflected in the prevalent discourse of most YOR participants. As illustrated throughout this book, almost all young people in the YOR study appeared to have absorbed this concept and used it to interpret and explain their attitudes and behaviours.

Representations of specific religions

Islam

Apart from their views on religion in general, young people provided unsolicited comments on how they thought specific religions were represented and perceived. Islam attracted far the most comments, with young people pointing to stereotypes that emphasised badness, extremism and terrorism. This presented challenges for young people who identified as Muslim in terms of how they would cope with stigmatising societal labels (Goffman, 1963). It seemed they were well aware of the persistence of stigma associated with Islam despite a general discourse emphasising mutual tolerance and respect, good inter-religious relations, and sufficient members of the Muslim faith within local populations to establish their legitimacy and give them what Berger and Luckmann (1966) term a plausibility structure. The majority but not all of those reporting these views were Muslim.

> 'When somebody says, "terrorism" or "terrorist", you will usually think of Muslims.' (NAOMI: female, Muslim, religion very important)

> 'On all the buses that I've seen round my area, they've got these big posters, sort of an advertisement for Islam on the side. And I think the website is something like "love for everyone, hate for no one", and it's sort of bad that they have to advertise themselves as non-hating . . . This just shows the stereotypical view that comes with sort of Islam now because of what's happened with the war and everything.' (JIMMY: male, atheist, religion important in some ways but not others)

'There's a prejudice towards Muslim people because terrorism is not a word for Muslims, it's a general word that can be (for) anyone who takes religion into extremist views. But people just think it's Islam but it's not.' (TAHIRA: female, Muslim, importance of religion not specified)

Two young Muslims in Bradford, one male and one female, linked the use of these stereotypes to particular class and generational groups, basing their arguments on principles that also happen to be central tenets of the symbolic interactionists and the notion that prejudice could be dispelled through direct interaction. They claimed that older generations were less likely to be prejudiced in Bradford because they had worked with Pakistanis in the factories, but that younger working class people living on estates did not come into direct contact with Muslims but only the negative stereotypes they heard about them. In Putnam's (2000) terms, many young people in Bradford did not have the opportunities available to members of older generations to develop bridging capital across different religious groups.

Alongside generalisations about different religious traditions was a recognition of the diversity of religious beliefs, adherence to rules, morals, practices and beliefs within faith groups. Differences between Muslims from different sects and different countries of origin, as well as individual differences within populations, were remarked on. Cultural and geographic differences were also seen as important. Young people contrasted moderates and extremists, sometimes arguing that extremists misinterpreted religious scripture and used this to justify actions that were destructive in society. A couple of young Muslims from Bradford used the 'misinterpretation of scripture' argument to explain how people justified things they considered wrong, such as being gay, or drinking.

'But even the Qur'an, like some people, like it's like terrorists, they'll interpret the Qur'an, like so they'll say we're allowed to kill people for Islam. But that's not true.' (SHEZA: female, Islam, religion very important)

'Sometimes right, what happens is, like just say for example, like gay people and so on, like in Islam, being gay is not allowed and like they'll say "oh in the Qur'an it says that you're allowed to be gay". But they haven't even read the Qur'an.' (FALISHA: female, Islam, religion very important)

Apart from differential history and exposure to Western culture, diversity within religious traditions was sometimes attributed to generational differences, particularly by those who identified themselves as moderately religious.

A few participants in Bradford and Newham also talked about how traditions themselves changed through successive translations of religious texts.

'Even then with the translations, not everything is accurate [. . .] and you won't get the exact meaning out of it.' (WAZIR: male, Islam, religion very important)

Other religions

Far fewer reported on perceptions of religions other than Islam, although members of other faith groups did think their religions could attract stereotyped views. Again reflecting diversity within the faith position, no consistent perceptions of Christianity emerged: some young people were unsure how it is viewed and others said that Christians could be seen as 'good' or 'not having much fun'. A few thought Christianity was associated with low levels of religiosity, although distinctions were made between different forms of Christianity. It was suggested that Catholics could be portrayed as particularly strict in observing religious requirements, even though young people insisted this was not always the case. A young male felt Pentecostal Christians were unfairly stereotyped as 'happy clappy', and a female Jehovah's Witness said stereotypes attributed to her religion included knocking on doors, not celebrating festivals and refusing to give blood. She felt there were legitimate reasons for these behaviours and customs and that portrayals were often false. Another young male said people expected him to be against contraception and abortion, and think women are second-class citizens, just because he is Christian.

Misrepresentations were also mentioned by two young Hindus who suggested Hinduism was incorrectly portrayed as a religion where people worshiped idols, and by a Buddhist girl who commented that Buddhists were often stereotyped as extreme in their views about not killing living things, to the extent that they could not blow their nose in case they hurt micro-organisms. A male atheist argued that the semitic religions (Christianity, Judiasm, Islam) were more strict and less accepting of others, while several participants (all from Bradford where the Jewish population is small) pointed to local anti-Semitism amongst people their own age. These examples related to minority religions within the research areas and might particularly reflect the lack of opportunities for these groups to attain a recognised status in the community or for individually expressed prejudice to be reduced through direct interpersonal contact.

Atheism and agnosticism

Young people, and particularly those without a specific religion, also talked about representations of atheism and agnosticism. Atheism was commonly constructed as something not directly comparable to religion. Rather than an active belief system that needed to be respected, it was seen by some as less sacred and militant and more apathetic and disinterested. This view was presented by non-religious respondents who, with one exception, bought into this construction themselves.

'If you're an atheist, you don't really, you're not really bothered whether there is or isn't a God. You just don't believe in it.' (JOHN H: male, no religion, religion not at all important)

Others reflected on how they felt atheists were seen as lacking in knowledge, ignorant or arrogant. A few recounted their reactions to how more religious people regarded them, and said they felt viewed as 'kind of breaking the rules and not a nice person', 'uneducated', 'a bit weird' or someone who 'just generally doesn't care'. One young male said he had been called a devil worshipper because he did not believe in God, which his friend said was 'a bit stupid because if you don't believe in God you won't believe in the devil either'.

It was, however, thought easier to be atheist or a non-believer than in the past, especially in areas like Newham where most people had one faith or another and where an emphasis on liberal individualism encouraged respect for all, whatever their religiosity. Many participants argued that atheists derive their morals from other sources such as family, society or particular philosophies. They said atheism was more open-minded than religion, and hence less likely to lead to conflict.

'If I was more religious I'd have set out boundaries already whereas being the way I am I can set my own boundaries about things that I find are morally incorrect.' (PENNANCE: male, religion not specified, religion important in some ways but not others)

'I think it means you're open to others' beliefs more and you're not like closed-minded on other people's religions, whereas if you're a particular religion then obviously you're gonna believe the stuff your religion tells you to and any other things you're gonna be "oh that's wrong".' (BOBBIE: female, no religion, religion not very important)

More religious young people did not always agree. For them, atheism could be constructed as less moral than religion and contribute to negativity towards religion through constant questioning and disrespect. Even in a context of practising liberal individualism, it may be a greater jump for a young person with strong religiosity to respect another religion than to respect the absence of religion.

'If someone came up, if a girl came up and said "I don't believe in religion" then I think that would put me off. They may not be a bad person but um . . . it's a stereotype that someone who doesn't have a religion doesn't have the moral values that someone who is religious may have.' (RUFUS: male, Hindu, religion quite important)

'I think if anyone doesn't get on with religious beliefs – I think it's the atheists and humanists that create more conflict than any other group.' (KATIE: female, Christian Protestant, religion very important)

Labels and assumptions

Young people talked about assumptions commonly made about faith position, many of which were misplaced, and suggested that religious labelling is commonplace. These assumptions were frequently based on visibility and linked to religious clothing, bodily presentation, ethnicity and skin colour. Muslims or, occasionally, Sikhs were most likely to make these comments.

A particular assumption seemed to be that White British people are generally expected to be Christian while Asians, who might be Hindu, Sikh or Buddhist, were commonly thought to be Muslim. As one young person put it, people often cannot distinguish between religion and culture and tend to think that 'Hindus, Muslims and Sikhs are all the same kind of thing'. Assumptions of Muslim identity were most commonly made, perhaps reflecting heightened awareness of this group following well-publicised instances of terrorist activity. More generally, it seemed that young people in diverse settings adopted typificatory schemes (Berger and Luckmann, 1966) based on probability. In the absence of better knowledge, they attributed others with the identity they thought most likely.

'I'm from Ethiopia and people think I look like a Muslim, but I'm not a Muslim. People on the street tell me "Salaam aleikum" but I tell them that I'm Christian, because for me it is important.' (PRINCE: male, Christian Ethiopian Orthodox, religion very important)

'Sometimes they just assume that I am Muslim because I am brown and it's just the easiest thing to assume.' (SHARON: female, Sikh, religion important in some ways but not others)

'Because like there's a Tamil community, so they think I'm Tamil first of all – because they don't really know what Sinhalese is because

Tamils are a majority. But I have never really had someone say I was Christian. They either ask me if I am Hindu, and because all my friends are Muslim, they assume I am Muslim as well. . . . When I tell them I am Buddhist they will be like in shock.' (NELI: female, Buddhist, religion quite important)

'Well it's funny because yesterday my little sister . . . goes "In my class there are five Muslims and 20 Christians". And I said, "but they're not all Christians". She goes, "But they're White". And I said, "No, they're not all Christians, they're probably not all Muslims". And she just assumes that if they're Asian, they'll be Muslims and if they're Christian, she thinks that also. So I don't know how she got that point of view.' (SHAZIA: female, Islam, religion very important)

Visible religious symbols, such as wearing the hijab or a turban, added weight to these constructions and conveyed the impression that some-one was particularly religious – even if 'you could be getting up to all sorts'. This view was held by young people from all faith backgrounds. Conversely, dress or behaviour could erroneously suggest that someone was not religious when in fact they were. One young female doubted that people often saw her as Christian as she wore 'quite random, quirky clothes' while another reached a similar conclusion 'because I just have a laugh all the time'. In other cases misplaced assumptions about religiosity seemed based on young people's school or college, or their friends. In all these cases, the significance of impression management, and the adoption of an identity kit (Goffman, 1959) comprising clothing or other religious symbols, is appar-ent where young people wish to indicate membership of a specific faith group. Nonetheless, as well illustrated, self-presentation does not always have the desired effect.

Constructions of religion as gendered

There were several ways in which young people drew on their own obser-vations to construct gendered perspectives of religion. Some, for instance, pointed to differences in the role of men and women within the church and mosque, stating that in most religions women have traditionally had fewer rights of religious preaching than men. Issues surrounding the appointment of female bishops, women priests and women being able to lead Islamic prayer only for other women featured among their concerns. One described inter-religious gender relations in the workplace of her part-time job, sug-gesting some division between rhetoric and reality.

'One of my bosses, he's a Muslim male. And he does think women are second class. And he's said that's not because he thinks women are bad, because he respects women. It's just he's been brought up to say that males are the more dominant sex. And that's how it is. I respect his opinion. He doesn't let it affect how he treats me particularly, he's not rude to me or anything like that. Whilst he doesn't make an issue of it, I don't make an issue of it.' (LILLY-MAY: female, Christian, religion very important)

Particular religious spaces were also regarded as gendered. Besides the large number of UK mosques that do not admit women, Sikh participants explained that men and women sit on different sides in Sikh temples, and two Christian participants suggested that young males and females do not stand together in church. Interestingly there was a great deal of support for the separation of men and women in places of worship on the grounds that it prevents both men and women becoming distracted from prayer. Everyone celebrates together much of the time, but private prayer is 'something you're sharing with God and so it's about not breaking that attention'. Or, as another young person said, 'It's just a good thing to show respect, that you are worshipping God'. Religious stories were related in support of the separation of the sexes.

'And in the Prophet's time, men and women used to pray side by side. But then when the Prophet passed away . . . because men used to always look at the women and they didn't concentrate on their praying, so the women were supposed to pray behind the men. And then I think when that Prophet died, another one came along, not the Prophet, the following halifa, and then they said, you know, women should just pray at home because it's just a distraction. Because they used to wear makeup and come all dressed up and that, and it was just a distraction for the men.' (ZARA: female, Islam, religion very important)

There was also talk about differential treatment and expectations of males and females within some religions. One non-Muslim female felt that Muslim culture treated all women as second-class citizens and said she knew many people who would not venture into Asian areas for fear of being 'hollered at, called names, wolf whistled at, that sort of thing, cars pulling up to them'. Nonetheless, a mixed group of Muslim students profusely argued against any gender divisions and professed that women were treated better than men. They felt their culture was under attack for treating women badly and needed to 'set the record straight'. They emphasised how girls were spoiled and protected more than boys, and that females were often better off as, although husbands and wives keep their own money and property, men have to use theirs to look after their wives. These comments highlight the shortcomings in mutual understanding between members of different religious groups within the research areas, and provoked rebuttals. Muslim females were eager to point out how many conceptions and assumptions about Muslim women in society are incorrect and stereotypical. One told how 'in the Qur'an it actually says that all women are seen to be more special than men' and that 'people think that the veil and the headscarf sort of brings women down but in actual fact it does the opposite'. Some non-Muslims acknowledged that they might sometimes make unwarranted assumptions even though 'if I just observed then I'd definitely say that women are inferior to men in Islam'.

Many participants pointed out that gender differences were often as much to do with culture as religion. Members of all religious groups claimed boys and girls are often treated differently and provided illustrative examples. Drawing on their own experiences, young people discussed how, in Muslim culture, boys are generally allowed more freedom than girls who are much more controlled by parents. The emphasis on the role of culture was highlighted by comments from Muslim participants suggesting that 'people in our culture use religion as an excuse to treat people differently' and that while Islam encourages equality between men and women, 'culture just plays about with it'. Others from Christian and Muslim backgrounds discussed the differing roles of men and women within the family and wider society, and again emphasised that patterns can be as much to do with culture and social norms as religion.

> 'But when there's people following the traditional religions, and still like having their wife at home looking after the kids, then people might think well that's because of their religion when it could equally be just because that's what they want to do, they're quite traditional in the way they live.' (JOANNA: female, no religion, religion not very important)

The politics of entitlement

Linked to constructions of different religions are issues of fairness and equality (Valentine, 2008). The politics of entitlement across religious groups, or 'who should get what', was debated in both discussion groups and interviews in relation to festivals celebrated in school, time off for religious observance, food options and choices, and school rules on religious clothing and jewellery. There was general consensus that these issues should be dealt with fairly, with equality between religious groups emerging as a very strong theme although, as one participant pointed out, schools would not exist if they closed for every religious holiday. The idea that England was a predominantly Christian country was also drawn upon at times. Some of the less religious young people had strong views on these questions.

> 'It seems unfair that non-Christians get Christmas and Easter holidays when we don't get days off school when many Muslims, for example, are celebrating Eid.' (ROSE: female, no religion, religion not at all important)

> 'But you kind of think if Muslims are allowed to wear head scarves that are like broadcasting their religion then maybe Christians should be allowed to wear something that represents their religion.' (ANGELA: female, agnostic, religion important in some ways but not others)

> 'Yeah, I think it's really unfair because like the thing in the news about Christians wearing necklaces with a crucifix where they're not allowed to because it's classed as a jewellery item. And I think that's really unfair because, say for people who don't know about Sikhism, they might think that bracelets are not for religious purposes. People don't understand that the cross can be religious. And I just think that it's unfair if it's just an expression of religion . . . Everybody has their beliefs so they should be able to show that.' (KYLIE: female, no religion, religion not at all important)

At the same time it was felt that clothing and other items may be more important for some religious groups than for others, and that this was what counted. Furthermore, and in line with Durkheim's (1912) belief that religion can in principle take on any form, even a civic form, some participants felt religion should not be favoured above other life and cultural choices, such as pink hair or 'different' clothes for punk rockers. Nonetheless 'it had to stop somewhere' because some people or groups might take advantage of the situation. The example was given of someone who said they were a Goth and came to school 'in all black clothes and dark eye liner because that's part of their beliefs'.

It is interesting to note, despite an emphasis on fairness and equality, how there were still instances in the research areas where understanding and knowledge between members of different religious groups was limited (see Chapter 8). This provides an early suggestion that there may be more than is immediately apparent behind young people's prevalent discourse of mutual positivity and respect.

The role of the media

Perceptions of religion, either in general or in relation to specific faith groups, reflect and are influenced by the media in its many forms. Ipgrave and McKenna (2008) found that the media were an important source of information about religion and other religions for young people, and Lewis (2007) points to the role of the media in creating pressures on, and potential grievances for, Muslim communities, including negative portrayals of Muslims. Recently Knott et al. (2013) replicated an earlier study from the 1980s examining media coverage in the UK, demonstrating that coverage of Islam has almost doubled in the interim with much current coverage focusing on terrorism, attitudes to women and other topics that present Islam as a problem. Reporting of Islam showed a clear change of direction since the events of 9/11.

It is likely that these representations played a part in the stereotypical views of religions expressed by some young people and outlined earlier in this chapter. They were also explicitly endorsed by YOR participants whose most commonly expressed view was that media coverage of religion was usually negative, one-sided and focused on extremes and sensational events. Several young people pointed out that religions other than Islam, or everyday religious events, were rarely reported on.

'I think the media just hates religion, they don't have anything good to say about religion at all.' (GORDON: male, Christian, religion quite important)

'I don't think people without religion are really portrayed that much, and it's always people on the extreme side. Like there's never any articles about just your average, everyday Muslim, or Christian or something like that.' (JOANNA: female, no religion, religion not very important)

'I don't think we get portrayed that much in the media and stuff. I think it's more Islam and stuff. I don't really see Sikhism in the media that much to be honest.' (SIMRAN: female, Sikh, religion quite important)

'They're not going to be interested in something they already know. Yeah, the Catholic Church believes this. Oh, we already knew that.' (CHUCK: male, Christian, religion important in some ways but not others)

Media representations of Islam were seen as particularly negative with a focus on radical extremism and terrorism. Almost every Muslim participating in the study made this comment as did others from different faith positions. Some respondents went even further, claiming the media were actually responsible for tension and conflict because of their representations. Most holding this view were Muslim and from Bradford, perhaps reflecting greater experiences of misunderstanding and mistrust due to greater segregation by ethnicity and religion, and fewer opportunities for different cultural groups to mix, get to know each other, and acquire bridging capital (Putnam, 2000). Further evidence on the question of social cohesion is provided in Chapter 9.

> 'The media is directly attacking Muslims, are thinking it's Muslims against the world basically [. . .]. They are presenting it as all Muslims are terrorists. . . . ' (HESSA: female, Muslim, religion very important)

> 'Um well like with the Muslim thing I think that's really bad. Because every time you read a newspaper there's something about terrorists and there's something about Iraq and there's something about like American fighting.' (RAJ: female, Sikh, religion important in some ways but not others)

> 'So I think it's the media that's starting it, conflicts.' (SHEZA: female, Muslim, religion very important)

On the other hand, a few young people mentioned the positives that can result from negative representations, such as different types of peaceful resistance or greater religiosity. Young Muslims might react to a negative press by finding out more about their religion in order to counter charges of terrorism and portray Muslims in a more positive light. Some of the female Muslims in the sample related creative ideas in this area, such as the creation of cartoon strips.

> 'Yes and despite what they're trying to do to bring people away from Islam, what they're actually doing is bringing people to Islam.' (PAPASMURF: female, Muslim, religion very important)

> '(There is a) young Muslim woman in Bradford who is trying to combat the negative press received by Muslims by creating a comic strip about the daily life of a Muslim woman. Apparently it is really funny. It shows the exact opposite of what people believe of Muslim women. I think it has affected other people a lot because if somebody's gonna try and shun your beliefs, some people do try to stick to them more.' (MIRIAM: female, Islam, religion very important)

Some non-religious young people reported how atheism was not represented at all in the media, due to a shortage of sensational stories, the perceived lack of conflict caused by atheism in comparison to religion, and
the invisibility of those with no specific faith. In a predominantly religious
environment, such as the neighbourhoods in which this study was undertaken, having no faith could be viewed as a potentially stigmatising, spoiled
or deficient identity, requiring appropriate coping mechanisms in response
(Goffman, 1963). Others talked about the portrayal of atheism in the media
as drawing on stereotypes and sensationalism, observing how the press does
not always appear to acknowledge the legitimacy of their faith position.
This can be particularly challenging for young women.

> 'I think we are shown to have no morals. Like if you are not Christian,
> you are going to sleep around and be disrespectful. But if you are, you
> are really upright and stick to your morals.' (KATHLEEN: female, no
> religion, religion not at all important)

Views on the media were certainly not all one-sided. Some respondents,
but no Muslims, felt the media did sometimes give both sides of the story,
presented positive reports of religion, and provided necessary coverage of
atrocities carried out by the minority. Others pointed to the potential of the
media to educate people and provide balanced representations of religion,
even if this did not always happen.

> 'They could show the good things about religion like everyone com-
> ing together like in religious events. It's actually good to see like so
> many people actually peacefully standing there and being together.'
> (SIENNA: female, atheist, religion important in some ways but not
> others)

Finally, going against the tide of the tolerance discourse, one young male
confessed that stories he had read about Muslims in the media had made
him more negative towards them.

Summary

Almost all young people are in accord with sociologists and others who
describe how the meaning and impact of religion have altered over recent
years and decades. YOR participants pointed to the role of population
movement, increased religious diversity in many areas of Britain, modernity
and a greater understanding of science in contributing to intergenerational
change in the expression of personal religiosity. Westernisation presented

pressures and had led to the emergence of 'modern Muslims' and 'liberal Sikhs' who adapted religious practice to fit in with the demands of contemporary British culture. There was some support for the secularisation thesis, particularly from Christians and those with no specific faith position who were most likely to suggest an overall decline in religious belief.

On the whole young people expressed more positive than negative views about the impact of religion in society, although many held balanced views. Muslims were more likely than those from other faith positions to hold both positive and negative attitudes. More positive attitudes were also held by young people in Bradford and Newham than in Hillingdon, suggesting the possibility of a *locality ethos*, and by those where fewer family members had been born in the UK, reinforcing a likely Westernisation effect. Those attending less ethnically diverse schools tended to have the most positive views of religion.

Religions, especially Islam, were often felt to be subject to stereotypical views. These were reinforced by religious clothing and linked to fear of terrorism. Young people with no specific faith commented on negative perceptions of atheists and agnostics, even though these positions were seen as easier to sustain publicly than in the past. Participants also commented on the relationship between religious and ethnic identities and the way that faith position can be presumed from outward appearance.

Less conclusive evidence of gender differences was found in survey data from this study than in much other research. Young people participating in interviews did nonetheless highlight a variety of situations in which religion-based expectations of males and females arose. Most discussion of the media reflected the predominant view that coverage of religion, and particularly Islam, is largely negative. Finally the concept of liberal individualism that runs through this book began to emerge. Young people were keen to endorse fairness and equality in the treatment of different faith groups not only according to gender and through the media but also in everyday life.

The next chapter examines young people's personal religious journeys within this overall context. It explores their reflections on religion from their earliest childhoods to the time of interview, as well as thoughts on the future. Particular attention is paid to factors that have influenced them along the way.

Note

1 The authors of quotations are identified by pseudonym, gender, self-described faith position and self-reported importance of religion in their life.

4 Religious journeys

The process of socialisation is key to symbolic interactionists as it accounts for how perceptions and understandings of the world develop through interactions with significant others as well as alternative sources of knowledge (Berger and Luckmann, 1966). Religious identity is an important part of this socialisation that evolves as the child grows up, develops cognitive skills (Piaget, 1936) and powers of moral reasoning (Kohlberg, 1976), and increasingly demonstrates personal agency and initiative (James et al., 1998). It might be anticipated on this account that young people would initially adopt the faith positions of their parents but later confirm, discard or adapt these as they achieve greater independence and engage in more rational thought. This chapter explores the trajectories of young people's lives up until the point of their participation in the Youth On Religion (YOR) study, looking particularly at the different pathways of participants from different cultural and faith backgrounds. Significant 'turning points' (Glaser and Strauss, 1971), identity transformations (Lindesmith et al., 1999), and 'switching, matching and mixing' (Putnam and Campbell, 2010) in faith position are of particular interest.

Although it is axiomatic that religious understanding increases with age, there is less consistent evidence that the same is true of religiosity. Some UK studies, for instance, have suggested a decline in religious beliefs and opinions as young people grow up (Francis and Kay, 1995; Kay and Francis, 1996; Francis, 2001) while American studies have suggested few differences (Smith et al., 2003; Mason et al., 2007) or even an increase in religiosity with age, albeit predominantly in the older age range of 18 to 30-year-olds. Nonetheless these studies tend to have a mainly Christian focus and the question arises as to how far similar findings might be found among those with different faith positions.

Despite inconsistent findings among younger groups, Voas (2010: 25) claims that 'age is far more important than any other characteristic in the strength of its association with religious commitment, easily trumping gender, education, employment, place of residence, denomination and so on' over the life cycle as a whole. The YOR study is not longitudinal but is able to examine the impact of age on religious identity in two ways. First, survey responses are compared by age of respondent, although only over the age span of 13 to 18 years and, second, young people taking part in interviews are asked to reflect on changes in religiosity experienced in their lives so far. By the teenage years, most have thought about their own religious positions and travelled some distance from where they started. Although every journey is individual, certain recurrent patterns emerge. A typology of religious exploration and adherence is proposed to highlight the main distinctions.

Age and religious identity

There is no clear-cut evidence from the YOR survey that age affected either attitudes or change in religiosity, although admittedly an age span of only about five years was considered. Any differences that were found are reported throughout this book. Nor was there any marked tendency for participants to believe that either 13 or 17-year-olds were more likely to be religious: there was, however, a small effect whereby those aged 16 years or more were slightly more likely than others to think that 17-year-olds were more religious than 13-year-olds (34% versus 25%).

The impact of age on religiosity emerged much more strongly from YOR interviews and discussion groups. Almost all participants, whatever their faith group or gender, described how their ideas about religion had changed from their early years when they had absorbed the faith position of their upbringing. In line with a symbolic interactionist account of primary socialisation, they pointed out that young children do not really think about religion much and tend to go along with whatever their family says. Of course these retrospective constructions may have been examples of identity transformations (Lindesmith et al., 1999) in which early recollections are influenced by subsequent experiences and perceptions of infancy and maturity. Whatever the reality, these accounts were nonetheless presented positively as offering young children security and guidance at an age when they are too young to be given their own freedom or really understand what religion is about. Participants said the benefits of a family socialising children in their own faith or culture is that it brings discipline, control and respect, and is a good grounding for later life.

The importance of upbringing for early faith position is supported by much other research demonstrating how attitudes are directly shaped by children's families and communities. Erricker et al. (1997) found that junior school age children expressed very different beliefs and experiences if they came from New Age, evangelical or Roman Catholic backgrounds, while Coles (1990) reported how young children of 7 years upwards from Christian, Muslim, Jewish and secular families revealed quite distinct understandings of the meaning and significance of religion. For instance, Christian children stressed Jesus dying for sins, Muslim children emphasised surrendering to God, and Jewish children mentioned morality and fairness. Often when children were asked who they were, they reflected God in their answers. Nesbitt (2004) suggested that different expressions of spirituality shown by children from different faith communities are in some ways distinctive and in some ways possess commonality, and that both formal and informal 'nurturing' is important. Thus while the language used by children might be specific to a faith community, most talk similarly about the importance of music, other people, morals, feelings of peace, sacred places, spiritual leaders, fear and enjoyment.

Although primary socialisation within the family would seem important, the development of personal agency is as well. Almost all young people taking part in interviews said that when children get to a certain age they become able to think about religion for themselves and make personal decisions about their faith position. They varied in exactly what they thought this age might be, but described it as a time when they begin to understand and question more. Most thought young people should be free to choose their religious identity for themselves, even if this is not always easy.

> 'I think for young people who are unsure about religion, it's a very daunting prospect because when you learn about it, it's like religion's for life and it's like you've always got to conform to that religion. So I think that some people are not so much scared, just nervous about being part of one religion.' (ALAN: male, religion not specified, religion not very important)

As young people grew older, religious journeys were affected not only by family and religious experiences, but also increasingly by personal exploration and significant life experiences along the way. Ceremonies, such as baptism, seemed to have little religious impact in the early years when children were too young to understand what was happening, but later ceremonies, such as confirmation or taking vows with an Imam, could strengthen beliefs. Going to church, praying and practising, Islamic classes, and nativity events or Christmas plays, were other things mentioned by participants that helped to make religion significant for them.

Other types of spiritual experiences were also mentioned. Dreams were important in the lives of a few young people who suggested they could be 'signs from God' and God's way of communicating.

'This might sound a bit crazy, but I have even had a dream where I saw Heaven. Because I had a cousin that died. . . . She was telling me about Heaven, and because of that I think that really made me think there is someone or something out there. So yeah, I do believe that there is something out there.' (SHARON: female, Sikh, religion important in some ways but not others)

'My life has actually been guided through her [my mother's] religion since I was young. . . . And she normally . . . sees dreams in the sense of responses to her prayers, that sort of thing. . . . She saw John the Baptist in a dream and he told her to leave the country. And after a week we actually packed up and we moved out of the country.' (CHARDANAY: female, Protestant, religion very important)

Seeing and hearing about miracles was important for a few others, as were messages from God. One young Sikh personally witnessed the sudden recovery of a severely disabled person in India and said 'This is definitely going to be the work of God. It's not going to be science or anything like that, because that's just not going to happen.' A young Christian told a similar story and said the experience strengthened his faith and led him to pray more. Another young person who regarded himself as an atheist described two spiritual experiences that made him question his beliefs.

'My Nan died ten days before I was born . . . When I was three I had an experience of her. I saw her but I didn't know who she was. And then I spoke to my Dad and he told me it was my Nan, and when he showed me a picture I recognised her . . . (When) my second sister . . . hit four, she had the same experience . . . It really makes me question whether there is a God and something higher than what we are. But then at the same time I sort of try to stick to what I think about the stars and think that God is sort of a man-made concept. But it's really difficult to determine between the two.

'I usually have a pendant that I wear. It's broken now but I used to wear it all the time . . . and I think it used to offer some protection. And I lost it and I really couldn't find it and I was getting really upset about it because it was just gone. And I hit down on something and then when I pulled my wrist back up, it was attached to my wrist. And I couldn't believe it. Like I was so happy and that made me question then where has it come from . . . I just thought that was God putting it there because he saw how distraught I was.' (JIMMY: male, atheist, religion important in some ways but not others)

The overriding impression from young people, whatever their faith group and whether or not they had changed their views and practices over their young lives, was that they were in personal control of their religious journeys. The significance of individual agency was linked to the widespread contention amongst young people that religion is a private matter and not for others to influence. It is important to take time to develop one's own ideas about religion, and young people should be given opportunities to question, explore and reflect. Young people did not appreciate being told what they should do.

> 'I actually get forced to go to church and I don't even have a choice and I'm 17 which is quite sad.' (INGRID: female, Christian, religion important in some ways but not others)

It is therefore not surprising that many participants regarded the idea of evangelism negatively, particularly when the aim was to convert or 'force' religion on others. They felt it was disrespectful and aggravating to evangelise and it was up to the individual to find their own private faith position. They also thought evangelism was likely to be ineffective. These views were expressed by young people from a range of different backgrounds.

> 'I think it should be more of a private thing to be honest. It's like spreading your view but it's not giving a balanced argument.' (JIMMY: male, atheist, religion important in some ways but not others)

> 'I think sometimes when people try and convert they try and put across that their religion's superior and I think that's wrong too because they should be seen as equal.' (FOON: female, Hindu/Sikh, religion very important)

> 'When the Jehovah's Witnesses come round knocking on doors, that really annoys me. You don't want to be lectured you know, and I think it's wrong just coming round knocking on doors and bothering people. If you are going to want to find out more about it, I'll find out in my own time . . . They [young people] don't need someone in their face telling them this and that.' (RHIANNA B: female, Roman Catholic, religion important in some ways but not others)

Some interviewees, although far fewer, felt it was okay to evangelise to a certain extent, particularly if just providing information, as it was an issue of free speech. These tended to be among the more religious but were far less numerous than in an American sample where more than half said it was acceptable to try to convert others (Smith and Denton, 2005).

'You shouldn't impose your views on other people. But then it is freedom of speech and you are expressing your views.' (SHEZA: female, Islam, religion very important)

'There's nothing wrong with spreading the word, like you don't have to force people to believe in it, but just as long as they know so they can judge for themselves.' (JANE: female, no religion, religion important in some ways but not others)

It was widely held to be more acceptable to evangelise to non-religious people or atheists than to those who were religious. According to one young male, and with reference to a current advertising slogan, 'You can't just tell people there's probably no God!' This comment illustrates the view that atheism is not always regarded as seriously as other faith positions (see Chapter 3).

Influences on religious journeys

The diversity of religious attitudes and experiences within the YOR sample was paralleled by the complexity of their religious journeys. The survey asked them about the most important influences on their religious beliefs and responses are shown in Figure 4.1. Comments from interview and discussion group participants on the role of many of these factors are considered in more detail in other chapters.

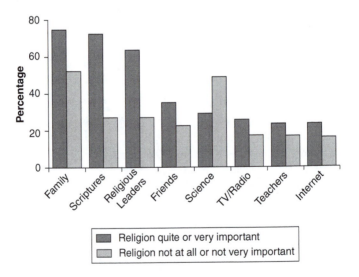

Figure 4.1 Influences on religious beliefs by importance of religion in life
(*N* = 8730–8970)

In line with young people's qualitative reports, family was the biggest influence overall on their religious beliefs whether or not religion was important to them. Nonetheless, religious leaders and scriptures came a close second for those, and notably Muslims, where religion was important in their lives. As might be expected, all possible influences under examination, except for science, were more important for young people who said religion was very or quite important than for those who said it was not very or not at all important. Furthermore, the biggest differences were found for scriptures and leaders, the only categories of direct religious influence. Generally speaking, Black, Asian and Mixed Ethnicity groups are more likely to be affected by all influences except science that has the greatest impact on the White group.

Age had some influence on these patterns, with family and religious scriptures showing a slight rise in importance for the older children, but teachers showing a decline as they are overtaken by the impact of television, radio and internet. Effects were nonetheless small. Some gender differences were also found with females influenced slightly more by family and slightly less by teachers than males.

Table 4.1 ranks the importance of the different influences for faith groups: this distinguishes Christians from White and non-White backgrounds due to the distinction between these sub-groups outlined in Chapter 2. The table confirms how family is a strong influence for all groups, but how science dominates the views of non-religious young people. Religious leaders and scriptures are in the top three for Muslims and both White and Other ethnicity Christian groups. It is important to note, however, that these findings relate to the relative and not the absolute importance of influences: more religious participants cited a greater number of influences than the less religious and, for example, were as likely to say that science had affected

Table 4.1 Ranking of influences on religious beliefs by faith group

No religion	White Christian	Non-White Christian	Muslim	Sikh
Science	Family	Family	Scriptures	Family
Family	Scriptures	Scriptures	Family	Scriptures
Friends	Science	Religious leaders	Religious leaders	Religious leaders
Teachers	Religious leaders	Friends	Friends	Friends
TV/radio	Friends	Science	TV/radio	Science
Religious leaders	Teachers	Teachers	Science	Teachers
Scriptures	TV/radio	TV/radio	Internet	TV/radio
Internet	Internet	Internet	Teachers	Internet

their religious beliefs. Further analysis shows how the media, internet and science form one distinct cluster of influences, while family, religious leaders and scriptures form another. Teachers and friends fall in between these clusters.

These patterns are interesting in the context of research that reports criticism of Imams by young British Muslims who say many do not speak English or understand the meaning of being young in Western society (Lewis, 2007; Mondal, 2008). Findings on the apparently small influence of the internet are somewhat surprisingly, particularly in the present digital age. Perhaps these reflect Singh's (2012) observation that young Sikhs tend to visit internet sites supporting their beliefs to confirm their faith rather than to seek alternative directions. Although it has been suggested that the media may be more important in developing secular than religious identities (Lynch, 2010), or that it is responsible for providing alternative 'religions' based more on popular culture (Beaudoin, 1998), these possibilities cannot be tested in the present study. Interestingly, teachers are most likely to influence those without a specific faith position. It could be speculated that the low ranking of teachers by Muslims reflects the lesser likelihood that they are taught by Muslims than that Christians are taught by Christians. Further analyses also highlight how the more family members born in the UK, the less strongly were any influences felt by participants; additionally, influences were generally felt more strongly in Newham than in Hillingdon, and slightly less strongly in Bradford than in Hillingdon. As in other areas of enquiry, these findings support the importance of both a generation effect, whereby families longer-established in Britain show lower levels of religiosity than the more recently-established, and a *locality ethos* that highlights differences between geographical areas. Patterns are considered further in the next sections.

A typology of religiosity

It is already apparent that young participants in the YOR study experienced very different religious journeys, were affected in distinct ways, and had varying levels of commitment to religious beliefs and expression. Influenced by the ideas of earlier researchers, a typology of religiosity was developed to describe identity status and associated attitudes and behaviour. As with other typologies, however, it is essentially exploratory rather than categorical.

Among earlier theorists of identity status and development, Marcia (1980) and his four-category model stand out as particularly pertinent to the YOR study. According to his model, Marcia proposed four levels of identity status that were identity diffusion, identity foreclosure, moratorium and identity achievement. Using his terminology, and in relation to religiosity, identity diffusion would suggest a disinterest in religion, foreclosure would indicate acceptance of the family faith position largely without question, moratorium would imply active exploration of different religions but without having made a firm commitment, and identity achievement would refer to an informed commitment to a faith position. Sahin (2005) has more recently proposed an alternative typology of religious identity, based on study of British Muslim adolescents, with a focus on commitment and exploration. According to this model, in which culture plays a strong part, young people were classified as foreclosed (not informed by any exploration, and without expectations that Islam should adapt), diffuse (no real interest in religion, even if they still believed in the basic teachings of Islam) and exploratory (trying to make sense of religion, and seeking to live their lives according to both their religion and their Western identities). Sahin concludes that Muslims are neither 'victims trapped between two cultures or able to switch effortlessly between cultures' but that they are engaged in negotiation of all the pressures upon them.

These categorisations bear some relevance to YOR participants, but do not fully represent the distinctions emerging from these new data. The young people in the YOR study live in diverse communities and come from a far wider range of backgrounds than those in either Marcia or Sahin's studies. Some are from families recently transported from other lands who may be particularly susceptible to competing pressures from their traditional and Western identities, and almost all appear to be influenced by the dominant discourses of liberal individualism and personal agency in modern Western society that emphasise the right of everyone to decide their life course for themselves. Indeed even the most devoutly and traditionally religious within the YOR sample would deny foreclosure, instead emphasising how their religious beliefs and practice are the outcome of their personal deliberations. These two factors of competing pressures and individual agency alone might predict variable personal outcomes within traditionally homogeneous groups. This possibility is well illustrated by Mondal's (2008) finding of divisions among young Muslims with some remaining or becoming strongly religious, others turning to alcohol and drugs and going 'off the rails', and yet others somewhere in the middle.

Opportunities to be 'somewhere in the middle', and perhaps to switch between identities, are undoubtedly present in the urban locations of the YOR research. As Goffman (1959) has highlighted, the ability to present oneself in different ways is partly a function of demographic complexity. Chances to experiment with different identities are scant within small static communities but increase as people move away, even temporarily, from the censorious gaze into either anonymity or contexts with consensual others. There were many instances in which YOR participants described how this was exactly what happened.

Indeed there seemed to be four broad categories of religiosity that subsumed the participants in YOR interviews and discussion groups. These are the Strict Adherents, Flexible Adherents, Pragmatists and Bystanders as described below. These categories overlap and do not always represent fully consistent behaviour on the part of young people, but they do nonetheless highlight some of the essential differences in perspectives on faith position.

Strict Adherents

A substantial number of the young people taking part in interviews, and particularly Muslims although also some Christians and members of other faith groups, portrayed themselves as strictly devout in their religion. These participants, who said that nothing had made much difference to their views on religion as they grew up, fell within the Strict Adherent category.

Unlike those in Marcia's foreclosure category, who adopt their family religion with little thought or questioning, the YOR Strict Adherents were similar to members of other categories in generally stressing how it had been their own personal deliberation and decision to remain devout.

> 'I think that's important for both religious and non-religious people, that even if you are born into, like even for me, being born into an Islamic household, I've still gone through that process of criticising things and wondering, "Am I right, am I wrong?" And then coming to that point where I can say, "Yes I do believe it".' (RASHA: female, Christian, religion very important)

One male Muslim commented how 'a true Muslim doesn't doubt' but added that the process of becoming a Muslim depends upon deciding for yourself that you do not doubt rather than just following your family's religion. A young Christian described how this is not without its difficulties.

> 'I think there are doubts. It's . . . as if the devil's trying to put doubts into your head to try and make you change your mind because he wants you to be on his side rather than on God's. And there are various scriptures in the Bible, I can't particularly quote one now, but that you should ask the devil to flee from you in those situations when you feel you're doubting, or you're starting to sin or come away from where you know that you should be. Then you just ask the devil to flee from

you and you can get on with things really.' (CHARLOTTE: female, Protestant: Baptist, religion very important)

Others, especially Muslims and Sikhs, said that questioning their beliefs and choosing their own faith position was not always accepted within the family or religious community. Belief was seen as an all-or-nothing experience in that either you are religious or you are not.

'It's almost like a forbidden area that you don't question religion, as by questioning religion you're actually going against it. Whereas I think the only way to learn is by questioning, because by questioning you're showing an interest in something. If you're being told something, you're never going to take it as well as if you'd actively wanted to learn about it.' (NAIHLA: female, Muslim, religion very important)

Despite frequent avowals of personal agency and choice, it was apparent that some young people felt under considerable pressure to follow family beliefs and not allow themselves to be influenced by other people, the media or anything else. Conversion to another faith was frowned upon and one participant felt strongly that changing religious views was disrespectful to parents. She asked if, in that situation, one should 'sacrifice what you believe is your parents' happiness or do you really have to go ahead with changing your views?' It was, however, a minority position that challenged the skills of moral reasoning valued by Kant and espoused by Durkheim (1961). More commonly, young Muslims, even if to a lesser extent than other faith groups, conveyed the impression of exercising personal agency in actively questioning their own religion. This was the case even when they devoutly maintained the religiosity acquired during primary socialisation.

'Oh yes I had to research it because . . . I'm the type of person that I need to know for myself. I can't go on what someone else is saying, and to live with myself. . . . I'm not thinking that Islam is not the right religion, but I'm just thinking that I need to establish my own like, affirm for why I'm in this religion. I can't just go on what my parents are saying. . . . You're not meant to say, "Why is this, why is that?" And I like to ask a lot of questions. And I like to – so you just learn to, you learn that things happen for a reason, you have your religion.' (SUMAYA: female, Muslim, religion very important)

Apart from the influence of parents, a minority of Strict Adherents (mainly Muslims and Christians) felt that guidance of religious leaders and scholars could be helpful in shaping beliefs or showing you how to be a good person,

'Like spend your money wisely, like give to charity, stuff like that'. Nonetheless, few mentioned specific examples of personal experiences, and several gave the impression that they did not always feel they could approach religious leaders with their questions. One participant described her reservations about creation-ism and how she felt unable to address this within the church. Others said that religious leaders can make one feel guilty, and one Muslim mentioned feeling isolated in the Mosque and not understanding what was being said. As another said, religious leaders are not necessary to have a relationship with God: this comment confirms the impressions of Lewis (2007) and Mondal (2008) on Imams in Britain who are often out of touch with young people.

Indeed young people more commonly referred to the importance of scriptures or written teachings in offering them guidance through detailing religious rules, offering answers to particular questions, and showing how to live life in a correct manner. One female Muslim referred to the Qur'an as an 'instruction manual' on how to live a good life to 'please our creator' and give proof of belief to God.

Religious events, such as baptism and confirmation as adults, and rites of passage were also important in this process, enabling young people to become full members of their religious group and gain a sense of belong-ing to a religious community, and acting as status passages (Glaser and Strauss, 1971). These were mentioned by many young people, although mainly Muslims in Bradford.

> 'One I see significant to me is when like in my religion, once you hit a certain age, you go through this ceremony where you have to take these vows, like how you'll stick with your religion throughout your life. And that was when you sit face to face with what you call the Imam . . . and you repeat after him, well we just had to say "yes" and "I'll follow all my religion, and I won't do anything bad and I will make sure that I wear the scarf everywhere". . . . And that's when you take the vows and you actually fully enter the religion.' (NAOMI: female, Muslim, religion very important)

Pilgrimages, or other reminders of religious significance, sometimes pro-vided spiritual experiences and helped young people reaffirm their faith. Wearing Muslim dress provided an identity kit (Goffman, 1959) and made one young male feel more in touch with God, while her mother's pilgrimage had a similar effect on a young female Muslim. Pilgrimages encouraged a small number of Muslim females to start wearing the hijab and hence put their religiosity in public view.

Many Muslims talked about specific festivals, such as Ramadan, that were reaffirming in helping them lead a moral life and feel better as a person.

Ramadan could be 'like a whole month of detox', according to one. Philosophy and theology could be important too, and compatible with religion.

> 'I study philosophy and theology and other things like that. And I can't just dismiss them because there are good arguments against and for religion. So I take them into my beliefs and I try to use them to make my beliefs stronger.' (GORDON: male, Christian, religion quite important)

It was also apparent that some Strict Adherents, as shown further in Chapter 5, followed their religion to the letter, even if they did not fully understand why.

> 'I mean most of my other friends, yes, they're like, "Yes we're Muslims and we go to the Friday prayer". But they don't know what to believe because no one's told them. I think it's an issue if you have to have someone there to tell you about everything, explain everything to you. And I've had that. And that's why I'm becoming more like, I'm believing more in it now than I was before.' (WAZIR: male, Islam, religion very important)

Few young people were entirely resistant to inconsistent presentation of self in different contexts, even if the changes involved were modest and not in violation of any key religious tradition or expectation. Where young people were, who they were with, and what else they might be doing seemed to be the main factors influencing the significance of context. According to Goffman (1959), performing back stage is distinguishable from performing front stage.

Strict Adherents were the most likely to strongly challenge the possibility that they would, under any circumstance, change their religious beliefs and behaviours. They expected friends and others to accept them how they are as religion is 'something built inside you, it wouldn't change no matter where you were in the world'. It is difficult to ignore your belief in God and despite pressures and sometimes hostility, 'acting differently with different people is not being yourself'. Although views were mixed, this included the view on the part of some that if you are a Muslim and wear the hijab, you should wear it all the time. Those taking this position felt that the main point is that you hold onto your own values and principles provided nobody is being hurt.

> 'I mean if you've got belief inside, and if you're not ashamed and you're proud of who you are, and you know what religion means to you, and you do know you're not what other people describe you as in the media or whatever, then it shouldn't affect you. It doesn't affect me.' (SYED: male, Islam, religion quite important)

Behaviour also depended on context, and participants referred to different expectations in different countries. A number of Muslims, for example, pointed out how festivals and ceremonies may be more spiritual and religious in countries other than England, and that it can be easier to observe in Muslim than Christian countries as things stop when it is time for prayer. All the same, even if going back to their country of origin did make them feel more religious than when in Britain, Strict Adherents could still feel outsiders in these settings. Conversely, being away from religious pressures could make observance more difficult as illustrated by one otherwise Strict Adherent. He related how he had not really thought about being a Muslim on one holiday where there was nobody encouraging him to go to the mosque and pray. As he said, 'I just wanted to relax and enjoy'.

Flexible Adherents

In contrast to the Strict Adherents, who gave the impression of following the codes and traditions of their religion as closely as they could, there was another group of devout adherents who were more flexible in the interpretation of their obligations. These Flexible Adherents were aware of multiple realities (Berger and Luckmann, 1966) and did what they could to accommodate them all. They often used their religion as a framework for formulating their own morals and modes of acceptable behaviour, saying that as long as one is a 'good human being', believes in God and feels comfortable, that is all that matters, and talked about being a bit 'wayward' with their religion or 'bending the rules a bit'. Others spoke about how they adapt their belief rationales to other forms of knowledge and understanding, such as an appreciation of science and evolution. Many felt that religious traditions were often outdated or did not seem to have any meaning behind them. If these did not fit with their own moral codes and opinions about equality, they felt it perfectly acceptable to make up their own mind about them. Types of forbidden food, and attitudes towards homosexuality and women, were some of the things young people mentioned.

> 'In terms of our religion, you can't eat meat. . . . I just think at the end of it, if we believe in evolution theory, we were like monkeys before and we obviously ate other animals. I don't know if monkeys eat other animals, a bad example, maybe bananas and stuff like that. I think we are mammals at the end of it in scientific terms. You have to eat meat, other mammals, to get the protein.' (ISHAN: male, Sikh, religion fairly important)

> 'I know my church laws and I know the Bible pretty well. But I do often stray against what I am taught on purpose. There are certain

things I don't believe in like homosexuality is wrong. There are some bits that I am not too fussed about like Jesus being married. And then there are bits which I'm not too sure about like abortion . . . When it comes to me and religion, I like to think I am pretty well adjusted, I am aware of the rules and I follow them as best as I can.' (MOZART: male, Catholic, religion very important)

Some Sikhs, Christians and Muslims exercised their own agency in placing an emphasis on questioning and choosing within the limits of the religious and family framework, and many said their parents were supportive of this approach. For Sikhs in particular, the emphasis was on liberalism. Despite many rules and regulations within their religion, they stressed that there was little pressure and everyone was able to choose for themselves how to interpret the obligations of religion. One participant commented that drinking alcohol was common among Sikhs, and a number of Muslims agreed that it was not necessary to follow their religion strictly as 'everyone has their freedom'. Another said that so long as she does 'what is permissible and refrains from what is forbidden', she can do what she likes the rest of the time.

Young Sikhs and Muslims recognised the distinction between what they called 'liberal Sikhs' or 'modern Muslims' and 'true' followers of these religions. There was much discussion (especially in Bradford) of modernised Muslims who will not necessarily pray five times a day, and acknowledgement of the difficulty of observing religion in a fully traditional way within a Westernised culture. Some nonetheless were critical of the token observation of peers who thought that, so long as they go to Friday prayers and believe, it did not matter if they take drugs and drink alcohol. Strict Adherents criticised Flexible Adherents for letting Western culture, and sometimes education, become more important in their lives than religion. They told how some of their peers might be a 'proper Muslim' for the month of Ramadan and then a modern Muslim for the rest of the year, whereas for the true Muslim it would be Islam before anything else. It was nonetheless acknowledged that most young Muslims living in Britain are modern Muslims up to a point as temptations abound and 'there's only very few that would actually stick to Islam and like not do any of the Western stuff'.

The complexity of identity for many young people from minority religious backgrounds has been highlighted by other studies. Jacobson (1998) reported how although young Muslims perceived Islam as a source of guidance that helped to structure their lives, their identities were sometimes more important than their practices, giving examples of males who went to the Mosque and then off dating females and drinking and taking drugs. Their complex identities reflected the conflicting pressures they faced from traditional and British cultures, and the multiple realities of their lives. Young British Hindus similarly have identities that are much more complex than those represented by ideas of a culture clash, often identifying strongly as Hindus to emphasise their family identity, rather than a drift to fundamentalism or strong teachings (Nesbitt, 2004).

Just as adherents to a religious position could be flexible about its interpretation, so too could those whose faith position was 'no religion'. These participants, who were clear about their beliefs, were under no specific religious obligations and had the freedom to follow their own inclinations as it suited them. Some within this category drew upon religion during difficult times, particularly to cope with death, or 'as a source of comfort'. Thus one male, who described himself as an atheist, found value and meaning for his daily life in a particular Bible verse. Lévi-Strauss (1966) might have described these examples as exhibiting a creative assemblage of symbolic elements for pragmatic purposes.

Young people developed agnostic and atheist identities in similar ways to those who were religious, and (apart from those who thought little about religion and who were more likely to say they had no religion than to label themselves as agnostic or atheist) actively questioned and explored their beliefs to reach these positions. Some had been brought up in religious families, but through a process of questioning had decided against following in the tradition. Sometimes arguments from philosophy and science had contributed to a sense of disbelief. Others, however, had no religious tradition to follow but had nonetheless thought hard about the issues involved. One young male describing himself as an atheist, and saying that religion is important to him in some ways but not others, exemplified this point. He indicated during interview that he had just thought he was atheist in his head at the time but that in fact he was more agnostic as he is somewhat confused by 'so many different sort of arguments and beliefs and stuff'. However their views had been reached, many young people without a strong faith position were quite clear what they thought but yet appeared to have some scope for taking other approaches on board – as witnessed by the fact that more called themselves agnostic than atheist. Although technically Bystanders, in that they did not have strong religious beliefs, they shared many characteristics with Flexible Adherents.

For Joanna (see below), being atheist or agnostic was indeed the only identity she felt accommodated a capacity for the questioning and exploring she considered so important, while for Sydney (also below), not believing in God gave him more freedom. It is interesting to note, however, that his Flexible Adherent status was affirmed by his comment that 'I suppose I miss out on having that comfort that there is something there to rescue me'.

'I went to like a Catholic primary school, and I was always told about Christianity, but I was always the one who was like 'well, if God is real then who invented God?' I've just always asked questions and nobody's ever been able to give me an answer. I just don't believe that there could be somebody who's always been there, I don't think I can get my head round that. I need answers for everything and I just don't think religion gives me those answers.' (JOANNA: female, no religion, religion not very important)

'I suppose I always feel free in the way I don't have to think about going to church on a Sunday. Or I don't have to look at God and think "how will you judge me on this?" And then it allows me to make choices I want to make. I never feel pressured into or obliged to do certain things.' (SYDNEY: male, no religion, religion not at all important)

A striking characteristic of these atheists and agnostics is how they felt that not identifying with organised religion relinquished them from pressures and obligations. Interestingly, whilst atheists felt they were freer to explore religious beliefs than religious young people, religious young people often felt it was the other way around. Religious young people believed they were more open to a variety of perspectives whereas atheists only considered the negative aspects of religion and consequently caused all the tension. Some religious young people felt it was more difficult for atheists to learn about different religions when they did not have direct experience of them, and it was being religious that made it easier to accept and understand other religions. It seemed those with these views were displaying a form of particularistic empathy across believers of different types. They were also expressing a variant of Rufus's comment (see Chapter 3) and the assumption that religion confers moral values in a way that being secular does not.

Flexible Adherents emphasised their status by saying they might change their 'point of view and everything' to mix in if they went somewhere else for a reasonable period of time. They talked about how some holidays were more 'about relaxing' than others that were 'for prayer', and that what you wore would not be what you would wear if you were going to India or staying at home, or if at home or at a place of worship. Nonetheless, some participants belonging to minority groups said that holidays could create anxieties even if they did try to fit in, particularly if they felt everyone was staring at them. These said they tend to go to India for holidays or else to places like Derby, Birmingham and Coventry where they have Sikh family and friends.

The social context is also influential. These young people overtly practised impression management (Goffman, 1959) and commonly said they were likely to dress differently if going out with friends or with family. They might also be more likely to drink alcohol with friends, even if family life is more permissive than in the previous generation. As discussed elsewhere, there was a common story among participants about how the pressures of the modern Western world could tempt even strongly religious young people away from full observance of the expectations of their faith. Some young people also mentioned that how the topic of religion was discussed also depended on company and setting. In these various ways, many participants suggested they might present themselves in one way when with peers and another when with family and other members of their faith. In many ways they were not unlike Jess in the film *Bend It Like Beckham* who had a much more open-minded approach to her Sikh identity than did her parents. It seemed that in a setting where keeping secrets was possible (Simmel, 1903), both others' expectations and one's own wishes could be met.

Pragmatists

In addition to Strict Adherents and Flexible Adherents are the Pragmatists. These are young people with less clear-cut views on religion who do not feel so committed to a particular religious framework even if they have, or have had, religious views and beliefs. Their views are more likely to fluctuate, particularly in response to significant events in their lives, and active exploration of their own beliefs was a key feature for many. Often this involved questioning the basic tenets of religion, such as how God can exist and allow such suffering in the world. One participant pointed to the contradiction in some religions between beliefs such as that God loves everybody and it is wrong to be gay.

Young people with a religious faith position (although generally not those for whom religion was very important), as well as those who referred to themselves as agnostics or atheists, might actively question the fundamental basis of belief. Typical comments were that scientific arguments seemed more convincing than religious ones, and how could any religion be the true one when there are several to choose from. 'It amazes me that so many people follow faith without questioning others', commented one female with no specified religion. A number of participants felt science raises questions and many felt convinced that it might hold the answers. Young people did not necessarily feel science was incompatible with religion but they did think it was likely to modify belief in some way. One person pointed out that believing in the big bang theory means looking for the catalyst for the event.

Several Pragmatists had made significant religious journeys through actively questioning and exploring ideas surrounding religion, morals and ethics to form their own individual faith positions. This had sometimes meant abandoning a childhood religious position or picking and choosing from different religions and other influences in their lives.

'Even though I was christened, I have never really been religious and as I grew older my belief in God completely vanished. This is partly because I choose to believe scientific arguments instead of religious ones, however it's also because each different religion has a different idea; they can't all be right and it amazes me that so many people follow faith without questioning others.' (ROSE: female, no religion, religion not at all important)

'Sometimes it's really nice just to join in with everyone and harmonise with everybody. But, yeah, I feel like I can join in with other people, I have my own opinion but at the same time I accept everyone else's opinion, like I know it's funny to say but I believe in the story about Jesus, I believe in the story about Guru Nanak and I believe in my own stories. So it's kind of weird to say yes I am a Hindu but I believe in like all the other stories as well.' (FIONA: female, Hindu, religion important in some ways but not in others)

'I have changed my mind, because I did come into this school as a Sikh and my family are Sikh, but I called myself a Sikh, but then I realise I don't do anything that actually is in the Sikh religion or like from . . . like I don't really understand religion, and I do cut my hair, and I do drink – stuff like that. So like as I like started to research into religion – all the religions, not just Sikhism, I just like kind of figured out that religion isn't for me. And then I don't really see the point of it, so that's why I've chosen not to be religious.' (SIENNA: female, atheist, religion important in some ways but not others)

It was most common for Pragmatists to question their religion when trying to make sense of difficult problems. Important societal issues, such as war, famine and personal suffering, that religion is not easily able to solve, fell into this category. These could cause young people to question their belief if religious or reaffirm their disbelief if not.

More than one in five young people interviewed, including both the religious and the non-religious, mentioned how death and illness of family members or others had tested their faith or made them question the existence of God. For them, this was often a key turning point (Glaser and Strauss, 1971) in their religious journey. Some expressed confusion and could not understand why God would let people they loved die, while others said witnessing death, or somebody who had been ill but had recovered, made them think about it and brought them closer to God. Even if not really religious, some young people seemed to find comfort in thinking somebody had gone to Heaven rather than they were just dead. In general, however, bad things tended to make young people believe less strongly, and good things made them believe more strongly. Would God let bad things happen?

> 'I think it's more like stuff in your everyday life that kind of impacts you a little more. Like a death in the family can make you believe less in God or have more faith in it. Because you need like something to depend on really. You know when you feel down, you need something to believe in. And then it kind of changes for me.' (GULZAR: male, Sikh, importance of religion not specified)

The process of questioning is not straightforward and young people, particularly those with no religion or for whom religion was not very important or important only in some ways, talked about the confusion and difficulties it led to. Pragmatists might point to the difficulty of knowing what to believe or which religion to follow. Picking and choosing bits from different religions could lead to contradictions, and active exploration within one's own religion could raise so many contradictions and issues that made acceptance much easier than further questioning.

> 'I were brought up a Christian. Like I've been baptised and confirmed but when it comes down to it, I'm questioning it now, some of that knowledge . . . Because do you know the whole entire argument of the existence of God, of how come if he's benevolent omniscient and everything, how come there's suffering in the world? . . . I don't know what I believe in, I just believe in something but I don't know what it is yet. So I'll just be Christian until I figure out what it is. I just believe in being good and spiritual and all that. I mean obviously there must be something, because the world didn't just think "Oh, I'll appear now". But I don't want to think . . . It's too mindboggling to think like where God is and what he is and all this.' (INGRID: female, Christian, religion important in some ways but not others)

> 'I am just looking for something that will try and tell me that there is a God out there. So I am just searching for an answer really. So I am just agnostic because I don't really know. A bit conflicted really.' (LEANNE: female, agnostic, religion not very important)

There were more instances of Pragmatists saying they had become less rather than more religious over time, usually through a process of exploration or because they encountered difficult questions they had not managed to answer. In other words, they were more likely to follow a cycle of belief-to-disbelief than the reverse (Berger and Luckmann, 1966). A couple implied they realised they were atheist when they learned enough to understand the meaning of the position. Sometimes it seemed they had never had very strong beliefs, but these had become even weaker over time. Science had been a critical decider for many.

> 'And then just sort of over time as I've looked more and more into it and got like more knowledgeable, it's just my belief has just dropped and dropped and dropped. I think about two years ago is when I sort of definitely decided for myself that there was no God.' (STUART: male, no religion, importance of religion not specified)

> 'Kind of made me have stronger belief that religion isn't true. Like I didn't think it was, but then science like kind of helped me, if that makes sense.' (JOHN B: male, Christian, religion important in some ways but not others)

More permanent geographical mobility also had an impact on religiosity. Coming to Britain, and the competing pressures of education and peer groups, and other practical reasons, led to less religious practice for many families. Moving from one community to another within Britain could also make a difference as illustrated by one participant in Newham who had previously lived in Bradford.

> 'I used to live in Yorkshire . . . where most people were atheist, and I sort of turned atheist as well. . . . But since I moved to East London . . . since then I've come closer to God. . . . Yeah, because I mean I didn't really care . . . I used to do like drinking and do anything, I didn't care. But since now, since I moved to East London, I've changed. I've stopped drinking and all sorts. . . . It's been really hard, but it's a good impact, I do feel better. Yeah, because I feel that I'm clean from the inside, whereas before I wasn't.' (SYED: male, Islam, religion quite important)

Bystanders

Bystanders are the final category in this typology and refer to young people who have thought little about religion and for whom it has little importance in their lives. They may witness the religious lives of others but, generally speaking, these do not impinge heavily on them. In practice, and probably because young people in our research were all living in multi-faith communities and often attending multi-faith schools, and because they had shown an interest in taking part in the research interviews on religion, there were very few who fell within the Bystander category.

Nonetheless there were a few participants in the interviews and discussion groups who said that religion had never really been significant in their lives and that they did not have strong beliefs about anything in particular. In these instances young people had followed their parents during the period of primary socialisation and had not subsequently encountered contrary significant influences. As one female with no faith expressed it, 'I suppose I've never questioned not being religious'.

> 'It's just because I'm kind of, I'm really kind of distracted and kind of wrapped up in my own life. So I just kind of, I don't know, I just kind of get on with stuff and just do it, and I don't, I'm not saying I don't stop and think, but just – if I see something, and I think, and it kind of makes me think, you know, realise – like when you see like wedding processions or a funeral car or something. But just kind of wandering around school like during the day, I'm just kind of – I've got a lot of other things on my mind that are kind of more important, because like exams are kind of at the front of your head and you're just kind of like focusing on those. And like religion, it's just, it's just not really important enough to me to be on my mind that much – just when it needs to be is when it kind of just wanders in.' (DEAN: male, Christian, religion not very important)

> 'I don't look at religion as being negative but I just don't see it as an important part of my life.' (RONALDO B: male, no religion, religion not very important)

It was interesting in this context that Bystanders were nonetheless interested in the questions raised by participation in the research, and that both the survey and the face-to-face sessions prompted thoughts about religion. A few participants may have become more involved in the issues raised as a result. They commented that 'I learned a bit about myself', 'It made you think about stuff, how your life is and that', 'When we write it down we think about our religious views', and 'This has actually got me thinking a bit more'.

Bystanders may, however, have other 'religions' or things they believe in. For Rose the football pitch could be said, in Durkheimian terms, to have assumed a sacred status:

'Tomorrow is the first day of the football season and I'm off to watch Leeds with my Dad. Going to Elland Road is the thing I would compare with going to a place of worship because really it's very similar; a group of people coming together because they all believe in the same thing and get joy from it. And one key thing that following Leeds United has taught me is to never give up faith! Even when we were 1–0 down and down to ten men on the last game of the last season, 38,000 people inside Elland Road were all cheering, hoping and praying for the same thing. Being a Leeds fan means I belong to a community, just like members of religions, so it just shows that even if you don't consider yourself religious, everyone believes in something.' (ROSE: female, no religion, religion not at all important)

Applying the typology to the survey sample

YOR interviews clearly suggested four sub-groups of participants differing in their religious beliefs, the importance of religion in their lives, and the extent to which their faith values influenced their everyday behaviour. This distinction is reflected in YOR survey data that demonstrate a similar division among those taking part. Table 2.5 (see p. 38) presents the model derived from these key variables and the proportions of the sample falling within each of the four categories. While this model inevitably has its limitations, it is illustrative of the divisions in the characteristics of YOR participants. Just over half the sample fell within the adherent categories, with three in seven of these Strict Adherents and four in seven Flexible Adherents. Pragmatists comprised just over a fifth of the total sample and Bystanders just under a quarter. Strict Adherents were typified as having strong beliefs, regarding religion as important in their lives, and being affected by these beliefs in their everyday activities. Flexible Adherents generally have strong beliefs and think religion is important, but their everyday behaviour is much less dependent on their beliefs. Pragmatists do not show any strong consistent patterns, and Bystanders do not find religion important, have beliefs in God or daily activities affected by religious beliefs (even though they may be fervent in their agnosticism or atheism).

Unsurprisingly, the profiles of survey participants in the typology categories are somewhat different. First, Figure 4.2 illustrates the links with faith group: Muslims are particularly likely to be Strict Adherents and unlikely to be Bystanders, while Christians, Sikhs and Hindus are most likely to be Flexible Adherents. Second, ethnicity is also important, as illustrated by a marked distinction between Christians from White and non-White backgrounds: the proportion of Strict Adherents in these two groups is 3% and 14% respectively and the proportion of Bystanders is 26% and 6%. Third,

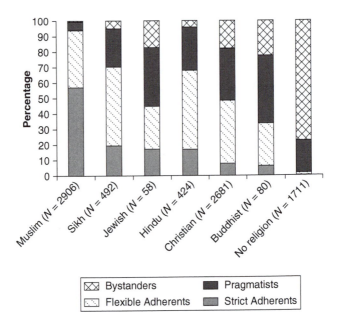

Figure 4.2 Members of the religiosity typology by faith group

membership of the typology shows a strong association with number of family members born in the UK: proportions of Strict Adherents range from 39% where only one family member was born in this country to 5% in the case of three. Interestingly, gender appears to make hardly any difference at all: there are almost identical proportions within each of the four categories among males and females. Once again these findings highlight the key influences of ethnicity and degree of Westernisation on the religiosity of young people in multi-faith areas.

Expectations for the future

Just as most young people had already been on religious journeys during their young lives, so some believed they had yet further to go. Flexible Adherents and Pragmatists in particular embraced the possibility of becoming more devout as they got older and settled down. In contrast to an Australian study that found many Catholic youth currently attending church expected to reduce their participation as they grew older (Rymarz and Graham, 2005), YOR participants talked about either becoming more religious or staying much the same. They partially, but not fully, confirmed the importance of age for religion (Voas, 2010).

'I have never attended a confirmation (and haven't been confirmed myself). This is because at the time, and still, I am unsure whether I want to make the commitment and agree to statements which I am still unsure of. Maybe in the future I will reconsider and get confirmed, but at the moment it isn't for me.' (LEON B: male, Christian, religion important in some ways but not others)

'I think the older you get, the more you are susceptible to believe in it because you want to think like this isn't it.' (JOHN B: male, Christian, religion important in some ways but not others)

Participants who talked about their own parental role, should they have children themselves, mirrored emphasis on their own personal agency: they said they would want their children to make up their own minds, although they would support them in the process. Muslim females in particular pointed to difficulties for parents should children reject family religion and 'go their own way'.

'I'm still thinking about my child and if he decides his religion it would be like he died.' (SUMAYA: female, Muslim, religion important)

'Despite respecting the fact my parents have given me and my brother total freedom to believe, I think if I had kids I would try to argue more for the scientific reasoning because I don't agree with religion as it could cause conflict. But, ultimately, if they felt so strongly for a religion I would allow them to explore it.' (ROSE: female, no religion, religion not at all important)

'With my children I think I would not pressure them into anything. I would like to teach them about the different religions. . . . I don't want to choose for my children . . . It is up to them. Whatever makes them happy I guess.' (BONO: female, atheist, religion not at all important)

'The only reason why we have children is that in that way our religion grows. If you are going to allow your child to become something else, converting from Islam to another religion, I'm not saying it's totally bad but, personally, I would feel as if I had failed as a Muslim and as a mother . . . At the end of the day . . . if he is going to go towards the wrong way, he is the one that is going to Hell.' (POPEYE: female, Muslim, religion very important)

Some concern was also expressed for the loss of knowledge, tradition and culture if members of the youngest generation do not have anyone to talk about their religion with once their parents have gone.

Summary

Religious journeys through life are very individual and personal experiences. Almost all young people nonetheless pointed out how they began in their families where they initially absorbed the beliefs and practices of their upbringing. As they grew older some continued to follow the religious doctrine they had been brought up with, but others actively questioned their faith and showed more fluctuating patterns of religiosity. They emphasised the role of personal choice and decision whatever pathway they took, but also acknowledged the role of family, friends, school, religious leaders and teaching, the media, science and philosophy in the process. Life events were also influential, with 'bad' things tending to make young people believe less strongly and 'good' things more strongly. These included the death and illness of those close to them as well as pilgrimages and trips to other places and settings. These findings provide some support for accounts of primary and secondary socialisation espoused by the symbolic interactionist school of thought.

A typology of religiosity was developed to distinguish between participants in YOR interviews, and was confirmed by patterns identified through responses to the YOR survey. The four categories in this typology are Strict Adherents (devout and largely following the teachings and traditions of their faith position), Flexible Adherents (also devout but more influenced by the Western context of their lives), Pragmatists (usually religious to a degree, but more exploratory than Adherents in their outlook), and Bystanders (for whom religion impinges little on their lives). A sense of personal agency featured strongly in young people's accounts whatever their status within this typology.

Most young people had not yet thought too much about the future, although those who were already the more religious expected to continue in their faith. Others were not sure or thought they might become more religious when they had more time.

Chapter 5 provides more detail on young people's patterns of religiosity, exploring their beliefs, religious affiliations, feelings of belonging, public practice and private prayer, and the relationships between the different elements. The importance of religion in young people's lives is also given a central focus.

5 Religious identity and expression

The previous chapter showed how most young people in the Youth On Religion (YOR) study, and living in modern multi-faith communities, developed religious identities as they moved into adolescence and early adulthood, but how they demonstrated several distinct patterns. Specifically there were Strict Adherents who were devout and practised their religion in its traditional form, Flexible Adherents who were similarly devout but less rigid in how they expressed their religiosity, Pragmatists who had some religious beliefs and disbeliefs but were less committed to any particular faith position, and Bystanders who had been largely bypassed by religion. This chapter looks further at the meaning of these religious identities, and how far heritage, modernity, setting and personal agency are influential.

Religious identity is regarded throughout as a complex concept embracing the religious affiliation or label a person chooses to give themselves, beliefs, a sense of belonging to a local, national or global religious community, acts of public worship, and private prayer or meditation. This notion of multidimensional religiosity has been advanced from the 1960s onwards (e.g. Glock and Stark, 1965; Stark and Glock, 1968) and is embodied in more recent discussion of secular Christianity and 'fuzzy religiosity' (Voas and Day, 2009), 'believing without belonging' (Davie, 1994), 'belonging without believing' (Robbins and Francis, 2010), 'believing in belonging' (Day, 2011), and vicarious religion (Davie, 2007b; Bruce and Voas, 2010; Davie, 2010), in which people may label themselves as religious but yet do not necessarily believe *and* belong *and* practise (Day, 2009). Religiosity has no unitary meaning even if commonalities are discernible.

The importance of religion in young lives

The significance of religion in daily life is an important index of personal religiosity, and the YOR survey asked respondents to say whether religion

Table 5.1 The importance of religion in daily life by faith group

	Muslim (N = 3422)	Sikh (N = 547)	Hindu (N = 455)	Christian (N = 3080)	Jewish (N = 84)	Buddhist (N = 93)	No religion (N = 1933)
Very important	79	44	37	27	27	25	1
Quite important	14	28	32	23	21	17	2
Important in some ways but not others	5	21	23	27	27	30	11
Not very important	1	5	6	14	7	11	23
Not at all important	0	2	3	8	17	17	63

was very important, quite important, important in some ways but not others, not very important, or not at all important to them. Responses by faith group within the study population as a whole are shown in Table 5.1. These show that religion was overwhelmingly most important for Muslim groups, followed by the Sikhs and Hindus, and then Jews, Christians and Buddhists.

The concept of *locality ethos* has already been introduced to account for differences between research areas, and Figure 5.1 examines the importance of religion for the two groups of Muslims and Christians in each of the three study locations. An interesting finding emerges. While there is near similarity in the pattern found for Muslims in Bradford, Hillingdon and Newham, there is much greater variability for the Christians: whereas fewer than 20% of Christians in both Bradford and Hillingdon said that religion was very important in their lives, this proportion was more than doubled in Newham. To explore this difference further, Figure 5.2 compares Christians from White and non-White backgrounds in each of the research areas. Striking differences were found that highlight the much greater importance of religion to the latter than the former group in all locations. It is noteworthy, nonetheless, that religion was most likely to be very important to White Christians living in Newham, reinforcing the influence of this *locality ethos* factor.

Further analysis confirmed these findings. Additionally, it indicated that religion was more important in older than younger participants' lives, and less important the more family members had been born in the UK, signifying a Westernisation effect. Religion was also more important to those who had more rather than fewer books at home, and to those attending schools

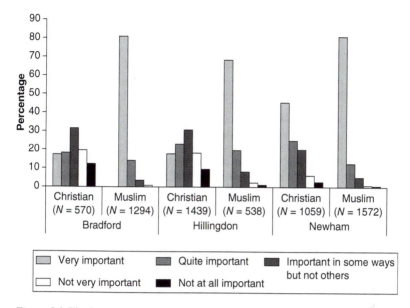

Figure 5.1 The importance of religion in daily life: Christians and Muslims by research area

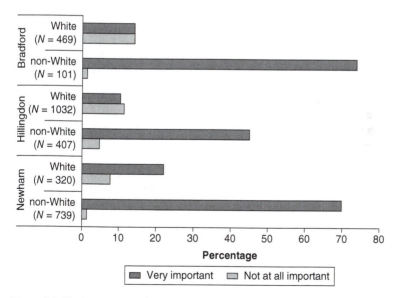

Figure 5.2 The importance of religion in daily life by research area and ethnicity, Christians only

with lower ethnic diversity. Consistent with other findings in this book, gender made no difference to reported importance of religion.

Durkheim (1912) advanced the view that religion gives meaning and purpose to life, particularly in its communal form by bringing people together and strengthening social bonds. Nonetheless it is clear from earlier studies that the interpretation and actualisation of religion vary considerably. At one end of the scale, the devoutness of many Muslims has been commented on by Jacobson (1998) who argues that young Muslims have a strong sense of identity because of the religious boundaries in place between themselves and others, and the demands of Islam in relation to practice and behaviour. By contrast, many 15 to 25-year-olds taking part in Savage et al.'s (2006) British study found little significance in traditional religious ideas and concepts, showed low religious knowledge and engagement, and did not reference religion in reaching ethical decisions. Both these groups found meaning in everyday life but drew on different sources of support. Other studies suggest that young people may find religion more important at some times than at others. Smith and Denton (2005) reported from a US study that religious beliefs and traditions were not very important in everyday life, but assumed more significance in times of crisis and, potentially, at a future time in adult life. In many ways religion was seen as a resource to assist in building a good and happy life. Similar conclusions were reached by Clydesdale (2007).

Participants in YOR interviews and discussion groups described the part religion played in their lives and reinforced clear differences between faith groups. They also confirmed a continuum in the salience of religion for everyday life. Strict Adherents, who were often Muslims but also sometimes Christians, saw religion as an all-encompassing way of life that affects them in everything they do from the moment they wake up, in the way they live, their dress, what they eat, their friends, their duties, and their preparation for marriage. 'You see everything through Muslim tinted glasses if that makes sense . . . you are your religion' said one female Muslim, while according to another 'It's like a major, major part of my life'. This was especially the case for those who prayed five times a day. For these young people it seemed that the most important significant other in their lives was God, and that the 'me' aspect of their social self (Mead, 1934) was chiefly validated through interaction with Him rather than others such as family or friends. God rather than anyone else was the most important point of reference (Shibutani, 1955).

> 'But God always comes first in whatever I do. And whatever I do, I have to put God into the equation.' (TEQUILA: female, Jehovah's Witness, religion very important)

'Because it's just part of us, like it's your name. I don't know, as much as your name is important to you, religion is as important to you. It's just like 99% of you. I think it shapes you as a person and it does everything.' (NADIA: female, Islam, religion very important)

'(God is my) very good best friend. You know, someone who is always there for you, always supports you, always there if you need to talk to them, always helps you. People always say you can tell someone by their friends and I think, you know, in that sense I think God is my friend. You can see God in me hopefully, and it reflects well.' (LILLY-MAY: female, Christian, religion very important)

Religious heritage was important in this sense. The survey data illustrate how almost four in five Muslims said religion is very important to them as compared to around a quarter of the Christians, Buddhists and Jews and over four in ten Sikhs, and interviews further highlighted variability in the importance of religion among those calling themselves Christian. There was a distinct impression, conveyed by Christians and non-Christians alike, that a Christian label has a less consistent meaning than a Muslim label. This is in part due to distinctions between Christians from White and non-White backgrounds (see above) and partly as many young people with some Christian beliefs preferred not to attach a religious label to themselves.

'I think a lot of people seem to say that, maybe it's with other religions as well, but you seem to know a lot of people who are like, yeah I'm Christian. Well, do you go to church? No, but I was baptised when I was like four. So they just say that they're Christian but like, they're not really, they don't follow the religion. Whereas Muslims seem to.' (JOANNA: female, no religion, religion not very important)

'I don't like to say that I am a Christian because I might not pray every day, and I might not go to church every day. I don't think it's right to go round saying that I am a real Christian when I don't know, I don't feel like I fit the criteria.' (JANE: female, no religion, religion important in some ways but not others)

Some Pragmatists confirmed how they called themselves Christian but were not necessarily very religious. It seemed they gave themselves this label because they had been to a church school, if their family called itself Christian, if they thought of being Christian as more about community belonging than personal commitment, or because they thought it was better to be called a Christian than an atheist. For others the label reflected either a level of belief, or occasional participation in church services. Sikh and Hindu participants said they used the religious description to describe belonging more than believing. In these instances it seems that a certain degree of impression management is in play to conform to the 'generalised other' component of the social self (Mead, 1934) and accord with key reference groups such as the family, peers and the faith community to which they are tangentially linked.

> 'I wouldn't say it's (going to church) majorly moving, but I suppose . . . it's a time when you're quiet and you're at peace and stuff and you can think about things.' (LIAM: male, Catholic, religion quite important)

> 'I think it's hard to say, because I'm not really as religious as I should be, kind of thing. I think, when I say Sikh, I class it more or less as just who I am rather than what I believe in.' (GULZAR: male, Sikh, importance of religion not specified)

Occasionally young people said they had no religion but still regarded themselves as Christian.

> 'I still class myself as a Christian even though I question it sometimes . . . I still class myself as a Christian which is weird when you think about it.' (ROSE: female, no religion, religion not at all important)

> 'I'm Christian . . . But to say that like I'm proper hard core Christian and I do all whatever Christians do, then I don't really do that.' (INGRID: female, Christian, religion important in some ways)

Bystanders and some Pragmatists outlined how it was not necessary to be religious to have a purpose in life. They explained the advantages of not being religious as not having rules or regulations to follow and being able to behave as they liked and in accordance with their own conscience. While they knew what is right and wrong they did not need to conduct themselves in any prescribed religious fashion. 'It's positive because it's just made me who I am' commented one female participant. Some, however, also mentioned the advantages religion might bring.

> 'I think if I was religious, although I'm not religious and I've never been religious, confidence seems amazing. A lot of Christians seem to be quite confident . . . Like one of my friends, she's religious and she's kind of stubborn and sticks up for her own ideas because she has to because everybody else isn't really religious. So I think confidence is quite a big thing in how I behave and stuff. I'm kind of not that

confident, so I don't wear clothes that are all crazy and stuff like that. I think that's an important part.' (JESS: female, no religion, religion not at all important)

'Maybe not having a religion, maybe some people would say it cuts out an option, a way to think about if things aren't going your way, you are having a bad time like. If you had a religion, people could say you could look to guidance from God etc. So maybe that's a negative aspect.' (JERRY: male, no religion, religion not very important)

Patterns of religiosity

Religiosity can be expressed in many different ways and the YOR survey sought to establish the relative importance of belief, belonging, public practice and private prayer. The frequency with which young people said these aspects of religiosity were very or quite important to them is shown in Figure 5.3.

Beliefs stand out as most important for all faith groups except Buddhists who prioritised praying or meditating, and those from a Jewish background who said belonging was slightly most significant to them. Attending religious services is marginally of least importance to all groups. Fewer

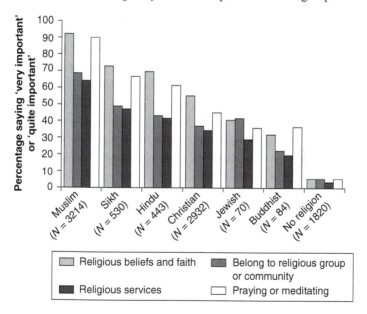

Figure 5.3 The importance of belief, belonging, public practice and private prayer: responses indicating 'very important' or 'quite important'

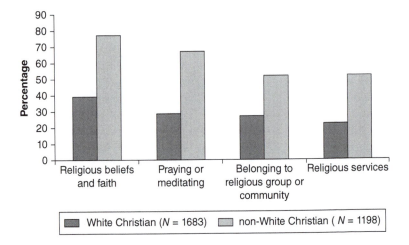

Figure 5.4 The importance of belief, belonging, public practice and private prayer for White and non-White Christians: responses indicating 'very important' or 'quite important'

participants from the 'no religion' group indicate any importance of any of these aspects of religiosity. Christians from White and non-White backgrounds show similar patterns although, in line with their lesser levels of religiosity, White Christians attribute less importance than non-White Christians to any of the aspects (see Figure 5.4). Further findings on beliefs, belonging, and public and private practice, are outlined in the next sections of this chapter.

Belief in God

YOR survey findings suggest that despite close inter-relationships between different aspects of religiosity, belief is usually paramount. This is true for all faith groups but particularly for young Muslims. To provide more detail on these patterns, survey participants were asked about their beliefs in God or a Higher Power. Findings are shown in Table 5.2.

Not surprisingly, there were striking differences in belief in God or a Higher Power by faith group. At one end of the scale the Muslims stand out with an overwhelming 89% of young people reporting certain belief in God. This is about double the proportion in any of the other main faith groups. Sizeable minorities of Sikhs, Hindus, Christians and, to some extent, Jews and Buddhists say they believe in God, but they have doubts. About one-third of both Jews and Buddhists say they do not believe in God or they do

Table 5.2 Belief in God by faith group (%)

	Muslim (N=3357)	Sikh (N=547)	Hindu (N=450)	Christian (N=3049)	Jewish (N=78)	Buddhist (N=90)	No religion (N=1917)
I know God really exists and I am sure about it	89	49	43	37	31	22	3
While I have doubts, I feel that I do believe in God	8	28	32	27	17	16	6
I find myself believing in God some of the time, but not at other times	2	13	15	18	14	23	10
I don't believe in God but I do believe in a Higher Power of some kind	0	2	4	3	8	3	5
I don't know whether or not there is a God	1	6	5	11	10	13	25
I don't believe in God	1	3	2	5	21	22	51

not know whether there is a God and, in some senses, more closely resemble non-believers than members of other faith groups. At the other end of the scale, only 3% of young people saying they have no religion have definite beliefs in God. Nonetheless still only just over half categorically state that they do not believe in God, and a quarter say they do not know whether or not there is a God.

Patterns were confirmed by further analysis. This also pointed to the importance of ethnicity with Asian and Black participants about three times as likely as White participants to have definite belief in God, even when adjusting for faith group. This highlights the distinction between the religiosity of White and non-White Christians: whereas 8% of the White group said 'I don't believe in God' and 21% said 'I know God really exists and I am sure about it', the proportions for the non-White group were 2% and 57% respectively.

Other interesting findings emerged. First there is again a *locality ethos* effect, with young people in Newham and Bradford more likely to believe in God than those in Hillingdon, even when adjustments were made for faith group and other key variables. This was confirmed by young people's comments discussed more fully in Chapter 9. Second, there was a *generation effect*, with diminishing religiosity over time, whereby the more family members born in the UK, the less likely young people were to be certain about God. Finally, and confirming findings from other studies (Francis, 2001: Wallace et al., 2003) there was suggestion of a small but significant link between socioeconomic status and belief: the more books young people report in their homes, the slightly more likely they are to have definite belief in God.

Interview data provided more depth on the ways young people viewed the significance of belief but also illustrated the complexity of the concept and the fact that God does not hold the same meaning for everyone.

> 'The problem is it's a game that you're always in control of because no one else can tell you what God's doing. . . . That's not saying he doesn't exist. It means that in every person's head inevitably it's different. Whatever you want God to be, or whatever you want him to do or whatever you want him to say is ok.' (DARREN: male, Church of England, religion important in some ways but not others)

Believing was nonetheless the main goal of religion, and much more important than public worship, for both Strict Adherents and Flexible Adherents. Having faith was viewed as total submission to God as a source of peace, a power to turn things from bad to good, and a presence that helps you make the right decisions.

'The Lord provides me with His peace. There are always days when I don't pray when I should and the way in which I take control of my life and my actions and do not submit everything to Him. On the whole the days when I don't give the day to Him first turn out to be worse days.' (CHARLOTT: female, Protestant: Baptist, religion very important)

'I believe there's a supreme being that's created everything. . . . I believe that something has to have happened to create everything. There needs to be some kind of supreme being for that to happen.' (ORIONTHI: female, Sikh, religion important in some ways but not others)

'I believe that everything I do, God's always there to help me. In the Qur'an it states a lot about God and God's existence.' (FATIMA ABDI: female, Muslim, religion very important)

The centrality of belief meant for many that public worship does not make a person religious and God will understand if practical difficulties prevent Muslims praying five times a day. Fervent belief could also override doubts and criticisms of certain aspects of religion.

'As long as it's in their heart and they truly believe it, then that's what makes the difference.' (SANEHA: female, Sikh, importance of religion not specified)

'In the sixth form, when we argue about religion, I am always the one who is reminding people that God isn't always good, and I think that frightens people because they always associate me with religion and the fountain of knowledge when it comes to Catholicism. They even call me The Church. And here I am saying that God isn't always good. But honestly, He's not. There is evidence of omniscience and His power, but not always good. We are talking about the Being who tried to totally wipe out humanity. . . . I mean what could we possibly have done to deserve total annihilation? And when Samuel, in order to please Adonai, hacked King Agag to death, this does not sound like a good God. Perhaps we are confused, perhaps God was never good and was never meant to be good but just on our side. He chose the Jews but created humanity, He was on their side and they mistook it for goodness and ever since we have mistaken it for goodness. Don't get me wrong, my love and fear of God is never ending. I am willing to look past all the painful things to see His radiance, but I just think we should know everything and stop ignoring the elephant in the room.' (TEQUILA: female, Jehovah's Witness, religion very important)

Other young people held different views, some stressing how the importance of belief lay in its basis for religious community.

> 'I think the belief is the most important because without the belief you're not going to have the rituals which follow. And then the rituals that follow, you're gonna be doing it as a community. So I think it stems from belief.' (MANISHA: female, Sikh, importance of religion not specified)

Some non-religious young people explained why they found it hard to believe.

> 'I couldn't like ever say that I believed in something when there's like flaws. In my opinion, there's flaws in every religion, there's not one that seems to explain everything.' (JOANNA: female, no religion, religion not very important)

> 'Well I wouldn't say I don't believe in God ... I wouldn't say I've found anything to say that there is a God. I haven't got faith, I haven't not got faith.' (JOHN H: male, no religion, religion not at all important)

Other types of belief

The YOR survey included a question on eight other types of belief that might or might not be expected to show an association with religiosity. Figure 5.5 shows the frequency with which participants overall said they definitely or probably believed in Heaven, Hell, life after death, karma (how you act now affects what happens to you later), miracles, reincarnation (being born into this world again as another being), ghosts or spirits of relatives who have died, and predicting the future from horoscopes and star signs. As can be seen, more people believed in Heaven than anything else, and fewest believed in horoscopes and star signs. Females were more likely to believe in these things than males, particularly karma and ghosts and spirits of relatives who have died.

Further examination of responses showed how young people's beliefs formed two distinct clusters. With the exception of a belief in karma (how you act now affects what happens to you later), which was associated with each of the two separate groupings, the more religious beliefs of Heaven, Hell, life after death, and miracles were highly correlated with one another, as were beliefs in reincarnation (being born into this world

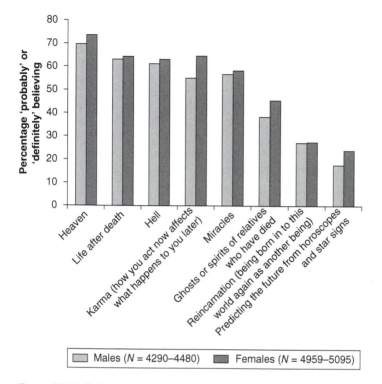

Figure 5.5 Beliefs by gender

again as another being), ghosts or spirits of relatives who have died, and predicting the future from horoscopes and star signs. Interestingly, there was hardly any correlation between the two clusters. Those from Black and Asian backgrounds were far more likely than young people from White backgrounds to believe in the first set of beliefs, while Sikhs were more likely to believe in the second. This is not surprising in the light of the traditional beliefs of the different faith groups (Morgan and Lawton, 2007). While Muslims as a whole believe in Heaven, Hell and life after death, Sikhs do not. They believe in reincarnation and also that individuality is lost after death. Most surprising perhaps is how beliefs in reincarnation and predicting the future from horoscopes and star signs are so closely linked.

In line with these findings, Muslims taking part in interviews pointed to the significance of belief in life after death, and how good deeds, however small, could help to wipe out sins and permit entry to heaven.

'You only follow Islam because when you die that's when the real life starts. It's like a test and we follow our Islam as best we can and after death our real life starts. So this test, if we fail then obviously Hell, then if we pass it will be Heaven. It gives us, it's guidance to follow the right path.' (ANYA: female, Muslim, religion quite important)

'I think it's important to me because obviously in Islam you think of life here as a temporary state, you're not here for that long. Obviously you die and you go back to God. So I think of it like I'm here to worship and then when I die, I go back to God. So what I do here is really important as it determines if I go to Heaven or Hell. What was the question?' (PAPASMURF: female, Muslim, religion very important)

Non-Muslims also talked about the after-life. A few, labelling themselves as Christian, showed some scepticism while others seemed to have some belief in it, especially when confronted by death.

'That there is no worries and no problems, your soul is just resting, it's just free from all troubles and hatred and killing and . . . ' (SHAKIRA: female, Catholic, religion very important)

'And that's probably the time in my life when I've most thought about religion in like a believing way (thinking someone close who had died had gone to a better place was a source of comfort)'. (KYLIE: female, no religion, religion not at all important).

Not many young people talked about karma although those that did generally recognised its importance.

'Well I'm quite a big believer in karma, and I believe if you do good, good things happen to you . . . I think it's all about a person's mindset. . . . You'll get what you deserve at the end of the day.' (STUART: male, no religion, importance of religion not specified)

'If you have dreams on sunrise, because that's the first prayer of the five prayers, if you have a bad dream or a good dream at sunrise, it's a sign for you, a sign for you that something bad is gonna happen, good is gonna happen. Or if you see a snake in your dream, for example, that means one of your friends or one of your own close people is backbiting you.' (SYED: male, Islam, religion quite important)

Belonging to a faith community

A sense of belonging to a faith community can occur at local, national and global levels. Most important might be the neighbourhood place of worship, a more overarching but still country-wide concept of affiliation with a group of people holding similar beliefs and values, or a global identification as typified, for example, by the worldwide Christian church or the Islam notion of the ummah linking Muslims worldwide. Young people in Mondal's (2008) study were sceptical of this notion, given the divisions within Islam and lack of unity. Even the most devout did not seem to feel an affinity with the ummah and one suggested it was because he felt he was a completely British Muslim. Another said how being around English people at work and in the community meant he did not particularly subscribe to a worldwide Islamic identity. One female said she felt more affinity with the ummah since she started wearing the hijab. In other words, she had a greater sense of belonging once she had her identity kit (Goffman, 1959) and her Muslim identity was made more visible. Lewis (2007) also challenges the frequent assertion that Muslims of different ethnicities feel they belong to one worldwide network.

To get some idea of the views held by the YOR survey population, respondents were asked directly whether or not they felt they belonged to (a) a religious group in their area and (b) a worldwide religious community. In terms of their responses, Muslims and Sikhs stand out in definitely feeling they belong to a wider group, in both the local and global context. However, once the impact of gender, ethnicity, family members born in the UK, research location, school diversity and books at home have been taken into account, there is little difference between Muslims and Christians. Figure 5.6 illustrates the differences in this respect between Christians and Muslims in the three research locations with Christians split into those from White and non-White backgrounds. Although Muslims are more likely to report belonging, the differences between them and the non-White Christians are not striking, especially in Hillingdon and Newham. Generally speaking, these data do not provide strong evidence that young people felt part of an 'ummah' that is distinctively different from what may be experienced by those from other faith groups, such as the global Catholic congregation.

Belonging to a wider religious community was nonetheless highly valued by many religious young people. They talked during interviews about how 'you feel united as one' and how it makes you feel 'part of something bigger' and 'like you've always got someone'. Being able to trust others who shared similar beliefs and values, and learn from those who were more knowledgeable, were important aspects. Overall, belonging to a religious community could make young people feel safe and supported within the community and give them a sense of identity and a reference group. In Mead's (1934) terms, their identity was reinforced and validated by the support of co-religionists who acted as significant others. Indeed

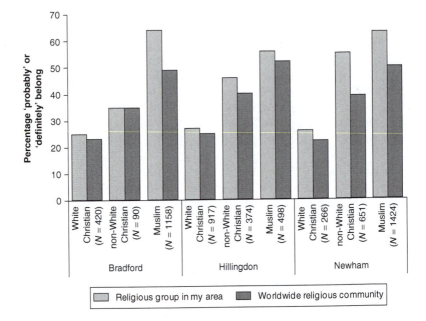

Figure 5.6 Belonging to a religious group locally and worldwide, by faith group and research area

for many it seemed to be the most important and best part of religion. This was acknowledged even by those who were not strongly religious themselves.

> 'The church is your family.' (GARY: male, Christian, religion very important)

> 'It gives you like a source of support. Like I know, well I don't know that much about Islam, but like if a young person in Christianity was having an issue they could go talk to the priest or whatever it is. There would be a definite source of support kind of thing.' (DEAN: male, Christian, religion not very important)

> 'Yeah but when I go back to the temple there's loads of Sikhs there. You feel really that you are integrated because they share the same sort of beliefs. It's really helpful as well because you learn things from them as well that you wouldn't know.' (RIDA: female, Sikh, religion very important)

'Generally because we're all praying, because we all face a certain way at the same time, and because it's at the same time like in Bradford then everyone's doing it at the same time. And it's just like on Eid and stuff, and people go to the mosque . . . people that you don't even know, you hug them and shake hands and wish them well. And it just gets rid of all this bad stuff and brings everyone together. It just feels really nice.' (SIFA: female, Muslim, religion very important)

It was fairly common for religious young people to discuss their own understandings, behaviours, beliefs and practices with reference to the wider religious community, often in a fairly uncritical way. For Muslim Strict Adherents in particular, there was strong emphasis on the collective ('We do this, Muslims believe that') with little recognition of their individual agency, and suggesting limits to accommodation between Islam and liberal individualism. For young people this religious community might be local, national or global, and connections could be strengthened by undertaking voluntary work or staging local events. As discussed in Chapter 4, young people's feeling of connection to communities could also be enhanced by travel to other places, such as their homeland.

Both religious and non-religious young people could feel that belonging to a religious group encouraged segregation from other groups in society, reinforcing a possible incompatibility between a specific religious identity and liberal individualism. Members of religious groups might not mix outside these groups and thereby isolate themselves from those not sharing their beliefs. Furthermore, as some young people pointed out, there could be divisions within religions as well as between religions. However, not all religious young people felt part of a wider community and a few specifically described feeling excluded.

'I think it's just mainly because of my background, because that's where I came from, that's why I feel like I have a link with Sikhism, and also because of the school, because I've come to a Sikh school. But I wouldn't really say that I'm part of . . . I wouldn't feel as if I am part of the Sikh group of people necessarily.' (ORIONTHI: female, Sikh, religion important in some ways but not others)

Others, in addition to Rose who 'worshipped' football (see Chapter 4), supported Durkheim's alternative view of religion in pointing out that belonging is not just about faith, but that activities such as music, sports and fashion could bring people together in much the way suggested by Beaudoin (1998).

'In general, like I think music you know brings a lot of people together, fashion, clothing, it brings people together. Things like football and sport. So it's not just religion. I think things like that, like other things, other hobbies and things that people have, bring you together. I think that's what makes a community because that's a local thing. It's not like you always meet up with people around the world that are just the same religion as you. You're probably more likely to see people in your area that support the same football team as you and that's what brings you close or you know, people that you see at the local library – it brings you close as a study group or something. So there's other forms of community, it's not just religion.' (SHARON: female, Sikh, religion important in some ways but not others)

All the same, non-religious people were particularly likely to feel they were missing out on that feeling of belonging.

'But um . . . one thing that I think I'm missing out on is . . . like you can't go to church to meet people, kind of things like that. So I may be missing out on like people of a certain religious belief who could be friends.' (JACOB: male, atheist, religion not very important)

'I was just about to say, like, for me would be, yes feeling like you're not really part of a community . . . Like I said before with the, with the sort of not being part of a community, sometimes. But mostly I just, I don't know, the freedom sort of tops that in a way.' (JOHN SMITH: male, no religion, religion quite important)

Public and private practice

Although some authors (Francis and Kay, 1995; Francis, 2001) have reported a clear correlation between church attendance and beliefs, young people taking part in YOR interviews often suggested that events at places of worship, whether churches, mosques or gurdwaras, were not just about praying but also ways of bringing the family and community together. They were about a shared identity developed through doing things together. This seemed particularly true through the shared celebration of festivals (e.g. Eid, Diwali, Hajj, Christmas Eve church service) and activities such as fasting. Some Sikhs were explicit in saying that coming together was more important than the religious meaning of events and 'we don't need to label religion as religion, if you are doing it for that family time'. Young people who had no specified religion still appreciated the value of religious festivals such as Christmas and occasions like weddings or christenings because they brought families together.

'I think we are the younger generation. It's like you forget why you are going, it's more we are going to be with our friends. And I think everyone just likes the atmosphere more and the vibe of it more than remembering more the whole principle of it and remembering that it is the Guru's birthday, or are we are doing it for the Sakhis?' (SHARON: female, Sikh, religion important in some ways but not others)

'I don't know, it's just like everyone gets together and you see like family that you haven't seen for a while. But then like there's people all over the world that celebrate it as well. So just like it's a worldwide thing, like there's not many things that a lot of people in the world are at like the same time.' (JOANNA: female, no religion, religion not very important)

Prayer was also important for most young people religious to some degree. Its many purposes and meanings included being a vehicle to ask for help, guidance and forgiveness, proof of the existence of God that helped to feel closer to him/her, a spiritual experience that encouraged well-being, an opportunity to show gratitude, and a way of bringing luck. A young Christian said there were essentially four types of prayer: to praise God, to give thanks, to ask for forgiveness and to ask God for things you might want or need help with. In common with public practice, prayer could reinforce feelings of unity with other members of the religious community.

'It's like when everyone's praying we're all doing it to one place across the whole world. It's not only in England, it's like the whole world is doing it to that one point in Saudi Arabia . . . And if you are having a rough time, say for instance someone was really ill and stuff, you can like pray for them to get better.' (ANYA: female, Muslim, religion quite important)

'I don't take time out to pray but in particularly bad situations, well not bad but stressful, like just before I sat an exam, I just sit there and just close my eyes. I think it's just a way of calming down for me. I feel quite bad sometimes really because I only ever do it when I am like in trouble, but never just say thank you for anything. It's just normally when I am asking for help.' (SARAH: female, Catholic, religion important in some ways but not others)

There was less consensus about where and when prayer should take place. Young Muslims were particularly likely to report the importance of prayer and the expectation that they should pray five times a day. Although most Muslims in the survey said they prayed, the qualitative accounts made it clear that they did not always manage five times every day. This is in line with findings from other studies of young Muslims in Britain (Sahin, 2005).

Many proponents of the secularisation thesis have proposed that religion has become more private in recent times, with people increasingly expressing their religion how and when they want to. This reflects the notion of individuation and Davie's (2005) thesis of a shift from obligation to consumption. Although the YOR study was cross-sectional and unable to examine trends over time, it did ask survey respondents about the frequencies with which they prayed and read alone and with others. Figure 5.7 presents the findings. There is a tendency for all groups to say they pray more alone than with others. Whereas Christians are more likely to read with others than read alone, the reverse is the case for the Muslims.

Further examination of the data revealed gender differences among Muslims but not among either White or non-White Christians. Among the Muslims, males were more likely than females to both read alone once a day (56% versus 48%) and read with others at least once a day (48% and 40%). These findings are complex and are not able to clarify the public versus private religion debate.

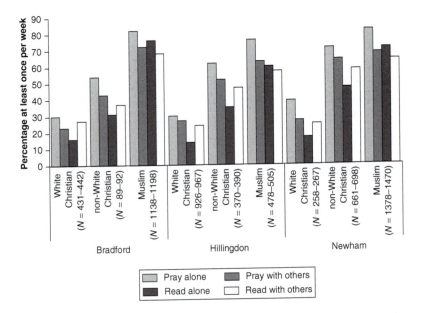

Figure 5.7 Praying and reading alone and with others, by faith group and research area

It is of course impossible to fully distinguish between public and private aspects of faith, and the view that religion includes elements of both was widely held. Religion generally has a communal aspect and, as suggested above, belonging can be central to religious identity. Nonetheless, many participants in interviews held views on the relative merits of public and private prayer, with proponents on both sides. Those who particularly valued public practice felt a more significant spiritual connection, and felt safer, when engaged in public practice than when they were praying on their own. They said it is 'easier' to be religious when you come together with others who share your beliefs, reinforcing both Durkheim's (1912) emphasis on rituals for shared values and collective identities, and the importance of other people for sustaining mutual identities (Mead, 1934). In these senses, religion has more personal meaning and can strengthen beliefs when enacted in company. Young people made comments such as 'praying with others motivates me to pray' and 'praying in a place of worship is more meaningful than praying at home'. Many also talked about the peacefulness of places of worship.

> 'The worship places, if you go there you feel connected with everyone that goes there 'cos that's like your religion. Like you're just with them people and so feel kind of safe in a way.' (KIKI: female, Sikh, religion very important)

> 'When I go I feel like all my troubles have gone. . . . It's just like going, spending a hour in church after like with the priest talking about God and all of that, I just feel that I have been released from everything. But I don't know if everyone else feels like that.' (RHIANNA N: female, Catholic, religion very important)

Not everyone agreed, and some participants thought there was no need to go to a place of worship to be able to pray and be religious. These said religion was experienced, for the most part, as a private and personal relationship with God, reinforced through personal prayer and rituals. As already mentioned, there are those for whom the most significant other appeared to be God. Private prayer could be more 'devout' and meaningful than public prayer that was more like 'showing off'. One young Sikh found it important to talk to God in her mind. Young people with these views talked about praying on their own at home even though they might sometimes have difficulties motivating themselves.

In these cases participants strongly rejected the notion that religious identity was determined by what you show through public practice (i.e. outer religion), and that showing religion equated to stronger faith. For them, private practice and a private relationship with God, or inner religion, was more 'authentic' or 'true'. This was especially the case for Sikhs who emphasised that God was all around, and for Muslim females.

> 'But really it should be your inner self, you understanding it yourself and you practising it yourself, not for anybody else and not proving to anybody else.' (SABEEMA: female, Muslim, religion very important)

Believing and belonging

The relationship between believing and belonging has attracted attention in the literature with claims of both 'believing without belonging' (Davie, 1994) and 'belonging without believing' (Francis, 2001). The YOR survey data provide an opportunity to explore these propositions. Table 5.3 shows that, overall, there is a strong association between believing and belonging among the young participants in the study. Almost eight in ten demonstrate a concordance between the importance of these two forms of religious expression and only one in five suggest discordance. Of those, the vast majority indicate believing without belonging, and only a very small minority report the reverse. Not surprisingly, the highest proportion of believers but not belongers is found among the Flexible Adherents while the greatest proportion of belongers but not believers are Pragmatists. Those who believe and belong are most likely to be Strict Adherents and those who are least likely to find either form of expression important tend to be Bystanders.

Whether or not religion was important in their lives, many young people taking part in interviews did nonetheless refer to taking part in religious activities without believing in God or some higher power. Some, even those with no religion or who claimed to be atheists, said they might attend religious services, either occasionally or regularly, to join in with their family even if they would not go on their own accord. It seemed as if they were taking part in these activities to keep others happy, to maintain family tradition, or because they enjoyed them, and not because they felt a commitment or sense of belonging to the faith group itself. Festivals and praying could

Table 5.3 Importance of believing and belonging within the survey sample (%) ($N = 8634$)

		Importance of believing		
Importance of belonging		*Yes*	*No*	*Totals*
	Yes	38	2	40
	No	19	41	60
	Totals	57	43	100

be important in bringing the family together and maintaining identity and cohesion, but this did not necessarily mean that rituals took on a sacred significance in a Durkheimian sense. Sometimes young people were open about their feelings in these circumstances, although at other times they said they kept the truth to themselves. A few specifically remarked that they were not sure people should practise if they do not believe.

'I have attended a few church weddings over my life – which are my favourite of all the religious festivals. It's a lovely occasion and even if the people, like me, aren't complete devout Christians and completely religious, the joining of two people who love each other is nice to see. Also, despite not being majorly religious myself, there still seems to be something much more special and committing about a marriage in a church rather than in the registry office – it just seems much more permanent in a church, as it is in the eyes of God.' (LEON B: male, Christian, religion important in some ways but not others)

'I've been to church before, even though I've never been forced to go like or anything like that, and I have enjoyed it. I don't think I'd go all the time. I just think that you should be able to go when you want to go, when you feel like you need to go, or anything like that.' (MIA: female, religion not specified, religion not very important)

'The main place of religious significance in my area is the church where every Sunday a service is held. I have only ever been in the church twice: the first time was for my sister's christening, an event which for me was important because all of my family had gathered to celebrate my sister's birth. This is a rare occasion where most of the family are together, therefore you have to enjoy it while you can! This event was also special to me because I got the opportunity to read out a poem about sisters, which I had personally chosen, to the congregation.' (ANNETTE: female, no religion, religion not very important)

There may also be an instrumental aspect to practice, and participants told of those they knew who were baptised to allow them to get married in church, or parents who attended church on a regular basis to enable their child to attend the Christian school. In these instances it is likely that neither believing nor belonging was predominant.

Following religious scriptures

For some highly religious young people, and mostly Muslim Strict Adherents, although also some Christians and Sikhs, personal identity and understanding of religion was closely linked to the scriptures. Reading the Qur'an was important to many young Muslims in strengthening their beliefs and sense of discipline, promoting calm and peace, and making them feel closer to God. One participant quoted extracts from the Qur'an to rationalise tragic events, saying that Allah (God) tests his people to see if they are continuing to believe or losing faith. Others challenged cultural rules and misconceptions about Islam, or justified wearing the hijab, through scripture. The Qur'an was also used to give identity to God.

> 'I think when you're reading the Qur'an, and you're reading an anasheed and stuff like that, you just feel that one step closer to your God. And I think that's what's really important, just to have that feeling. I think that's what keeps some people going, because, you know, sometimes I just think people that don't have a religion, I kind of feel like, you know, they don't have that.' (MUNISA: female, Muslim, religion very important)

> 'I think the best way to describe him (God) is one of the hundred and fourteenth chapter of the Qur'an which is Zurid Laas which says he is the "one and only".' (MALCOLM: male, Islam, religion very important)

It was not uncommon, however, for some Muslims and Sikhs to read holy books in languages they did not fully understand. For example in Islam the Qur'an was written in Arabic or Urdu and for Sikhs the holy book was written in variations of Punjabi. Some young people took great pleasure in the experience of reading or listening in these languages because they felt it was more 'authentic' and gave them the pure intended meaning while the English translation was only an interpretation. Others, however, pointed to practising without understanding and sometimes said they found this personally problematic: it allowed room for individual interpretation when they wanted to be able to get the meaning right to follow the teachings correctly. These, who tended to be Muslims or Sikhs, indicated they had never had the meaning of certain practices explained and so followed rules, and carried out rituals or practices, without fully understanding the purpose or meanings behind them.

> 'I think this one is more important, I think this Eid is called Eid al-Addha, so there's a story behind this Eid um um it's about . . . I'm not really sure about the story.' (FATIMA: female, Islam, religion very important)

> 'I never used to really eat beef but I never knew why. And now it's like my mum says if you are gonna eat meat you might as well eat all types of meat. Don't pick and choose, you know you either eat it all or nothing sort of thing which is fair enough. You can't pick and choose, you can't say my religion says you can't eat this but you can eat that.

And it's like no, you are either a vegetarian or you are not.' (SHARON: female, Sikh, religion important in some ways but not others)

A few young Muslims felt that obligation often overrode consumption for young people like themselves when it came to praying and the scriptures. They acknowledged that agency was unlikely to be involved and that the consequence could be a lack of understanding or personal meaning.

> 'There is like practice and then there's believing. Like some people will go on like a pilgrimage or like even read five namaz, but they don't know why. They just do it because they're told to. They don't understand properly and like if probably they had the choice not to, they wouldn't.' (SHEZA: female, Islam, religion very important)

> 'I think it's beneficial to be within a group because you don't feel alone and that people will be experiencing similar feelings at the same time, also. But I think sometimes, especially within some of the Christian celebrations, there's often things that turn into like a mass hysteria when there's maybe like hundreds of people gathered together and you sometimes wonder if people feel like they're forced to act in a certain way, because there's just so many people doing the same thing. You know, for instance, some people raise their hands in worship and some people begin speaking in tongues and you wonder if it's just a mass hysteria rather than people actually feeling it. They feel obliged to join in.' (KATIE: female, Christian Protestant, religion very important)

Whilst there was often emphasis on pure or intended meanings of scripture, many young people indicated that everyone has their own individual interpretations, particularly when applied to the contemporary context. For example Muslims felt the Qur'an could be used to justify killing or other acts of extremity whilst other people interpreted the same passages in very different ways. A Christian female voiced the view that some young people may be influenced to adopt extremist views by reciting texts they do not fully understand. Another also found a focus on scripture unhelpful.

> 'Like people who really, really follow it, I think it does make them a little bit know it all. They think they are exactly right and anything that is not what they are doing is wrong.' (DEAN: male, Christian, religion not very important)

Gender differences and religiosity

Davie (2007a: 231–2) reports how differences between men and women in the Christian West is 'one of the most pervasive findings in the literature', but that the significance of gender does depend on the specific religion in question. So far as Christianity is concerned, she says that differences pervade belief and practice and are found in most denominations. These emerge from empirical study of young people in both the UK (Francis and Kay, 1995; Kay and Francis, 1996; Francis, 2001), the US (Smith et al., 2003; Wallace et al., 2003), and Australia (Mason et al., 2007). Research findings also suggest girls are more interested in Bible stories than boys (Freathy, 2006), Anglican girls are most likely to enjoy Sunday school, probably because of the type of 'girl friendly' activities on offer and the female profile of the staff (Levitt, 2003), and junior school boys from New Age religious groups and Evangelical Christian groups are most questioning of these religious beliefs and their implications (Erricker et al., 1997).

For religions such as Islam the picture is more complicated. Because of a lack of engagement and/or exclusion from many mosques, young Muslim women inevitably show different patterns of religious expression from their male counterparts, and may engage in prayer less frequently than boys (Sahin, 2005). Religious practice may be gendered for other reasons too. Several female Muslims from Bradford and Newham, for example, told how females were not meant to pray during menstruation as prayer should be a pure and clean practice. They told how girls sometimes pretend they have periods to avoid having to pray, and that teachers and relatives are usually too embarrassed to question the reality.

YOR survey data found less conclusive evidence of gender differences than many other studies. Almost three-quarters of both males and females believe that boys and girls are equally religious and, among the rest, there was a small but insignificant tendency for boys to report that boys were more religious and for girls to say they were more religious. There were no major differences in perception by either religious group or ethnicity, although members of all religious groups were slightly more likely to say that girls were probably or definitely more religious than boys. Few significant differences also emerged in relation to differences between males and females in responses to questions about their own religiosity.

Changing times

The discourses of modernity, with attendant values of liberal individualism and personal agency, and consumption rather than obligation, were recognised by most YOR participants even if devout followers of their faith. Society and its values are changing, many young people are confronted with competing pressures from friends, family and the community, and schoolwork and other activities are time-consuming. Moreover, science and technology are ever more prominent, as highlighted by a thoughtful e-Journal account of changing times by one YOR participant (Figure 5.8). Becoming or remaining a Strict Adherent requires conviction and determination and many young Muslims in the YOR sample could better be described as Flexible Adherents. This was a contemporary response to Westernisation and, authorised by prevailing values of freewill and liberty, allowed them to remain true to their religion but also concordant with their peers and current youth culture.

'As a general rule, the following of religion is declining and liberal, secular attitudes are increasing as we go down the generations. My grandparents are deeply religious – going to church every Sunday, and to some weekday services, and religion plays a big role in their lives – but this is likely a result of their more strict religious upbringing. My parents do seem to have a belief in God – but their following of religion seems to be slightly less strict, for example they won't go to church every Sunday – just occasionally. Finally, my generation (me and my brothers) are much more liberal in our views and much more lax in our following of religion – my older two brothers never attending church, and me only attending on special festivals/occasions, e.g. Easter and Christmas.

'Also, views on matters which religion gives "moral guidance" on (e.g. abortion) change as we go down the generation. My grandparents agree with the Catholic view of no to abortion, euthanasia and homosexuality. However, my parents take a more liberal attitude, saying those who need an abortion/euthanasia should get one in extreme circumstances. Me and my brothers are much more liberal yet in our views. I believe if somebody has a terminal illness and they have no quality of life – euthanasia should be allowed. If a woman is raped, the baby will have no quality of life – abortion should be allowed (although I don't agree with women who just didn't use protection, get pregnant then have an abortion). And I think people only live once and homosexuality is not a choice and people should be free and happy to have a partner to love whatever their gender. Therefore it can be seen that down the generations attitudes have become much more liberal – probably because of a more religious upbringing and a broader education. I imagine the grip of religion will continue to weaken as we go down the generations.

'Furthermore, my generation has been born into a time period of immense scientific research and discovery and receive excellent science education in schools (compulsory up to GCSE). Some of the things taught – such as the theory of evolution – lead to questions being raised. Whereas years ago, when these things were kept off the curriculum, people had less of the full picture in the information they got to make their own informed and balanced decisions about religion and God.' (LEON B: male, Christian, religion important in some ways but not others)

Figure 5.8 Changing times: one participant's view

'Well I think for a lot of people there's this one thing where like a lot of people don't follow. You know, like prayers, five time prayers is like compulsory for Muslims to read, and a lot of Muslims like in the Western culture, you know, like Western society now, are struggling to follow and to pray their five time prayers, and because when they're in school they'll be like, "Oh we're in school so we don't have time", and when they're in work, "we're in work and we don't have time". And they'll be out shopping and then they'll say, "Oh we haven't got time", so basically they'll just be making excuses and stuff. But personally I've kind of like, from a young age, I've always kind of adapted to reading my five prayers. So I don't find it much of a problem. I'll just read it wherever, anywhere. And, but I think for a lot of Muslims, that is like a major problem for them.' (FALISHA: female, Islam, religion very important)

There was much discussion, especially in Bradford, of differences between modernised Muslims and those referred to as true Muslims. Modern Muslims did not necessarily pray five times a day, and although they might be 'proper Muslims' for the month of Ramadan they were modern Muslims the rest of the year. Many modern Muslims use drugs and alcohol, which are banned by the faith, but still go to Friday prayers and believe. Some young people thought modern Muslims, whether or not this term described themselves, might become more devout as they got older. There was a general feeling that it was everyone's choice how they practised their religion, and where there was criticism it was as likely to be by modern Muslims of true Muslims as the other way round. The modern Muslims might criticise the true Muslims for not joining in with friends while the true Muslims might be critical of modern Muslims who seemed to think saying their prayers was what mattered, but who ended up doing more Western than Islamic things. Education was said to be the most important thing for the modern Muslim whereas for the true Muslim it would be Islam before anything else.

'Modern Muslims think that being a Muslim is just praying five times a day, and it's just like reading the Qur'an and stuff. But it's actually a lot more than that. It is more about faith and what you actually believe. A true Muslim has to be described as someone who's got faith in Allah, but no doubt at all in their mind, and you can't say that for a lot of people nowadays. Because the stuff that's on the news and stuff, it makes you doubt why that evil suffering and stuff, it makes you doubt like the existence of God. But a true Muslim doesn't doubt that at all.' (WAZIR: male, Islam, religion very important)

It was generally agreed, however, that most Muslims are modern up to a point as 'there's only very few that would actually stick to Islam and like not do any of the Western stuff'. It was suggested some use the word Muslim more for identity than to describe their way of life. Going to work clean shaven to make a better impression was also seen as Westernisation. Nonetheless it is always a question of balance.

> 'Religion holds more importance because I have an element of freewill and control. You know, it's my spiritual journey, my decisions and sort of I'm not going to make a decision on my ethnicity, it's not that I can change from one to another. But with religion, I will make mistakes, I will learn from them, I will grow as a person. It's something that's very sort of personal and it's always growing. Even if you've got no religion, you're always going to grow and hold on to that belief or change it later on.' (RASHA: female, Christian, religion very important)

> 'So then in the Qur'an or in the books and stuff, it will say, if you're smoking you get all the problems like heart problems and all that stuff. But then, as I say, if you still choose to do it, it's for your own good, it's your own choice. And that's when it will, it will give you everything, give you the good side and give you the bad side to it and then you make the choice of what you really want to go in to. And that's what it's like, in fact you still make a choice with your free will.' (HAMMERA: female, Muslim, religion very important)

The YOR study is cross-sectional rather than longitudinal and thus not able to chart the degree to which views and expression of religion, especially for those identifying with minority faiths such as Islam and Sikhism, are undergoing change. There were indications, nonetheless, that many young people in these groups were to some degree picking and choosing the elements of religion they liked and suited their lifestyle, and exercising both rational thought and personal agency in the process. At the same time it was evident that the power of religion remained strong and that additional constraints operated. While perhaps the majority of young people show signs of becoming consumers of religion (Davie, 2007a) in a very real sense, it may be a statement too far to say they treat religion as a supermarket of choice (Bauman, 2000).

Summary

The concept of 'being religious' has no unitary meaning. There is no necessary match between the affiliation young people may give themselves, whether they practise religion in a public and/or a private way, their sense of belonging to a religious community, and their beliefs in God or a higher power. Religion underpins the whole life and existence of some young people but assumes a lesser or minimal significance for others. Many young people in modern day Westernised society are best described as religious 'in their own way'.

Overall, religion is most important for Muslims in the YOR sample. Ethnicity is also significant, particularly in distinguishing between Christians from White and non-White backgrounds. As suggested in the previous chapter, there seems to be an additional *locality ethos* whereby religion is more important in Newham than the other research settings even when other factors are taken into account.

Religious labels also have more significance for some groups than others: it is suggested that they can often mean more for those from Muslim than Christian backgrounds. Public and private forms of religion appear to serve different purposes. Some young people value private prayer as an opportunity to engage in a personal relationship with God, while others emphasise the importance of practising publicly to bring family and the religious community together and feel that they 'belong'. Nonetheless, and for all religious groups, believing is what appears to be most important. The basis for belief is, however, variable and a distinction can be drawn between young people (mainly Muslim Strict Adherents) who show a strong reliance on religious doctrine and teaching as a rationale for everyday life, and others who give prime importance to individual agency and personal experiences. Believing without belonging is much more common than belonging without believing.

Times are changing and the impact of Westernisation and modernity on young people is apparent. The prevalent discourse of liberal individualism, and the growing presence of 'modern Muslims', suggests that neither public nor private practice in its traditional form readily fits into a modern lifestyle.

The rationale for everyday behaviour is taken up in more detail in the next chapter that considers three areas that can be influenced by faith position. These are morality and purpose in life, bodily care and presentation, and dating and expectations of marriage.

6   Religion and everyday life

While Durkheim was most concerned with the function and impact of religion, Weber (1965) was more interested in its content. In particular he examined how religion influenced the daily lives of followers and how behaviours associated with a particular faith position changed as people moved into different contexts and spaces. This aspect of his theorising links closely to Goffman's (1959) account of the presentation of self in everyday life and how setting affects impression management. In relation to young people in multi-faith areas, these theories give rise to key questions such as similarities and differences between and among members of different religious traditions in patterns of everyday life, and whether indeed individuals behave consistently whatever their faith position. Moreover, what might account for observed behaviours?

Earlier chapters have already charted many of the ways in which the everyday lives of young people in the Youth On Religion (YOR) study were influenced by their faith positions. For some religion was all-encompassing and strongly linked to beliefs, public practice and private prayer, while for others it was linked to only some of these things or perhaps simply to observance of specific religious rituals at particular times and on particular days. For yet others it meant very little. Later chapters consider the influence of religion on schools young people attend, friends they make, areas they live in, and people they mix with. There is a myriad of ways in which religion can affect everyday life.

This chapter focuses on three areas of everyday life that can have strong links with religious traditions (Morgan and Lawton, 2007): morality and purpose in life; bodily care and presentation including dress, treatment of the body and diet; and dating and expectations of marriage. Young people's reports on their attitudes and behaviours in these areas are examined in relation to the impact of religious and cultural heritage, modernity, agency, social pressures and setting, with distinctions drawn between Strict

Adherents, Flexible Adherents, Pragmatists and Bystanders. The ways in which gender affects the daily expression of religion is also considered.

Morality and leading a 'positive' life

Almost all young people taking part in YOR interviews, whatever their age, gender or faith position, talked about how they led their daily life and the values they followed. A largely consistent story emerged in which thinking about and helping others, and doing the 'right' thing, featured strongly. This finding underlines the discourse of liberal individualism permeating young people's accounts throughout this book and mirrors the conclusion of other studies. The concept of Moralistic Therapeutic Deism (Smith and Denton, 2005; Smith, 2010) has been introduced to reflect the prevailing posture of American teenagers who seem to believe that being a good, moral person is central to living a good and happy life. Smith (2010: 41) writes how 'This "religion" . . . consists of a God who created and orders the world, watching over human life on earth. This God wants people to be good, nice, and fair to each other, but does not need to be particularly involved in their lives, except when he is needed to resolve a problem. Being happy and feeling good about oneself is the central goal in life.' The authors highlight how Moralistic Therapeutic Deism is a position between strong traditional faith and no faith, and that it represents the metamorphosis of Christianity rather than secularisation.

Similar findings were reported by Savage et al. (2006) who studied 124 young people, aged between 18 and 25 years and from mainly White backgrounds, who were attending youth clubs, colleges and universities. These authors coined the phrase 'happy midi-narrative' to describe the predominant characteristics of the sample who were concerned with being happy and with the here and now. They showed communality, although largely on a small-scale and in relation to 'me, my friends and my family'. Although they might identify with Christianity, religion remained predominantly in the background of their lives.

The YOR survey explored these notions further among young people living in multi-faith communities, first asking participants how important it was to them to have a purpose in life. Durkheim (1912) is amongst those to advance the view that religion gives meaning and purpose to life, and it was hypothesised that more religious members of the sample would be particularly likely to ascribe importance to this notion. The survey findings by faith group are presented in Figure 6.1.

More Muslims than any other faith group saw having a purpose in life as very important, although differences between faith groups were not marked. There was no difference between Christians from White and Other ethnicity

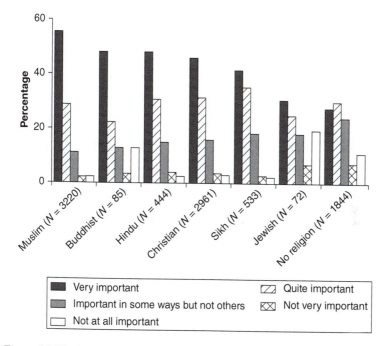

Figure 6.1 The importance of having a purpose in life by faith group

backgrounds in this respect and, with the possible exception of those from Jewish backgrounds (who represented only a small part of the overall sample), religious young people were somewhat more likely than those with no religion to stress its importance. There were no significant differences between males and females, but age did have some effect, with older participants finding a purpose in life more important than younger participants. A generation effect was also evident: the more family members born in the UK, the less important was having a purpose in life. The number of books at home made an additional difference, with more books associated with greater importance. Given other reported associations, these findings are in the expected direction.

Table 6.1 confirms the clear relationship between importance of religion and importance of purpose in life. Most young people see a purpose in life as either quite or very important, but this becomes more likely the greater the importance of religion. This supports other similar findings of differences in the strength of purpose in life between young people from a variety of Christian denominations and those without a specified religion (Francis, 2008). Other writers have pointed to the significance of religion, among

Table 6.1 Purpose in life in relation to importance of religion (%)

Purpose in life	Importance of religion		
	Not at all/not very important (N = 2528)	*Important in some ways (N = 1484)*	*Quite/very important (N = 5440)*
Not at all/not very important	18	8	4
Important in some ways	22	23	11
Quite/very important	59	69	85

other factors, for identity as 'the frame within which they can determine where they stand on questions of what is good, or worthwhile, or admirable or of value' (Taylor, 1989: 27).

Whether or not having a purpose in life was seen as important, almost all young people, regardless of religiosity, stressed the importance of leading a positive life. They also talked about morality or other comparable concepts and many, mainly Muslims but occasionally also Christians, Sikhs and Hindus, listed moral guidance among a range of personal benefits associated with religion. It could serve as a guide to behaviour and self-presentation in society, a purpose in life, a comfort zone, someone (God) to talk to and share burdens with, and a source of pride. It might also help in being a better person and doing good deeds.

'I think it's probably my upbringing as well. Just going through primary school and everything. It's how people treat you. I think you kind of know what's right and wrong anyway, without having religion there to tell you.' (JESS: female, no religion, religion not at all important)

'If I wasn't a Muslim, I don't know, I'd just be sat here not knowing what to do. Being Muslim, it gives me a whole list of rules and everything that I need to follow and how I need to talk . . . As a Muslim, you're supposed to be good to the other person and, like she said, a duty. It's a duty but then again it's your own responsibility and it's your own personal choice. So as a Muslim, I'm given a choice, but within that choice, I'm given the rules so that I should just choose the right path . . . And the right path will lead me. In this life I'll get the good things, and after I die I'll get the good things.' (HAMERRA: female, Muslim, religion very important)

Both religious and non-religious young people told how their everyday life was guided by a personal sense of right and wrong, with the main difference being that whereas the first group attributed their values to their religion the second group stressed the influences of society, upbringing and family. To explore this question further, the YOR survey asked participants to rate the importance of a number of possible influences on their decisions about what is right and wrong. Parents were most often said to be very or quite important (87%), followed by friends (66%), God (62%), scriptures (53%), religious leaders (48%) and teachers (44%). Apart from parents who were important to everyone, members of faith groups, as well as those from Asian and Black backgrounds, were particularly likely to mention God and scriptures, and females and White participants were more likely than males and Black participants to cite friends. In addition, Asians cited teachers more than other racial groups, and older pupils mentioned teachers less often than younger pupils. These findings are in line with what might be expected, and are particularly interesting in highlighting the widespread manner in which God is regarded as a significant other by many of the more religious participants.

Participants in YOR interviews elaborated on these findings. Strict Adherents would follow religious guidance and rules very strictly, and Muslims frequently drew values from religion and stressed how it was important to follow the prophet and do as he tells. They told how the Qur'an states what is right and wrong, sets values and norms, and leads one on the 'right path'. The afterlife is a crucial consideration and it is important always to be on one's best behaviour as 'if you're religious you're supposed to think or fear that judgement day can happen any second'. Many Christians expressed similar views, saying they learned about right and wrong from the Bible and the Ten Commandments and that religion provides limits, boundaries and very practical guidance in everyday life.

> 'As a Jehovah's Witness, many things that other people wouldn't think twice about, I do. For example, today I went to stay at my friend's house . . . (and) we decided to watch a film. But a film which is morally right. Films that don't have sex or violence in them. Films that don't use swear words . . . Some people would say that we are being over cautious and they are right. But by being over cautious I avoid doing things that may displease God.' (TEQUILA: female, Jehovah's Witness, religion very important)

There was again an emphasis on how religion helps one to 'grow up to be a good person, kind and caring to others' and that 'good behaviour makes sure you go to Heaven'. According to one female Christian for whom religion was very important, '(it's) no good just thinking that (you) can make up tomorrow for what (you) did wrong today, because tomorrow may never come'. Some Flexible Adherents were less adamant. A young Buddhist stressed how her religion provides teachings rather than rules, and that their purpose is to make her a better person.

Non-religious Bystanders, and some Flexible Adherents, did not attribute their moral codes to religion but were just as clear about their personal distinctions between right and wrong. These young people emphasised how they set their own boundaries and follow a morality that comes from within and is influenced by society, family, school, friends and particularly parents. Many stressed that they may have the same values as religious young people, such as 'I'm not going to kill someone', but that they had not come directly from religion. Their moral values may have come from the law, which in turn had roots in religion in the past, but behaviours such as not stealing were also 'common sense'. Non-religious young people greatly appreciated not having to follow religious guidance as it gave them the opportunity to learn from their mistakes, develop their own moral codes, and decide on what they personally think is right and wrong. They suggested their values were freedom, living life to the full, justice and happiness. In many ways they reflected a pragmatic philosophy of life (Rock, 1979) whereby the development of understanding occurs through actions and a process of trial and error.

Many links were made between religion, morality and caring behaviour, particularly by Sikhs who told how they were taught to volunteer and help others from a young age. Muslims too said that religion encourages them to engage in voluntary work and that helping others will increase reward later. Christians made similar comments, and it was noted that the Bible tells one to give to charity and provide for poorer people. One female Christian did much voluntary work with an 'extra little push' from God. These associations were explored further in the YOR survey where participants were asked how religion influenced their everyday behaviour in relation to treatment of others and treatment of the environment. The findings are shown in Figure 6.2.

A considerable proportion of young people in religious groups, notably Muslims, said that their religion affected how they treat other people and how they treat the environment. For all groups (apart from the small Jewish sub-group), treatment of other people was more affected than treatment of the environment. Moreover, and when everything else was accounted for, both types of behaviour were more likely in Newham than in Hillingdon or Bradford, more likely the more books there were in the home, and less likely the more family members had been born in the UK, confirming the association between these factors and religiosity. They were, however, less likely among pupils attending the more ethnically diverse schools, supporting the general conclusion that, within multi-faith areas, greater inter-faith mixing is linked with weakened adherence to religious tradition.

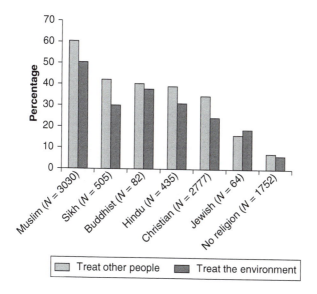

Figure 6.2 Treating other people and treating the environment: affected by religious beliefs 'quite a bit' or 'a lot'

Issues of morality are nonetheless complex, and young people charted the conflicts they could face in reconciling traditional religious views on matters such as gender equality, homosexuality, euthanasia and the role of women in the church, with the more liberal values they encountered on a daily basis. Furthermore, moral issues are not always clear-cut, as recounted by one devout Christian. Is moving something at home in fact stealing, and what should the response be to a direct question about whether you like someone? She pointed to decisions surrounding telling a lie or the truth and commented 'And I know that I've gone wrong in places before with lying with just simple things when put under pressure'.

Bodily care and presentation

Young people, from a range of religious backgrounds, described how religion influenced the way they presented and treated their bodies. This could mean wearing the hijab for Muslim females, not cutting hair and wearing a turban for Sikhs, wearing a cross for Christians, carrying a sword for Sikhs, not drinking or smoking for those from a variety of faith positions, cleansing the self before prayer for Muslims, and not eating certain types of food for several groups. The mechanisms mediating religion and behaviour varied and included enhancing the visibility of religion with the aid of an identity kit comprising dress codes, behaviours and other props to construct and display the desired impression (Goffman, 1959), following traditions prescribed by scriptures and other religious teachings, family and cultural expectations, and personal values and agency.

As Tarlo (2010) vividly illustrates in her book on *Visibly Muslim*, religious symbols and dress serve an important role in maintaining and conveying identity. She charts the recent history of the hijab in Britain, highlighting the complexity of motives shown by Muslim women who choose either to wear or not wear it. Reflecting 'politics, ethics, aesthetics and belonging' as well as faith, the hijab can be a fashion statement that allows the wearer to both observe modesty as required by Islam and reflect modern Western fashion (Lewis, 2013). Tarlo points to the relevance of Goffman's (1959) concept of impression management when wearing the hijab and relates how multiple identities are reflected in changing dress according to setting. The importance of the hijab for visibility is emphasised by women who are not straightforwardly Muslim but who still decide to wear it: 'For them, looking Muslim is a question of invention rather than conformity to inherited tradition'. Both Tarlo (2010) and Mondal (2008) agree that reasons for wearing the hijab are changing, and that tradition is giving way to personal identity and choice. In Davie's (2007a) terms, religion is becoming something to be consumed rather than followed through obligation.

Change is also underway among young British Sikhs who may or may not conform to traditional cultural and religious values in relation to identity, hair and the turban (Singh, 2010). As with the hijab, young men may wear the turban to be like their friends, to act as an ambassador for their culture and religion, because it makes them feel more like a Sikh, to keep their families happy, or because they feel comfortable with it. Others however may choose not to wear it if they think it may lead to ridicule or mistaken identity as a Muslim, or because they do not feel 'ready' for it.

The YOR study investigated patterns and meanings of adherence to religious tradition in relation to bodily care and presentation. Figure 6.3 presents findings from the survey on whether what young people eat and drink, and what they wear, including clothes, jewellery and other adornments, is affected by religious beliefs. Muslims were most affected by their religious beliefs in these areas, with six in ten influenced in what they ate, and almost half in what they wore. Those from Jewish, Hindu, Sikh and Buddhist backgrounds were affected to a lesser extent, and Christians to a very limited degree. In line with the findings for treatment of others and treatment of the environment, the more ethnically diverse their schools, the less young people's religious beliefs affect their everyday behaviour in these ways. More family members born in the UK had a similar impact. Once again this

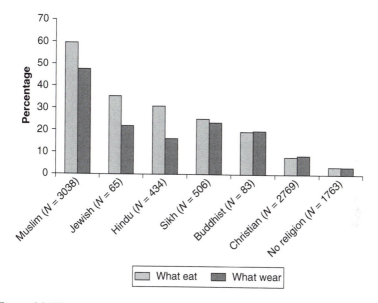

Figure 6.3 What young people eat and what they wear: affected by religious beliefs 'quite a bit' or 'a lot'

provides suggestive evidence of a Westernisation effect and a weakening of religious tradition in multi-faith settings.

Participants in the interviews and discussion groups elaborated on these findings, particularly in relation to clothing. Many described how practices related to dress and religious symbols were important signifiers of their personal and religious identity. These items of dress and religious symbols were, according to Goffman (1959), their identity kit.

> 'I wake up in the morning, the first thing I do is reach over, glasses, cross on, there you go, and then I can get up and get dressed. I can't go out of the house without my cross on. But then, after that, it's usually pretty much the same thing, converse trainers, jeans, sweatband, hat, t-shirts, a shirt, a tie . . . ' (TED: male, Christian, religion very important)

Several reasons for displaying religiosity were given. Many young people said they liked to express their own religious identity in a visual way as a reminder to themselves of their own religiosity: a visible religious symbol or item could help the wearer think before they act. It was also important for displaying identity to others. According to several young Muslim females, wearing religious dress enabled them to present themselves as ambassadors 'speaking up' for their religion. It also meant that they, as well as Muslim men wearing full beards, were likely to be seen as more religious. Nonetheless, as several pointed out, it did not necessarily follow and a person wearing a hijab 'could be the biggest drug dealer in Bradford'. Styles of dress also distinguished between groups or sects within Islam.

> 'People are judged by image. There was a girl who wore the hijab and she's covered and everyone thinks "wow, she's an angel". Whereas if they saw someone with their hair open . . . they'll think "oh, she doesn't pray, she's more Westernised".' (SIFA: female, Muslim, religion very important)

Those who valued the visibility of religion fell within both the Strict Adherent and the Flexible Adherent categories. In the first group were Muslims who felt strongly that if you wore a hijab you should wear it all the time. It did not make sense to them to be religious one day and not the next, or alternate between front stage and back stage. Interestingly, this view was echoed by participants without a specified religion who were critical of Muslim women who sometimes wore the hijab and sometimes did not. They felt that religious clothing should be worn either always or never, and seemed to feel that it was not fair otherwise. They suggested that some people took the hijab off if they felt their hair looked particularly good, or if a specific outfit seemed better without it. This clearly caused tensions for young people who felt Muslims were being treated more favourably but were taking advantage of their privileges. One female complained that a Muslim had not explained her inconsistent behaviour and said that 'if they were just to explain it and the reasons why, then that would promote more understanding'. There could be resentment if certain young people were allowed to wear religious jewellery, such as the Sikh bracelet, while others could not wear a Christian cross, for example. In these ways young people experienced the politics of entitlement in their everyday lives.

It was, nonetheless, argued that religious clothing is sometimes worn for practical rather than religious reasons. It was pointed out that the hijab and full veil were designed to be worn in Arabic countries to counter the 'sun, dust and the sand', or that kara bracelets were sometimes worn to hurt others or offer protection rather than for any real religious reasons. Sikhs themselves intimated that bracelets can be worn as a symbol of authority, to show off, and as an aggressive symbol. Some young people clearly valued the fashion element of the hijab, personalising their scarves with decorations and matching them to their outfits.

For Flexible Adherents, however, practices depended on where young people were. They lived in multiple realities and it was common for them to say they would wear religious clothing in particular contexts, such as to

Friday Prayers for Muslim males or to church for Christians. It was considered respectful to dress appropriately in religious places, whereas there was much more scope for choice in other settings. In particular, some young Muslims said they preferred not to wear the hijab if they were with friends, particularly if these were mainly White friends as they did not want to stand out. A few said they would do their hair, rather than wear the hijab, and dress up for weddings and other parties. Others said they preferred not to look visibly Muslim in non-Muslim places where they could feel much more self-conscious. For some it was a case of experimentation.

'I don't always dress like this. I'll dress, I'll have loose fitting clothes sometimes, and then other times I'll just wear normal jeans or whatever. It's kind of like I'm trying to make that effort of doing what my religion says, but I can't kind of like throw myself into it straightaway. I'm seeing how it's like and what people's reactions to it are, but at the same time I wear my normal jeans and whatever as well. So it's kind of like I'm experimenting, you know, type of thing.' (FALISHA: female, Islam, religion very important)

These Flexible Adherents tended to think it was fine for a Sikh to cut their hair or for a Muslim not to wear a hijab and did not think these outward signs were important. For many, it was what was 'within' that was far more significant. One young Sikh said it was not necessary to show everyone and say 'Look at me, I'm so good and stuff'. As reported elsewhere in this book, participants often felt their relationship with God was private and only He should be the judge. Young people said things like 'God's looking, he knows if I'm religious or not' and 'I'll wear it (hijab) for God, not for anyone else. I'm not going to wear it because you tell me to'. They stressed how everyone is individual and it is hard to jump to firm conclusions simply on appearances.

'I know people who don't wear a scarf, but read namaz five times every day without fail. I know people who do wear a scarf and do not read any namaz. I know people who wear a scarf and read all their namaz. I know people who don't wear a scarf and don't read any namaz.' (HESSA: female, Muslim, religion very important)

Strict Adherents would not be flexible in these ways and a small number were adamant they should dress and treat their bodies as set down in biblical texts. As one female put it, 'the Prophet describes that (women) should just show their face, hands and feet and nothing else' and so if you were not wearing a hijab and die the next day 'what are you going to say to your

Lord?' They did not allow for multiple realities and did not distinguish between front and back stage.

Many participants from all religious backgrounds discussed how religion informed how they treated their bodies. Muslims, Hindus and Sikhs talked about foods they were not supposed to eat, even if they were not always quite sure what they were not allowed and why, and young people from all backgrounds discussed drinking alcohol and smoking. Again it seemed that the most devout restricted themselves to varying degrees. So-called Strict Adherents tended to observe the edicts of religious texts and explain their behaviour by saying such things as 'we're not allowed to drink alcohol because God gave us our body as healthy and purified', or the Bible says 'treat your body like a temple', while Flexible Adherents tended to admit to being liberal in these respects.

Although Tarlo (2010) suggests that dress decisions taken by young Muslim women are influenced by much more than issues of modesty, protection from male attention does undoubtedly remain important for many. A strong theme emerging from the Muslim sample in the YOR study was that religious clothing covering the body, and which was not tight or figure-hugging, protected them from the male gaze. Only family, fathers or future husbands should be able to see them without religious clothing, and participants who chose to wear a hijab commonly felt better treated by other men as a result. Employing an identity kit to portray their religiosity served a positive function in this instance.

> 'The way Muslim women dress reminds and advises women to cover beauty except for what appears naturally. So when I go outside, I cover my body. And we believe it's not for men to look at. Personally, when I'm covered I feel that when I'm spoken to, it's for my opinions, thoughts and values and not because I happen to be displaying the idea of beauty that the West blasts on television.' (NAOMI: female, Muslim, religion very important)

This feeling was not restricted to females, and one young male specifically said that men should also wear loose fitting clothes as 'like it stops us from temptation'.

Strong cultural expectations, particularly in Bradford, for Muslim females to wear a hijab and Muslim men to wear religious dress at Friday Prayers, reinforced these views. Young people were not entirely sure where this edict emerged from, and did not think it was explicitly mentioned in the Qur'an, but talked about the pressures placed on them. Some felt other religious people, particularly older age groups, would look down on them and think 'shame on you sort of thing' if they did not conform. These pressures were not always fully tolerated.

'The people in my community would view me taking the scarf off as a sin, whereas people of my generation, we kind of are a bit more flexible.' (NAIHLA: female, Muslim, religion very important)

'It's not something I personally experience ... I don't wear a headscarf ... but if I'm walking down the street from school or something and other women will see me, she'll be like "Oh my God, look at her, she's not wearing a headscarf". And then they'll start talking and gossiping ... It's a bit stupid because it's like women do that – Asian women do that a lot. They see you walking down the street with a boy and "Oh my God, she's talking to a boy", "Oh my God, she's doing this, oh my God, she's doing that". It's just like, you know what, it's a modern society, just get over yourself. I think the rules need to be changed.' (ZERINA: female, Muslim, religion very important)

In line with increasing Westernisation and the personal agency discourse, individual decision-making on when, where, how and why young people begin and continue to wear religious clothing was in evidence. There was a prevailing feeling that wearing a hijab was a personal decision and something that should be done only from choice. As one young Muslim said, 'I believe that until you're truly from your heart, that you're wearing it with the right intention, there's no point in wearing it. If somebody's forcing it upon you to wear it, what's the point of that?' Although participants identified adulthood as a time when a Muslim female would be expected to wear a hijab, and pointed to the family and cultural pressures on them, they were generally keen to emphasize that it was their own choices that were paramount.

'Um, the headscarf, I started wearing it quite late. I was supposed to do it as soon as I reached puberty, like when I started my menstrual cycle, that's when we have to. You know, it's compulsory. Basically, if you don't wear it, there will be punishments for us. I started wearing it when I was in Year 10, when I felt more comfortable about it and not because my parents were always telling me "Oh, you know, you have to wear it".' (FATIMA: female, Islam, religion very important)

It seemed that parents generally supported personal choice, often because they had wanted to take their own decisions when they had been young themselves. All the same, there did seem to be some illusion of choice in the implicit expectation on the part of parents, particularly mothers, that daughters would at some point wear the hijab. Comments such as 'Well you'll wear it when you find that you want to wear it, when you wear it for God, not for anyone else really' were reported.

Despite these assertions, there were a number of Muslim females who felt that others were being forced to wear the hijab by their parents. They agreed it was common for girls to wear it to school but take it off and put on make-up as soon as they arrived. Nonetheless some young people said others assumed they were forced to wear religious dress when in fact the decision had been their own. As has been observed throughout this book, young people are keen to justify their actions through recourse to personal agency.

Dating and marriage

Religious and cultural expectations play an important part in opportunities for dating members of the opposite sex (Jacobson, 1998; Lewis, 2007; Yip et al., 2011). This was particularly true for Muslim young people in the YOR study. As dating was forbidden by 'rules', Muslim girls rarely talked about boyfriends and one female specifically said she would not be allowed to hold hands with boys. Young Muslim males described how hard they found these restraints, one noting that asking a girl out would mean losing your own and the girl's respect. This was challenging for young men as there are girls 'all over the place'.

> 'Like you'd walk through a street and you see a pretty nice girl, and you know you should actually shield yourself, you shouldn't actually look back at her . . . There's a saying from the Prophet, he said you're only allowed the first glance at a girl, the second glance is not allowed. So like when you look around the corner and you just notice someone, you can't look back a second time – if it's a girl especially.' (TAZEEM: male, Islam, religion very important)

Although Sikhs were more liberal, young people were discouraged from dating too young and, when they did, faced strong pressures to go out with somebody from a similar background. As Simmel (1903) might have predicted, participants reported difficulties of meeting somebody in a tight-knit community without everybody knowing and gossiping about it, but could maintain secrets in the greater anonymity of the city. As a result it was common for Sikh young people to meet boyfriends and girlfriends at some distance from home. Similar findings are reported from other research (Watt and Stenson, 1998).

> 'It's like a big deal to like have a boyfriend, or be like going out with boys. So because you know you don't normally bump into people in London, it's just the easiest place to go to get away.' (MAYA: female, Sikh, religion fairly important)

This Sikh girl disregarded cultural expectations and had a white boyfriend but said she would be in serious trouble if her parents found out. She had visited his family but keeping him secret from her parents had caused some tensions between them.

Young people from a range of faith positions intimated that they would date or marry only somebody with similar beliefs. A Christian female quoted the Bible as saying that 'unbelievers shouldn't be unequally yoked together', and another female without a specific religion said she would not marry someone from a different religious background as her family was more important to her than whom she might date. Some young people emphasised the importance of marrying within the faith for the sake of future children. They said both they and their parents felt it important that children grow up with similar views to their parents.

> 'My mum thinks so. Mum says it (my future husband) has to be Catholic otherwise you're obviously going to have different views on how to bring up the children and just how you live overall. So I don't know, because, I don't know.' (EMMA: female, Catholic, religion important in some ways)

For their own part, young people did not always see religion as an important factor in choosing a marriage partner, and instead stressed aspects such as love and personality.

> 'Most people I speak to about this particular issue always want to marry someone who is Muslim. But I feel kind of different really, because in my head I don't agree with that. I would want someone I want. I wouldn't really mind what religion someone was, because there are people out there who are really religious but they are not the best of people. And there are other people who don't believe in God at all and they are really nice talented, really good people.' (MIRIAM: female, Islam, religion very important)

Mondal (2008) highlights the issue of marriage as one producing particular tensions between young Muslims and their parents, and this seemed confirmed in the present study. Young people had absorbed the idea that 'marriages between people of different religions simply don't work' as 'a common religion establishes a broad base of commonalities and prevents a number of potential problems'. They reported that parents were commonly very concerned about whom they might marry and would 'go mental' if they wanted to marry outside their religion. This was as true for males as for females.

The issue of gender inequalities between men and women in choosing marriage partners did however arise during discussion with a group of

Muslim females. They said that while men are allowed to marry out of Islam, and the women they marry must convert, Muslim women cannot marry outside their religion. There was, however, some confusion during a discussion group about whether or not a Muslim man could marry a Christian woman. Young people explained that gender inequality followed from expectations on a family to follow the father's religion, and a wife to follow her husband's. One female Muslim suggested 'they think men would have it in them to get the wife to convert but women wouldn't have it in them to get men to convert'. Some participants also felt there would be an impact on the children if a woman married out of Islam, and that the Muslim tradition would not easily live on. Nonetheless, and although men are allowed to marry out of Islam, they are supposed to marry women who are religious (Christian, Jew or Muslim) rather than those who are not.

> 'Yes, and basically if they do, she didn't have to convert, but she has to be a good Christian or a good Jew, or a good Muslim who he marries. And then she doesn't have to convert, because their family can follow his religion. So typically, you know, you do follow your dad's religion. So that's where the logic is. And then for a woman to marry a non-Muslim, because obviously the kids are going to go with the dad's side or whatever, and it's going to be too complicated.' (NADIA: female, Islam, religion very important)

Marriages are still arranged for many young British Muslims in contemporary Britain (Mondal, 2008; Sardar, 2008; Malik, 2010), and several YOR participants reported that finding partners for children, to ensure they do not marry out of caste, is a strong topic of conversation when parents get together. As found in other studies (Din, 2006), none of the young people in the YOR study said they were in favour of an arranged marriage for themselves, although they did know people whose partners had been found for them and seemed to joke about the possibility of it happening to them. Overall they seemed to have vicarious experience of both positive and negative outcomes. They thought some young people still accept arranged marriages because they are reluctant to challenge their parents' wishes. This is supported by Baumann (1996) who found that although almost four in five young people in his study said people should marry the partner of their choice, only a quarter said they would actively go against their family's wishes and marry either cross-caste or cross-religion. In practice it appears, as Lewis (2007) suggests, that the close family is very significant when it comes to determining marriage matches. Nonetheless times are rapidly changing and young people in the YOR study suggested arranged marriages were becoming less common, in part because families are smaller and there are fewer cousins or other appropriate suitors to marry. One Muslim female summed it up by saying 'We've got more Westernised views, we don't believe in that as much as the older generation do'.

Summary

Religious identity is often demonstrated in everyday life, not only through religious practices but also through a sense of morality, clothes and personal presentation, treatment of the body, and the food and alcohol consumed. Views and experiences of dating and sexual behaviour, as well as expectations of marriage, are also relevant. Young people reported how religion could influence their lives in all these ways. Apart from the sense of morality, these respondents came mainly from Muslim or Sikh backgrounds, and to a lesser degree from Christian and other faith groups. Young people also reported on some of the ways in which religion impinged differentially on males and females.

The findings on morality endorse the account of liberal individualism and its adoption by young people. Being a moral person, understanding the difference between right and wrong, and respecting others, characterised participants whether or not they were religious. The distinction was that the more religious tended to attribute their attitudes to God whereas the non-religious said they stemmed from society, family and upbringing. Similar findings have emerged from other studies in less diverse settings and it is noteworthy that they also arise in multi-faith locations.

Many young people report how much everyday behaviour, such as how they choose to dress, serves to make their religiosity visible. They say how this could act both to remind themselves of religious rules and to let others know of their affiliation. Others, however, provide different reasons such as keeping others happy or feeling comfortable. Strict Adherents are more consistent in following religious tradition in their everyday behaviour than Flexible Adherents. These are more influenced by context, peers and personal choice and say that what is most important to them are their faith values and 'what is inside'. As in other areas of religiosity, many young people say they exercise reason and agency in deciding how to present themselves and conduct relationships with members of the opposite sex – even if expectations and pressures to conform to religious tradition are apparent.

In the next chapter the theme of negotiation is taken forward with a focus on the realm of the family. Particular interest is paid to family patterns of religiosity and ways in which faith position is or is not passed on. Five case studies of young people from mixed family religious backgrounds are also presented.

7   The family and its influence

The family is the context for primary socialisation (Berger and Luckmann, 1966) and parents are significant others during the early years for most children. There is clear research evidence that this key role of the family extends to the religiosity of children as they grow up, and before the influences of friends and society gain in importance (Hyde, 1990; Kay and Francis, 1996; Gunnoe and Moore, 2002; Smith and Denton, 2005; Mason et al., 2007). As illustrated in Chapter 4, the Youth On Religion (YOR) study also found the family to be a key influence on religiosity, at least for the early years, when young people acknowledge they are strongly influenced by their parents' faith position. For many it continues to be important as children become teenagers and make their own more personal explorations and commitments.

Young people growing up in multi-faith communities are subject to a wide range of influences besides the family, stemming from their interactions with peers as well as their immersion within the real and virtual modern-day society. How far do they maintain the faith positions of their families or develop their own identities within these contexts, and are intergenerational continuities more evident among some groups of young people than others? The answers to these questions provide incidental evidence for the reality or otherwise of secularisation in modern day Britain. This chapter examines the many ways in which religion has a family focus, and the impact of parents on their children, from the perspectives of young people taking part in the YOR study.

The role of the family

It has already been shown how families are almost always critical for children's early faith positions, and how 42% of YOR survey participants say their families influence their religious beliefs (including not having a religion) either quite a bit or a lot even in their teenage years (Figure 4.1). In addition, 64% of respondents report how families are important in helping them understand about religion. The significance of the family in this respect is second only to Religious Education (RE) lessons, and slightly ahead of friends, who come a close third. Ipgrave and McKenna (2008) also found that family, alongside school, was cited most often as significant for hearing about religion/other religions.

The strong role of the family was also evident from what young people said in YOR interviews and discussion groups. Talking about religion was a case in point and emerged as 'a natural thing' for many, particularly those who were strongly religious. These outlined how family discussion was often about their own religion, although sometimes about issues that arose from different faith positions. Discussion might be about messages from the Bible, Qur'an or other religious text, and the purpose seemed often to reaffirm belief. One young male Sikh would ask parents for 'basic stuff' about religion but his grandmother for 'proper religious stuff' because 'she just knows everything'. Some participants talked about discussing different religions to seek understanding of similarities and differences, while others were more focussed on attitudes associated with religious creeds.

'So the older you get, the more you try to debate and you get to know your religion more. So it makes you more aware of your religion.' (SHAZIA: female, Islam, religion very important)

'Some nights I just sit down with my Mum and Dad and we talk about everything. We talk about God and I ask questions. And my Mum teaches me. And she buys me books and tells me to read to know more about my religion.' (SHAKIRA: female, Catholic, religion very important)

'Yes – it [religion] probably gets a passing mention every so often and an in-depth discussion monthly. We talk about a range of things such as how much we actually believe and how many Catholic "policies" (attitudes towards abortion, homosexuality, euthanasia etc.) we agree with.' (LEON B: male, Christian, religion important in some ways but not others)

Practising religion together was another way that family experiences were shared, again particularly for those where religion was very important. Praying together, or taking part in religious occasions and celebrations, were regular occurrences in some families but restricted to special occasions for others. Religious festivals and activities could also be appreciated by those without a faith position.

> 'In my family we all go to the same mosque to pray and the days we don't go then everybody prays at home . . . When it comes to namaz time at home we all pray at the same time and the house is quiet and peaceful. My brother who is 5 and sister, 7, they don't know how to pray yet but because the rest of us in the family are praying they are not allowed to make noise until we have finished. Therefore, listening to music or watching TV is banned during that time.' (NAOMI: female, Muslim, religion very important)

> 'My grandparents practise their religion together, but without the rest of the family, attending church every Sunday. The rest of the family only really attends on the big festivals/occasions (e.g. Christmas and Easter). At these times there is a more community feel and the whole family gets together to celebrate at Church for the occasion – we worship together.' (LEON B: male, Christian, religion important in some ways but not others)

> 'Yeah 'cos I think, practising a religion as a family, you're all doing something together, so you're all closer and spending more time together.' (JOHN H: male, no religion, religion not at all important)

Patterns of beliefs

Even if families practise religion together, a key question is whether they share attitudes and beliefs. The transmission of religiosity has long been a topic of interest, particularly in relation to the future of religion. The issue is, however, complex. Brown (2009), for instance, argues that secularisation in Western society is largely due to parents failing to pass faith values on to their children, while Hervieu-Léger (2000) proposes that religious socialisation and transmission are not simply dependent on the family but involve a 'chain of memory' linked to tradition and a vision of the past. Much research in the field has largely bypassed these broader arguments and focused on the similarities and differences in such matters as the frequency with which members of different generations read the Bible or go to church (e.g. Myers, 1966), distinct patterns of intergenerational religiosity within families (Hopkins et al., 2011), or ways in which younger generations influence older generations as well as the other way around (Gallaher, 2007; Hopkins et al., 2011). Many recent studies have concluded that, on the whole, young people tend to be quite similar to their parents in beliefs and practices (Smith and Denton, 2005) even though considerable 'switching, matching and mixing' is likely to occur over the trajectories of their lives (Smith and Denton, 2005; Mason et al, 2007; Putnam and Campbell, 2010).

To contribute to discussion and debate in the area of intergenerational continuities, and their implications for the secularisation thesis, the YOR study explored religious beliefs across family generations. Specifically, the YOR survey asked how similar or different young people's beliefs are to parents and grandparents they see at least once a year. Figure 7.1 shows that there was a high level of concordance. The greatest similarities were shown with mothers, followed closely by fathers and then, not far behind, grandparents: apart from girls and their grandparents, at least half the participants said their views were 'very similar' to those of their relatives. Slightly higher levels of concordance were shown by males than females throughout, although differences were minimal in the case of similarity to mothers.

Looking in more detail at concordance between participants and mothers, Figure 7.2 further shows that 'very similar' views were the predominant pattern. While 57 and 58% of females and males said they held 'very similar' views, only 17 and 14% respectively said they had 'quite similar' views. The

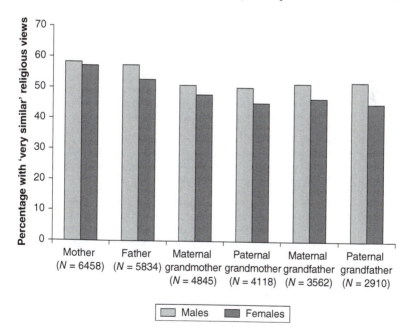

Figure 7.1 Survey participants with 'very similar' religious views to parents and grandparents

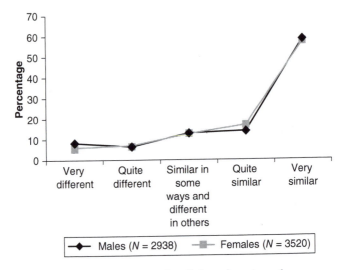

Figure 7.2 Similarities and differences in religious views to mothers

frequency of other responses was even less. Comparable findings have emerged from other studies. Crockett and Voas (2006) found that 59% of young British adults reported similar religious affiliation as their parents, with 54% showing similar attendance levels and 56% reporting similar levels of belief, and Sahin (2005) found that 54% of a sample of 16 to 20-year-old Muslims had a similar understanding of Islam as their parents, whereas 24% did not.

   The qualitative data support the notion of considerable continuity in religious belief and expression between young people and their parents and grandparents, with similarities emerging among those with strong beliefs, less strong beliefs or with no particular faith. In many cases, participants acknowledged the significance of primary socialisation (Berger and Luckmann, 1966) and told how their own faith position was determined by their upbringing, adding that it might have been quite different had they grown up in other families. One young male, who had not yet decided which university he wanted to go to, told of a friend who had been so influenced by his father that he had his whole religious life mapped out while still a teenager. Where participants were not fully clear about their parents' beliefs, or in families without a strong faith position, religion was not a common topic of conversation, and views were not explicitly voiced. Young people in these families nonetheless seemed to think they had broadly similar beliefs and attitudes to their parents.

'I wouldn't be a Catholic if my parents weren't Catholic and my grand-parents weren't Catholic. But at the same time I'm quite free to choose. I don't have to be Catholic if I don't want to, but it does depend on the rest of your family. . . . So it would be strange to be anything else, for starters.' (LIAM: male, Catholic, religion quite important)

'It would have to be my family, because um well if I didn't grow up to be with a religious family, I wouldn't be religious now, like I wouldn't be an Islamic teacher. I wouldn't have bothered to go, I wouldn't have bothered to learn more about my religion.' (AVRIL: female, Islam, religion very important)

'I just think for me like not even as far back as my great grandparents I don't think – nobody in my family is religious. . . . So I've just sort of like developed into not believing in God, if you know what I mean. Because it's never been something that I've had to think about.' (KYLIE: female, no religion, religion not at all important)

'Like obviously if they weren't religious, I would not be religious now. I'd probably be, I don't know, I'd probably be atheist or agnostic or something like that, but I'm not sure.' (INGRID: female, Christian, religion important in some ways but not in others)

'My mother is an atheist as well as all my brothers. So I think that I was very much, yes very much influenced by them probably on this different way of looking at life.' (BONO: female, atheist, religion not at all important)

Not all young people, however, reported religious similarities to their parents. Often this meant that they were Pragmatists who talked about growing up and learning more about the different ways that people led their lives, and were 'just thinking about it and having a look' or cur-rently 'kind of in the middle'. In other cases young people were asserting personal agency and much more actively rejecting the family position or 'going their own way'.

'Cos my parents are Albanian, they're like Muslim, but I'm like Christian. . . . No one's gonna change my mind, but I'm an example of someone who's not the same as everyone else in my family.' (JANE: female, Christian and Muslim, religion very important)

'When I was younger . . . I went to church and everything through my parents. . . . Now I just find it hard to believe that there is anything because there are so many different religions and everything. I find it hard to believe that there is one set of beliefs that everyone should follow or anything like that, or any like supernatural being like God. I can't like get my head around it really.' (RICK: male, no religion, religion not very important)

YOR participants talked about discrepant patterns within their families, such as differences between brothers and sisters. They also said that some family members had more of an influence on them than others. More young people suggested that mothers were more important than fathers in this respect, although there were varying views. Siblings were occasionally mentioned, as in the case of a Muslim female who had been interested only in music until her sister got her to watch a DVD that confirmed her in her faith. Grandparents were also important in many of the young people's families. They were variously said to have stronger beliefs, uphold strong values and traditions, practise their religion more fervently, and have more free time. Some young people said grandparents (almost always grandmothers) were continually telling them to pray and putting pressure on them to go to worship. This is an interesting observation in the context of Durkheim's (1893) descriptions of mechanical and organic solidarity. Might it be that some members of older generations are trying to maintain the common religious traditions found in their homelands and encourage their grandchildren to remain religious despite the pressures of the dominant culture of the country in which they now reside?

'The reason my parents took me to church is because my grandma was really strongly religious and she said he needs to be, he needs to be brought up religiously. But now, that thing might carry on through parents who don't necessarily believe but are still taking their children to church. They're still doing the thing that was done to them and they disliked.' (DEAN: male, Christian, religion not very important)

'I think like if anything my Nan has played a huge part when it comes to like me and religion, not just me actually but with all the grandchildren in my family.' (SHARON: female, Sikh, religion important in some ways but not others)

'My Nan is from the Caribbean so she's really religious, but my mum and my uncles were born in England and they're not that religious. But like my Nana is praying for everything. Like say we're about to eat, "let's pray", before we go to bed, "let's pray", before we go out, "let's pray", when we come back in from where we've just gone, "let's pray", before we go on a plane, "let's pray". So we're praying everywhere.' (RHIANNA N: female, Catholic, religion very important)

'I remember my Nan telling me when she was, she used to be part of the Brownies, the club Brownies, and she said, she joined and then she was told that they had to kind of read things from the Bible. And after that she instantly left because she didn't believe they should be forced to do things. I think a lot of my family members are normally quite critical of it and don't believe in, don't like some aspects of religion. So I think that probably influenced me quite a lot to think that. Yes, be atheist.' (EDWARD: male, atheist, religion not at all important)

Related to similarities in religious belief in young people and their parents and grandparents is the direction of change where this is apparent. The ongoing secularisation debate (Berger, 1999; Brown, 2009) focuses on a decline in religiosity in successive generations but, as already pointed out, this is largely a Christian-based observation. Indeed different patterns have been found for other groups. Snow (2007) mentions research for a TV documentary suggesting young Muslims are more radical and religious than their parents, and Mondal (2008) reported a stronger interest in religion among the young Muslims in his study than among their parents.

YOR survey participants were asked how similar their beliefs were to their parents and grandparents, but not specifically whether they were more or less religious. This latter issue was addressed in face-to-face interviews where a wide variety of patterns was found.

'The way it works in my family is through the generations you are more religious as you go on.' (GORDON: male, Christian, religion quite important)

'Religion in my family is basically, it's like a scale of religions . . . Mum and Dad most religious, grandparents maybe a bit more religious than that, brothers, sisters, religion going down a bit. But we are all religious in our own sense . . . And my nieces, they're still quite young, so I don't know what their generation is going to be like.' (HESSA: female, Muslim, religion very important)

'My parents and grandparents and us, the younger generation, there's no differences . . . because what our grandparents taught our parents is like just passed on to us like the same way. And yes we don't believe in anything else but God.' (ZARA: female, Islam, religion very important)

Influences on transmission

More than half the YOR survey participants report strong familial similarities in religious beliefs while others suggest weaker continuity. Many factors are likely to be responsible for these discrepancies. Smith and Sikkink (2003) review the literature to suggest that greater religiosity of parents, strong relationships between parents and children, and traditional family structures, increase the chance of religious retention, while socially disrupted life course transitions (e.g. marriage, divorce and geographical relocation), and family disagreements about religious beliefs, tend to increase the chance that young people will switch religion or take a non-religious stance. Interestingly, these authors further suggest from their own data that different religious traditions respond to a range of social factors (such as gender; educational attainment; RE experiences; marital status; number of children; location; mobility; strength of faith in family) in distinct ways.

Other commentators believe that parents are decreasingly likely to transmit their religious beliefs and practices to the younger generation (Brown, 2009; Woodhead, 2010) and, although there is no baseline comparison, a report from the British Household Survey (Voas and Crockett, 2004) suggests two non-religious parents are likely to produce non-religious children, but two religious parents only have an even chance of passing on their religion. The YOR study cannot address all these issues but explores associations between familial transmission on the one hand, and faith group, the importance of religion and family generations in Britain on the other.

Links between faith group and mother-child similarity in religious views are shown in Figure 7.3. Muslims stand out as having the highest

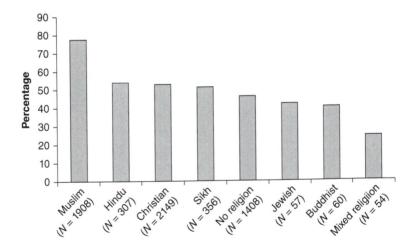

Figure 7.3 Self-reported faith group and 'very similar' religious views to mother

correspondence with those from mixed religious backgrounds showing the least correspondence. (Young people whose parents have different faith positions are considered further later in this chapter.) These findings are of interest in comparison to friendships with peers that also show high levels of concordance for faith values (see Chapter 8). Muslims report the highest levels of similarity (78% for mothers and over 70% for friends) but all faith groups show the same pattern of slightly lower levels of concordance for friends than mothers (see Figures 7.3 and 8.1).

To understand family patterns better, Figure 7.4 further compares the similarity of views between young people and their mothers by both their faith position and the importance of religion in their lives. This analysis is restricted to Christians, Muslims and those with no reported faith, and distinguishes Christians from White and non-White backgrounds. It emerges that similarities are greatest where religion is most important, and this holds within Muslim, White Christian and non-White Christian groups. Effects are, however, strongest in the first of these groups and weakest in the second, confirming the importance of considering more and less orthodox forms of religion separately (Kaufmann, 2010). Further analysis confirmed this pattern whereby the most strongly religious young people report the most concordance with mothers' religious beliefs.

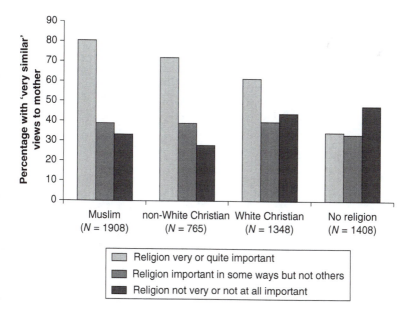

Figure 7.4 'Very similar' religious views to mother by importance of religion and faith group

These findings suggest that strong beliefs about religion, including a non-religious position, are more consistently passed on than equivocal views. Indeed the 8% of males and 6% of females with very different religious views to their mothers were likely to be living in Hillingdon, White, from families where they and their parents were born in the UK, without a specific faith position, and reporting that religion is not important in their lives. This notion gains additional support as both Strict Adherents and Flexible Adherents show more intergenerational similarity in their religious beliefs than Bystanders who, in turn, show slightly more similarity than Pragmatists. Although we do not have parents' views to confirm the thesis, all these findings support the idea that stronger religious beliefs are most likely to recur in successive generations.

The considerable intergenerational similarities found in some families, especially where young people say religion is important in their lives, should not detract from the corollary of the many young people who do not hold the religious beliefs of their families but have developed their own faith positions. Patterns of transmission are only rarely direct and uni-directional, and are more commonly complex and fluid. Hopkins et al. (2011) identified four broad patterns of parent–child religiosity in the current climate, describing these as correspondence (views and values are shared), compliance (young people forge their own path within the family religious tradition), challenge (young people openly question and negotiate religious attitudes and values) and conflict (views and values are not shared). For Woodhead (2010), the notions of challenge and conflict are particularly important, pointing out that young people are not the conformists they once were. She suggests young people often rebel against religion, and are characterised by autonomy and individuality. This analysis applies not only to young Christians but also to young Muslims too who may reject aspects of the religion and culture of their families and communities as well as Western culture.

Length of time a family had spent in the UK seemed to be an important factor influencing the transmission of religiosity. YOR survey participants were asked where they, their mother and their father, were born and a variable was constructed to measure the number of these family members (none, one, two or three) born in the UK (see Chapter 2). Figure 7.5 presents information on the impact of this 'generation' factor on similarities of religious beliefs between young people and their mothers. A clear pattern emerges with a trend away from familial concordance as more family members are born in the UK.

While these findings can be partly explained by the likelihood that less devout groups overall, such as White Christians and no faith groups, are among longer-established families in the UK, and that the reverse is the case for more devout groups such as Muslims and Sikhs, there is an

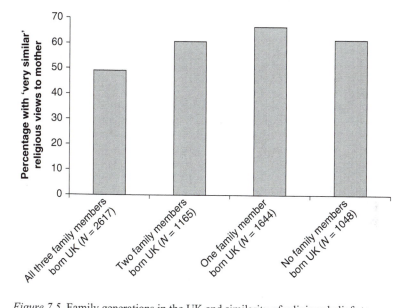

Figure 7.5 Family generations in the UK and similarity of religious beliefs to
    mother

additional 'generation' effect that emerges even when these and other factors are taken into account. This is supported by a trend among the three
most numerous faith groups in the study away from strict adherence as the
number of family members born in the UK increases: the respective proportions of Strict Adherents with one and three members born in the UK are
15 and 3% for Christians, 57 and 48% for Muslims, and 22 and 10% for
Sikhs. These findings provide suggestive evidence that the longer a family
has been in the UK, the more individuated young people become in terms
of their religiosity. There is no direct evidence from the study on whether
members of the younger generation in these families are necessarily less
religious than their parents, although the qualitative data would suggest this
is usually the case. Regardless of specific patterns, it can nonetheless ten-
tatively be concluded that these findings underlie the effects of Westernisation on a tendency towards greater secularisation among minority faith
groups in Britain. Other authors have also discussed differential experiences for successive generations within Muslim groups in Britain (Lewis,
2007). As Mondal (2008) comments, generational change does not simply
reflect pressures from parents or the community, but is also a response to
young people wanting to be different from their parents and having the
opportunity to make their own life choices.

Choice or pressure?

Despite divergent patterns, a striking finding from the YOR qualitative data is that most young people engaged in a discourse of personal agency, emphasising that it had been their choice to follow family practices. Even if they closely adhered to familial patterns of religiosity, they stressed personal agency in determining their identity status. It would have been hard to place many in Marcia's (1980) category of identity foreclosure with the implication that identity was transmitted with little conscious thought on the part of the younger generation. As one young male explained, 'it's kind of silly to believe in something because someone else told you to or someone else believes in it or anything. You should really think of it for yourself.' The prevailing view was that parents taught them about their religion, set an example, and encouraged them to follow family beliefs and practices, but still allowed them choices in the matter.

> 'My Mum and Dad brought me and my brother up with a choice really, they brought us up in a way until the age, I think, of about 12 or 13 with good Christian morals, but . . . they were never going to turn round and say to us "You are a Christian and you're not allowed to be anything else". They were always going to give us the choice.' (TED: male, Christian, religion very important)

> 'My parents have never told me or my brother or tried to influence our opinions, which I think is really important because often people feel like they have to agree with their parents but we should all be free to choose what we want to.' (ROSE: female, no religion, religion not at all important)

It was frequently implied that parents 'showed' young people what to do rather than 'forced' them, perhaps giving 'a little push here, a little push there' but letting the young person work it out on their own. One Christian female said her non-religious parents are 'a bit like "why would you want to?"' about her choice to convert, but let her get on with it. Often, however, the reality appeared more complex in the context of implicit (if not explicit) pressures from families. Young people talked about religious families who say their children can choose but still seem to force them to go to a place of worship, engage in prayer, or be christened into something they dislike. A female Muslim distinguished between families, saying you can tell the difference between girls who are forced to wear the hijab and those who are not. Some take it off as soon as away from home, illustrating how they live with multiple realities (Berger and Luckmann, 1966) and manage their impression differently in family and peer settings (Goffman, 1959).

'In Ramadan recently, this last year, I think you had to get up at like three o'clock in the morning, to close your fast and stuff, and mum would be like, "Oh just read a bit of the Qur'an before you go to sleep," and I'm like, "Oh I want to sleep," so I was forced to read then. But yes, I used to sneak upstairs and go to sleep.' (SHAZIA: female, Islam, religion very important)

Family tolerance might, moreover, be limited. As discussed in Chapter 6, parents often raise strong objections if their child wishes to convert or marry out of their religion or faith position. One Muslim said her father had not spoken to her brother for several years because he married someone he did not approve of, and that he told a cousin who married outside her caste that 'you're not part of our family'. Others expressed frustration at the way parents could interpret religious values, such as staying at a friend's house or having a boyfriend, as described in other chapters. Some were fully aware of the ironies that could arise, and how parents who proclaimed otherwise were themselves affected by Western culture.

'And I sort of saw the bigger picture because it's funny like my mum, she says "Oh, I don't cut my hair" but then she'd like get her waxing done or her eyebrows done. When you're young you don't understand that, but now that I'm older I say to her "You're still removing hair from your body, so you're actually doing it". So I kind of understand it a bit more now.' (MAYA: female, Sikh, religion quite important)

Parents appeared more censorious of girls' than boys' behaviour, particularly when it comes to going out and dating. Sisters told how their brothers got away with more things than they did, and are allowed out in the evenings when they are not. Two Muslim females discussed how 'guys' will also tell you off for doing the same things as them. They did acknowledge, nonetheless, that they faced more potential dangers than males if they did go out alone. A Christian girl queried why women but not men wear hats in church.

'I am seen as more religious than my brother, and I am treated differently because he still gets away with more things than I do. And that's not fair as I don't do anything wrong. So I think they kind of punish me more for doing a little thing (when) they don't punish my brother for doing something big.' (AMINA B: female, Muslim, religion quite important)

Participants tended to be sympathetic to parents who wanted to keep their children within the faith, and acknowledged that it can be quite hard for a parent not to try to enforce their beliefs. One said that parents of any faith position would be unhappy if their child did not share their views, particularly as 'it's quite understandable . . . because if you had a religion that makes you very happy, you probably would want that for your child'. A female Muslim advanced a different argument, talking about the heritage of families moving to Britain from Bangladesh, and how parents forced religion on their children to ensure it was passed on. 'It was like a panic', she said. Another appreciated her mother's feelings but also her patience.

> 'With my family, Mum probably does wish we were all more religious because being descendants of the Prophet, we really should be. But she knows we'll all come round to it eventually, because that's just what most people tend to do. When you're younger, you want to mess about and you want to just think "I've got my whole life ahead of me, blah, blah, blah". When you're older you think, "Right, I do want to get into Heaven, let's try and work for it".' (HESSA: female, Muslim, religion very important)

In general young people understood the pressures on them, even if they might rebel against them at the time. A few even suggested that parents should be more forceful in ensuring that young people followed family tradition in practising religion.

> 'I think again it's the Western way, the Western way that we've become too accustomed to it, because I think our parents weren't probably traditional enough in raising us to be proper devout Muslims. So maybe that's why . . . they send you to mosque and stuff and say to learn about Islam, but I think they don't enforce it as much as they should. I don't think it's just my parents, but any parents should like enforce it more and teach their kids, because most of my knowledge I get from my friend, not my parents, but it should be the other way around.' (WAZIR: male, Islam, religion very important)

> 'When I stop doing my prayers and stuff like that then I notice I become really lazy and just start goofing off at home, stuff like that. And it's just like I might get shouted at by my parents or something like that, you know "You're going to go to Hell. Go round to the mosque, do your prayers" and you know just be a good person, stuff like that. . . . Yeah, they just want to make sure that I'm a good person . . . And I just want to make sure that by being a good Muslim, hopefully I should be a good person through doing that. So yeah just make sure that I stay religious. So yeah. And also they don't get sent to Hell. It's like if your kids mess up, that's your fault. Yeah they drag you down.' (LUCAS: male, Muslim, religion very important)

Many, however, agreed that too much pressure from parents could be counter-productive and lead to rebellion or covert behaviour. The reality was illustrated by a Sikh participant who had a White boyfriend and met him in central London rather than risk comments and disapproval within her own community. 'It's really common for like people to sneak around, and go see their boyfriends or girlfriends . . . But I think it's getting a little bit more lenient, slowly it might fade away'. Implicitly she acknowledged the ability to become anonymous and maintain secrets in Western urban contexts (Simmel, 1903) and took advantage of these possibilities.

The tensions between choice on the one hand and pressures and expectations on the other, were described by many young people from a variety of faith backgrounds. One young person said the onus was on the younger generation to smooth the way and that 'It's the way you handle the situation' that is important, while another suggested that you have to have the courage to tell parents if you feel really strongly that you do not want to be religious any more. A more common strategy, however, seemed to be to go along with aspects of religion to keep families happy. Young people told how they followed family religious tradition to avoid upsetting their parents even if they did not believe themselves. They often felt they owed it to their parents to conform. According to one young male Sikh, not following your religion of upbringing 'would kind of wipe out all the efforts made'.

> 'Actually I was just thinking the only time I would go to church is for family reasons . . . If my Mum is going there or my Dad is reading in church . . . because I know it means a lot for him for me to be there. He watches me play sport and whatever and he likes me being there. And it's like we all go to church with my granddad, not because we have any particular urge to go there, but because he likes, you know, essentially showing off his grandchildren. It's just nice for him to be there. So it's like the family reasons for it.' (DARREN: male, Church of England, religion important in some ways but not others)

> 'I think like religion is followed a lot in my house at home . . . Like my Mum prays so then like we . . . as the girls, we know we have to pray as well now. So when my Mum prays we all pray as well. But like if my Mum doesn't, then we'll just kind of just sit there and just try and get away with it, if you get me.' (ZERINA: female, Muslim, religion very important)

The case of mixed family religious identities

Census data reveal increasing trends in the UK towards unions between partners from different faith groups, and a rise in the children and young people growing up in these families. From the limited research available, it seems that different parental approaches in these cases are to instil a child's sense of identity in an individualistic way, without a focus on their mixed background, or to stress the faith position of one parent over that of another (Caballero et al., 2008). None of the 35 families in the study in question stressed the child's mixed identity in relation to religion. In other research, however, young people from mixed-faith backgrounds valued the multiple realities available to them (Arweck and Nesbitt, 2010).

Young people reporting more than one religious identity numbered only 74 in the YOR survey, and it is therefore not easy to draw firm conclusions on this group. The majority (54) were in the Hillingdon sample, with only 6 and 14 in Bradford and Newham respectively. Half were Asian, compared with 10, 12 and 25% classified as from White, Black and Mixed Ethnicity backgrounds. Most were Flexible Adherents or Pragmatists, and almost six in ten said religion was important in their lives. Seven in ten were female and, interestingly, there was no clear pattern according to the number of family members born in the UK. Not surprisingly, these young people with mixed family religious identities were considerably less likely to report strong similarities in religious views to their parents than the sample as a whole. Although there was a slight tendency for them to report closer similarities to fathers than to mothers (33 versus 24%), the most numerous response was that they were 'similar in some ways but different in others' to both parents.

More information on the implications for young people from families reflecting more than one religious tradition came from the qualitative part of the study. Although hardly any participants initially described their backgrounds as 'mixed', more identified themselves in this way as interviews progressed. Mixed religious identity was more common in the London than the Bradford samples, and most participants from Hillingdon and Newham in this group talked about issues such as the dilemma between choosing one religion or maintaining affiliation with different religions, taking part in multiple religious practices, the commonalities or differences between religions, possible identity confusion, and mixed religious identity as a possible source of tension within the family. The case studies given in Figure 7.6 illustrate some of the issues they raised.

These participants exemplified the role of personal agency in religious identity formation. Although confronted by certain family pressures amid multiple realities, all gave the impression of being consumers rather than constrained by obligations. If anything, perhaps having a 'mixed' identity gave them more opportunities to exercise personal choice than were experienced by peers from backgrounds with more consistent faith values. Other young people reiterated some of the points made in these case studies,

JANE (female, Christian/Muslim, religion very important)

Jane identifies herself as Christian, and has a Christian mother, but also has an Albanian background with her father and relatives on his side of the family 'properly' Muslim. As she says, 'I'm a bit stuck in the middle. But I'm a Christian'. Nonetheless, and even though 'it's not like I'm pressurised to like be Muslim or anything', she does practise aspects of Muslim religion, and had fasted this year of her own free will even though 'I only lasted for about ten days'. Jane is, however, constantly told that she should choose one religion, with even her parents saying 'you can't do both'. Her reaction is 'Oh my gosh' as she says she has seen both sides and finds the religions 'really similar'. She does not see being influenced by more than one religion as problematic and cites her grandfather who 'is like me, like one day he'll be reading the Bible, and the other day he'll be reading the Qur'an'. She also says that her brothers and sisters are Christian and not at all Muslim and that 'they're not confused at all'.

BOB N (male, Islam, religion important in some ways but not others)

Bob's mother is Hindu and his father is Muslim, and he considers himself an agnostic Muslim (although he wrote Islam on the research consent form). His parents are divorced and he lives with his father. He says he followed what his parents said when he was younger but that as he gets older, 'you start questioning these kinds of rules and regulations and then you kind of grow your own opinion on religion and whatever'. He said that things were difficult when his parents were getting divorced as his mother wanted him to be Hindu, and took him to a temple, while his father wanted him to be Muslim and regularly took him to the mosque. In his words, 'it was all mixed up and everything.'

Bob now celebrates Diwali with mother but also celebrates the Muslim festivals of Eid and Ramadan. He has tended to follow his father more as he lives with him, and goes along with fasting and celebrating the festivals. To complicate matters, his older sister decided not to follow either Hinduism or Islam and has converted to Christianity. His father no longer speaks to her.

Bob concludes that all the different religions in his family have 'led me more towards the fact that I disbelieve in God. . . . I would say family (has most overall influence on my religious views) because of the way my family is totally separated into three different religions. I think that's made me think Islam says one thing, Hinduism says one thing and Christianity says another. So I think I just form my own kind of thing where I just think (it is fine) as long as you're a good person from the heart and you help other people as well as yourself'.

KATY (female, Christian/Hindu, religion very important)

Katy was born into a Hindu family but moved with her mother from India to London to live with her uncle, aunt and cousins who had converted to Christianity. Staying with them, she went to church and learned about God and Jesus although, like her mother, retained links with Hinduism and now

(continued overleaf)

goes both to church and temple. She does not think this matters and says: 'I always thought there is only one God and he may have different forms or names for different religions. For me, there's only one greatness up there who I can talk to and ask for help.' Nonetheless she does say she finds much more in Christianity than Hinduism.

CHRISTIANO (male, Christian, religion quite important)

Christiano lives with his aunt who is Christian and uncle who is Muslim. He says: 'So there's always like some sort of tension in the family. However, when it comes to just like basic stuff of like living your inner good life, it's all the same ... If I was to turn atheist, they would be a little bit disappointed in me that I'm not following God. And they'd be disappointed that okay they'd probably think I've lost all the moral values I had following the religion. So it's just basically worship God and try to live your life in a good way.'

FOON (female, Hindu/Sikh, religion very important)

Foon tells how she has grown up with a mix of Hindu and Sikh in her families and does not really see any strong differences on the surface, although there are more if you go into it 'really deeply'. She acknowledges that she is a bit of both religions, even though she follows Hinduism more: 'In Southall there's a mandir and gurdwara right next to each other, so whenever I go to one I always go the other as well. . . . I do follow Hinduism a little bit more than Sikhism, so I do tend to go to mandir on a lot more of the occasions.' She says she perhaps sits for ten minutes at one and then goes to the other. Apart from mosques, where she thought she probably wouldn't be allowed, she also likes going into Christian churches.

Figure 7.6 Case studies of young people with self-reported mixed religious identity

talking about similarities between religions, such as that Hindus and Jains hold similar values on vegetarianism and peace. Several spoke of the benefits of more than one religion, saying things like 'I like having that mix . . . I get to experience like everything', or how living with different views means you experience tolerance towards other religions. One participant, however, thought that growing up with a Christian mother and Muslim father was confusing for his young cousin: both parents wanted him to follow their religion and this had led to arguments in the past.

Summary

Families are very important in young people's lives and play a significant role in the development of their religious views and behaviours. Often this may be in transmitting their own attitudes and beliefs, but in other cases it may be through the support they provide as young people negotiate their own personal religious journeys. Young people valued family discussion of religious issues and values, but were clear that force or pressure to conform to particular ideals was not helpful and could be counter-productive.

There was considerable concordance between the religious positions of young people and their families, and this held whether families saw themselves as essentially religious or non-religious. Nonetheless, transmission appeared strongest in families where young people reported that religion was very important to them. Transmission was also most marked where more family members (of young person, mother and father) had been born outside the UK: these findings are suggestive of a secularising role of Westernisation. Alongside these instances of intergenerational continuities were many young people who, despite taking on their parents' values during childhood, had made their own decisions on their personal positions by the time of the study and did not report close family similarities in religious beliefs. It seemed that for some religion had become more important than in their parents' generation whereas for others it had become less important. The role of personal agency was stressed by all these young people, whether or not they grew up to share their parents' religious beliefs.

A small number of young people from mixed faith backgrounds took part in the YOR survey and/or the face-to-face interviews. While no strong conclusions can be drawn on this group, they were more likely to emphasise the advantages than the disadvantages of a dual identity.

The next chapter looks beyond the family to interactions with, and influences of, friends and peers. It also considers the role of schools and RE lessons on the development of knowledge and understanding of the beliefs and traditions of different faith positions.

8 Friends and schools

The previous chapter has demonstrated that the family has a key impact on developing religious identity, but that other influences and pressures become significant as children grow older. Friends and peers constitute an important part of young people's social environments and are among these other influences. This chapter explores friendship patterns among Youth On Religion (YOR) participants, examining the levels of mutual understanding and knowledge these reflect. The question of whether some friendships are closer and more durable than others is also considered. Furthermore, do friends and peers contribute to informal education on the diverse faith positions found in the research areas?

The character of schools and whether, in multi-faith areas, they represent a microcosm of the diverse communities they are located within or a relatively segregated section of society, affect opportunities pupils have to mix and make friends with others from similar and different religious backgrounds. They do not, however, determine the nature of friendships that emerge and how far these demonstrate 'boundary maintenance' along religious and cultural lines (Barth, 1969) or extend beyond the school gates. Nonetheless, the extent to which the school milieu enables new cross-cultural associations, and aids bridging (Putnam, 2000) between religious groups, has important implications for social cohesion at school as well as integration across religious and ethnic divides within neighbourhoods. The school also plays a vital role in promoting understanding of religious diversity through the curriculum and other experiences, and providing a setting for the development of moral reasoning and moral values. The prevailing discourse in modern Western society espouses liberal individualism that, as demonstrated in other chapters, is widely adopted by participants in the YOR study.

Friendship patterns

There is limited research evidence on friendship patterns among young people in multi-faith areas and, in part, this reflects the difficulty of collecting information. Despite an almost universal discourse of tolerance, respect and integration running through the commentaries of YOR participants, the nature and quality of friendships is not always easy to discern. Findings from other investigations are also variable. G. Smith (2005) found that despite a certain amount of mixing in school, friendship circles were often ethnically and religiously homogeneous among primary school aged children. It was rare for children to have friends of different religions and ethnic backgrounds outside school, and it seemed that both religious commitments and parental discouragement of inter-faith friendships were contributory. Other studies too have found that many White young people have no contact with members of minority ethnic groups outside school (Finney and Simpson, 2009). Baumann (1996) on the other hand found that almost half of a sample of 324 teenagers in a community comprising five cultural groups (Sikh, Hindu, Muslim, Afro-Caribbean, and White) said their out-of-school friends represented a range of faith backgrounds. The complexity of patterns is illustrated by Mondal (2008) who reports a 2006 poll in which 87% of Muslims said they had a non-Muslim good friend while only 33% of non-Muslims said they had a close Muslim friend.

The YOR survey asked respondents how many of their friends have religious beliefs similar to their own. Figure 8.1 presents the findings by faith group. Overall, Muslims were particularly likely to say that most or all of their friends were from similar faith backgrounds. Almost half the young people from Sikh or Christian backgrounds gave the same response, while those from Buddhist or Hindu backgrounds were most likely to have friends with a mix of faith positions.

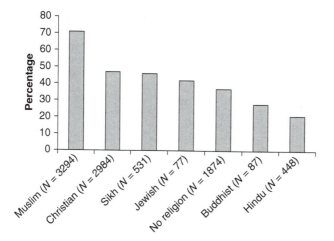

Figure 8.1 Friends (most or all) with similar religious beliefs by faith group

Further analysis confirmed, when other factors are taken into account, that participants who report a specific faith, and those from minority ethnic groups, are most likely to have friends from similar backgrounds. Ethnic diversity at school or college also makes a difference to friendship patterns (see Figure 8.2) although, even in schools or colleges with mid or high diversity, 43% and 42% of participants say they have similar, religious beliefs to most or all their friends. Patterns were not affected by gender, books in the home or family members born in the UK. However, there was a link with free school meals in that those at schools with the highest levels of eligibility were most likely to share beliefs with all or most of their friends. This may reflect neighbourhood factors and school location.

Variations in friendship patterns across religious, ethnic and cultural boundaries were discussed by young people during face-to-face interviews. While some said they had friends from a range of backgrounds, others suggested most of their friends were similar to themselves. As also suggested by the survey data, friendships tended to reflect opportunities for mixing with others from different faith backgrounds and, in turn, areas and localities where young people lived and attended schools, as well as hobbies and interests they might have. As most went to schools close to them, school populations broadly reflected community populations. Greater residential segregation between Asians and Whites

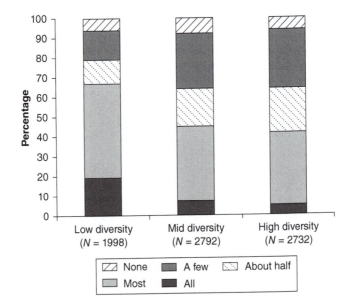

Figure 8.2 Friends with similar religious beliefs by school/college ethnic diversity

in Bradford than Newham was, in this way, linked to more limited opportunities for inter-faith mixing both at home and at school. Two participants from Bradford described what could happen.

> 'Often the area around the faith school is largely built up of that particular faith, again meaning that the children from that area are not mixing with other children outside of school in their home area. Although there is the possibility of children mixing with other children from different backgrounds in extra-curricular activities which they may partake in, it can generally be said that children spend most of their time in school and playing in the area they live in. . . . ' (ANNETTE: female, no religion, religion not very important)

> 'You don't get into a situation where you get the chance to mingle. I have many friends that are Muslim and Sikh and Christian, but you tend to find them in specific groups.' (JON: male, no religion, religion not at all important)

Sikhs in Hillingdon and Muslims in Bradford were particularly likely to say all their friends shared their religion. Sikhs and Muslims also tended to make friends through the mosque or gurdwara, again reinforcing the likelihood of friendships within their own faith group. Some pupils, despite living in multi-faith areas, seemed hardly integrated with other cultural groups. This was especially true of pupils at the Sikh school who might have only ever attended the one school and consequently had mainly Sikh friends. They might have a wider social circle if they had a job, joined groups such as St John Ambulance, or had sociable parents with wide friendships, but otherwise tended to remain largely isolated from other religious groups. A young Sikh illustrated this well.

> 'I've joined work and I met this white guy. And like I've literally never spoken properly to a white person before. And when you're talking to them, you just assume they know what you're on about. Like I'd be talking to them about religion or whatever and assume that they know. But they actually don't.' (MAYA: female, Sikh, religion quite important)

The importance of schooling for friendship patterns was widely acknowledged, and pupils who had attended primary and secondary schools with different patterns of diversity described a different mix of friends in the two settings. Two young Sikhs said their friends came from a range of backgrounds only because they had been to multi-faith primary schools. Similarly, a young Muslim had mainly Catholic friends due to attending a Catholic school at both primary and secondary stages.

Is a friend's religion important?

It has been suggested that the religiosity of friends can be important in reinforcing personal identity and group membership (Nesbitt, 2004; Rymarz and Graham, 2005), an account that fits with the interpretivist thesis and the significance of personal interactions for identity development. To pursue this line of enquiry, the YOR survey asked participants how important it was for them to know about a new friend's religious beliefs. The vast majority said religion was not important in this respect, or important only in some ways. Faith group however made a difference and, overall, 37% of Muslims, as compared to 28% of Sikhs, 26% of Hindus, 22% of Christians and only 12% of those with no religion, said it was very or quite important for them to know. Taking everything into account, patterns did not differ between research areas. Females and those with more family members born in the UK, attending schools with greater ethnic diversity, in receipt of free school meals, and reporting fewer books in the home, were all more likely to want to know the faith group of a new friend. These findings are difficult to interpret but perhaps reflect the greater opportunities that more Westernised young people with more diverse peers have to mix with, and find out about, different faith groups. They are also interesting alongside the finding that young people tend to choose friends from similar backgrounds to themselves.

To explore this issue further, the YOR survey also asked how people from the same and from different backgrounds get on together at school or college. Findings for the sample as a whole (Figure 8.3) revealed some interesting patterns: in particular, while some 45% overall say that all those from different religions get on well, 28% say the same for those from different religious backgrounds. These patterns are, however, much more striking when the proportions saying that most or all get on together from similar and different religious backgrounds are examined by faith group. As illustrated in Figure 8.4, all groups, but particularly Muslims and Hindus, thought that young people are more likely to get on with peers from similar than different religious backgrounds.

While these findings suggest different faith groups attach differential importance to the religious background and beliefs of friends, the prevailing discourse among the majority of interview participants from all backgrounds was that religion was not a prime consideration. Quite a number of young people, and mainly those with no specific faith position, said they might not even know the religious background of friends they were not particularly close to. A few said they did not always believe friends who depicted themselves as religious or non-religious: they thought they might, in effect, be acting front stage and engaging in impression management in order to fit in with their friends and not stand out as different.

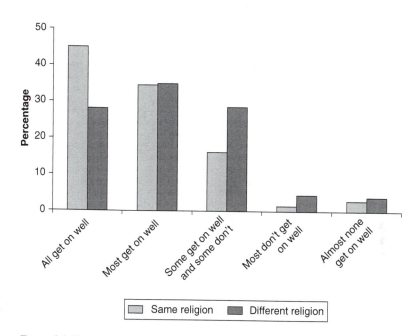

Figure 8.3 How young people from the same and different religions get on together at school/college (*N* = 8903)

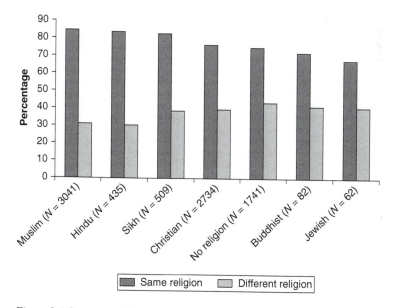

Figure 8.4 Survey participants saying all or most young people get on at school with people from the same and different religions, by faith group

In general participants stressed the importance of having friends you like and get along with, and said that friends can have different things, such as music, movies and hobbies, besides religion in common. Friends interested in football and girls, or those who were hard workers and did their homework at lunchtime, were among the examples given. Religion did not always form part of a key typificatory scheme (Berger and Luckmann, 1966) influential in determining friendships for these young people.

> 'I don't think it would be a problem really for me to have friends of different religions or different races. I think I don't find it a problem because even though we are Muslim we share the same age groups, we share the same culture, so we can find similarities other than religion.' (MIRIAM: female, Islam, religion very important)

> 'Overall, I think people do tend to realise more that people are just people at the end of the day.' (PLUM: female, Sikh, religion quite important)

> 'Religion isn't a big factor in who we become friends with . . . I don't go "Oh I'm Kylie, what religion are you? Let's be friends because we're the same religion".' (KYLIE: female, no religion, religion not important)

Participants in interviews and discussion groups did nonetheless discuss implications of friendships within and across faith groups. They saw advantages to friendships with people from similar backgrounds, but mixing more widely had its benefits too. Furthermore, the term 'friend' could have varied meanings and refer both to classmates and closer intimates. One participant illustrated this difference by talking about 'Hi Bye' friends to describe the more transitory and superficial, although amicable, relationships with peers. Overall it did seem that even if young people reported a mix of friends from different backgrounds, the more enduring friendships were between those with most in common. Although bound together with most of their peers by core moral values including liberal individualism (see Chapter 6), they might differ in religious adherence and norms. While the former seemed important, it was not always enough.

> 'And like I got to know different people (at a mixed primary school) (but) I haven't kept in touch with them as well since I left primary. So I guess even though like sometimes we're in a mixed-faith thing, you still become friends with the same sort of people.' (SANEHA: female, Sikh, importance of religion not specified)

> 'I don't let it consciously influence me, but I think everybody subconsciously, you go to people who are a bit more like you and have a bit more in common. It's just that natural way to go. You don't consciously

try to do it, like I try and be friends with everyone, but . . . the friends that you tend to do more things with and spend more time with tend to be the ones who you've got the similar values and cultural beliefs and some things like that.' (LEON B: male, Christian, religion important in some ways but not others)

The YOR study confirmed that the religiosity of peers influences the degree of conformity to social and religious norms (Hopkins, 2004). A commonly mentioned advantage of friends from similar backgrounds is that they are easier to turn to for advice, or to talk about religious matters such as praying and whether or not to wear the hijab. Several Muslims said it is good to have friends with similar inclinations so that, for example, 'if you walk past a mosque you can all go in together'. Others said it is easier because of similar cultural aspects such as clothes or food. Indeed culture was often likely to be more important than religion in this context. Sarah, for instance, was a Catholic but all her friends at school were Church of England: 'So they don't have the same Catholic beliefs, but they have the same kind of view of church and going to church. And then out of school some of my friends are Catholics with similar views again.' It was easy both to relax and to respect religion if friends had faith position in common.

'Whenever I'm with my friends we have fun, but whenever we have to go to the mosque then it changes completely. We become really religious, we change how we act and stuff. Also, whenever we are only Muslim we are completely different. When it's time for prayer, then we become religious and stuff like that.' (LUCAS: male, Muslim, religion very important)

Not everyone agreed that friends from a similar faith background were necessarily 'best'. It was emphasised that people are not all the same just because they are Muslim or Christian, and some take their religion much more seriously than others. Mixed friendship groups provided the chance to discuss religion more broadly and learn something different. 'I don't think religion should define who your friends are, because you'd just get stuck with the same people all the time' claimed one female who said religion was not very important to her. Almost everyone seemed clear, nonetheless, that direct experience of different religions was positive. They mentioned how getting used to mixing makes it easier to get on with a range of people in different settings, such as at university. Young people suggested it was best to mix as young as possible as it gets harder to change attitudes later. To illustrate the point, one participant mentioned feeling a bit 'strange' at a Jewish wedding where she met people from a Jewish background for the first time.

Ipgrave and McKenna (2008) found that friends were a significant secondary source of information about other religions, after home and school, and many YOR participants described the opportunities provided by friends from different cultural backgrounds. They enjoyed the experience of multiple realities and developing new understandings, and mentioned learning about other religions at first hand through their friends. Trying traditional foods, observing and finding out about different religious customs and practices, experiencing alternative places of worship, and visiting friends' homes, were among the things they reported. A young Christian reflected on his perceptions of an atheist friend's house.

> 'They have a laid back life and it was refreshing to see how they led more of a guilt-free life without religion. However, they were still good and nice to others, obviously, as you don't need religion to do that. Just basic human morals and kindness.' (LEON B: male, Christian, religion important in some ways but not others)

He also mentioned Muslim friends and how their way of life differed from his. As he wanted religion to be only part of his own life and not his whole life, he concluded that Islam was not for him. Additionally, he regarded Sikh and Hindu friends as laid back and not very restricted, especially in the younger generations.

There were many other similar reports. A non-religious female talked about a Hindu friend whose home was similar to the house next door 'apart from the shrine upstairs'. Her friend belonged to a large extended family, and she was able to observe the different praying patterns of grandparents, parents and children, noting that religious practice seemed to be changing over the generations. Another participant talked about going to the gurdwara with a Sikh friend, and finding it very beautiful, even though she does not agree with religion herself. A Christian boy attended the marriage of his best friend's (Muslim) sister and was interested in the difference between a Christian and a Muslim wedding. It had not been how he had expected, and he was impressed by the centrality of the family and the big party afterwards. The experience increased his understanding of the religion and made him want to learn more. Yet another was shocked when a Muslim friend said she was not allowed to listen to music and was glad her own religion (Hindu/Jain) was not so strict.

Awareness contexts, or understanding of both one's own and another's identity, as well as how one is regarded by the other (Glaser and Strauss, 1964), depend on reciprocal understandings, and it was evident that interfaith friendships were important both for learning about other people's religion and for being an ambassador for one's own. Several Muslim females pointed out how they were able to show first-hand how Muslims were 'not as bad as people think', and a Sikh reported how she had been able to convey something of Sikhism to her boyfriend's White family. Practical experiences, such as taking a non-Muslim into the school prayer room as an observer, accompanying a friend to a place of worship, or informal talk about special religious days or reasons for praying, helped young people learn about other religions. Serious discussion was also important.

> 'It's not just that we're talking to Muslims, because we've got Hindu friends, a friend that's atheist and stuff like that. So we sit down and we have quite deep conversations about religion and what we think is right. Obviously sometimes religion does raise conflict, but . . . as we grow older we've learnt to avoid those conflicts and just rise above it.' (NASHWA: female, Islam, religion very important)

It was generally agreed that it is best to learn about religion from those your own age rather than an elderly priest who tells you what you should or should not do and makes you think 'how can I tell this person it's the 21st century now and you need to really adapt to changes and stuff?' Young people also appreciated learning about different religions from friends 'instead of reading it off the paper'.

Friendships across faith groups and cultures could, nonetheless, present challenges, restrictions and boundaries. For example, religion could alter what you did with friends. Going out to eat might mean having to go to certain restaurants and, according to a female Muslim, social gatherings and parties might be 'out of bounds' if alcohol is on the agenda: 'it might spill on you, you might smell of it'. One Christian Strict Adherent said she does not see friends out of school as she disapproves of drinking alcohol, does not like swearing, and has been taught the 'evil influences' of much music. Saying prayers at regular intervals could present difficulties for young Muslims who preferred to pray at home. Ramadan, and going to worship on Sundays, also restricted activities with friends. More generally, religion could also be used as a reason to prevent activities with friends.

> 'It (religion) restricts people from living their lives. Like my Dad . . . doesn't allow me to do the things that I want to do . . . Basically he says "no, you can't do that". It restricts people because now we are in a modern setting and we are in a different era to where the Bible was set like 2000 years ago. . . . I wanted to stay over at my friend's house because we were having a barbecue and it would be too late to walk home. But I was made to walk home at 2 o'clock in the morning on my own because I wasn't allowed to sleep over at someone's house when it would have been safer in the first place.' (RHIANNA B: female, Roman Catholic, religion important in some ways but not others)

Despite some suggestion that religious practices could push friends apart, it was more common to find that friends from different religions accommodated one another in much the same way as friends from the same religion might. A Muslim girl who was friends with a boy who smoked told how he went outside when he wanted a cigarette and, as she said, 'we can be friends inside'. Similarly she would not join him when he went to the pub but would go to other places with him. She commented that 'it's not as though we always have to be together'. Although young people generally respected the differences between them, they nonetheless felt it might sometimes be easier if religion was not in the equation.

> 'With me, most of my friends are non-religious. And I think that's a lot easier in the sense that we can go out and just have fun and not really worry about that sort of religion.' (JOHN SMITH: male, no religion, religion quite important)

Peer pressure and faith tradition

Friends can indeed exert pressure on one another, whether intentionally or not. It has clearly been shown that peers do both influence religious attitudes and practice (Regenus et al., 2004; Smith and Denton, 2005; Mason et al., 2007) and contribute to competing pressures from religion and the wider youth culture (Hopkins, 2004). Similar findings emerged from the YOR study.

Some of the ways in which friends affect each other's religiosity through conversation and experiences have already been described. In addition, participants (mostly female Muslim Strict Adherents) talked about telling each other to pray more and discouraging smoking, breaking a fast, eating non-Halal food, wearing tight clothes, going out with people they do not know well, taking the hijab off when going out, or wearing 'skinny jeans, short skirt and something that shows all your arms'. Peers seemed as likely as parents to encourage friends to maintain appropriate cultural and religious boundaries (Barth, 1969). However, living in a Western society could present multiple realities, particularly for Muslims who felt under strong pressure from their religion but nonetheless wanted to fit in with peers and have 'fun'. Others play a crucial role in sustaining personal identity (Mead, 1934) and friends were often there to encourage their peers to follow their religion. Nonetheless temptations abound in Western culture in the form of alcohol, smoking, drugs and sex, and young people gave the clear impression that being a Strict Adherent can be difficult.

> 'Sometimes it's more about what you feel yourself, because you want to do that stuff, but you can't do it. But in the end your body tells you to do it, but your heart tells you not to do it.' (KHUSHTAR: male, Muslim, religion very important)

'Yes, like for example I have a lot of friends that are Muslim but their faith isn't strong and they indulge in all this wrong stuff . . . Yes, so like my friends, like they'll get together and they're my cousins as well, and they'll ring me and they'll say "come over". And then they'll have spliffs and alcohol and everything there. And I get really tempted . . . and now I'm never ever going to because my faith got stronger. But then it's really hard on me because I sit there with them, like I'll go out with them . . . And it's really hard for me because I've been smoking since I've been little, and it was really hard for me to stop. . . . I think about it that as a Muslim I shouldn't smoke, but then everything else is telling me to smoke.' (NADIA: female, Islam, religion very important)

These young people gave the impression that there were many Flexible Adherents in their midst. This did not mean they did not believe or pray, but that being liked and approved of by their friends was also important. Members of mixed friendship groups could face a choice between 'temptation' and the dictates of their religion. Flexible Adherents often demonstrated agency in deciding how to deal with competing pressures, and were generally able to justify their actions through their own moral reasoning. They pointed out, for instance, that smoking was not specifically forbidden in the Qur'an and was therefore permissible. Moral justification was not always consistent: two girls spoke of a friend who told one of them off for wearing tight clothes but smoked herself, justifying her own behaviour by saying 'this is different'. According to one female Sikh, 'you have to be really strong, like mentally, to be able to follow everything 100%'. Some Strict Adherents accordingly developed techniques and strategies to enable them to follow their religion but still join in with friends. A devout Muslim, for instance, would read namaz at a party or in the changing rooms of shops when trying on clothes. Others developed techniques to resist pressures from friends, such as thinking 'that's them and I'm me'. Nonetheless much depended on the significant others in their lives at the time as some might lead you away from religion while others can encourage you 'to do the right stuff'.

Single-faith and multi-faith schools

The majority of young people in YOR interviews and discussions advocated diversity and inter-cultural mixing, whether or not they had friends from a range of backgrounds themselves, and favoured multi-faith over single-faith schools. Baumann's (1996) Southall study found that 88% of the 185 young people interviewed were against single-faith schools and, although interview data are not quantifiable in the YOR project, the impression is that at least this proportion expressed a similar view. Nonetheless most participants, and especially those at faith schools, did see some advantages of both.

Issues surrounding young people and multi-faith education were explored further. First, as described in more detail in Chapter 3, links were examined between attitudes to religion and the degree of ethnic diversity within young people's schools. Interestingly, it seemed that YOR survey participants were less likely to agree with positive statements about religion and more likely to agree with negative statements the more ethnically diverse their schools. This is at some variance with Torstenson's (2006) finding that levels of belief in God tend to be higher in Swedish schools with a multi-faith intake than in those that are less diverse. Jackson (2004) also asks whether faith schools produce less 'tolerant' citizens than community colleges. At first sight, these new YOR data seem to provide some contradictory evidence. Nonetheless, the ethnic diversity measure employed does not distinguish between faith schools and others in any strict sense, and many faith schools in England do not restrict intake in the sixth form. Moreover, as suggested earlier, it may be that pupils exposed to different groups are likely to witness both positive and negative aspects of religion and present a balanced perspective.

Whatever their attitudes to religion, almost all participants saw the overarching advantages of multi-faith schools. The most common reason for this view was that mixing with young people with a range of beliefs and customs is good preparation for meeting people from diverse backgrounds at university or in employment. The real world is diverse and sharing ideas with people from different backgrounds is not only interesting but helps to break down prejudices and encourage tolerance. Multi-faith schools expose pupils to different practices and traditions, such as fasting, and could raise interest in learning more about different religions. The general view seemed to be that a diverse range of faith positions at a school, including atheism, agnosticism and secularism, make it easy for anyone to retain a personal religiosity. For instance, some nonbelievers told how listening to peers telling religious stories confirmed them in their own views. Furthermore, anybody's position could be challenged. A student at a mixed school in Bradford pointed out that when you are so diverse, religion does not matter. At the same time, and in line with other findings (Ipgrave and McKenna, 2008), there were a number of participants who expressed a certain reluctance to discuss religion or atheism in contexts where it might not seem relevant and where others might be sensitive to their comments.

> 'There's too much attention so like everyone's too cautious around it. You can't really be friends because of all the tension and because everyone's so cautious, you don't really want to open up to each other. . . . It's just hard to overcome all the tension and you know just trying to be cautious, trying to be all politically correct with them because you don't want to offend them. You know they probably don't want to offend you, but if they do it's probably going to cause a big fight.' (HESSA: female, Muslim, religion very important)

The fact that different faith groups are educated together does not mean they are fully integrated, and participants in several multi-faith schools reported how different ethnic and religious groups tend to congregate. As they put it, they told of Muslims or Asians sticking together, Christians and Catholics forming a sub-group, and pupils from the Czech Republic keeping themselves to themselves. Typificatory schemes, or the ways in which young people classify their peers in contexts of diversity (Glaser and Strauss, 1964), may or may not be based on religion.

'Yes they all know their table. Even if nobody is sitting on it, we know that's their table and don't sit there or an argument breaks out. . . . It's not that we don't get along, they just choose it, they just don't like talking to us. They're speaking in their own language which is different. We don't understand.' (SARAH B: female, Islam, religion very important)

It was concluded by participants in a YOR discussion group that culture was as important as religion in this context. It was also pointed out that these sub-groups were not necessarily cohesive but could display divisions and tensions. It appeared there was more integration in the sixth form when there is more choice in the curriculum and common interests are likely to be shared with fellow students. One participant commented how at his stage 'you have people who you would have never of thought would have mixed and you see them talking and learning'. Nonetheless, introducing diversity into the sixth form of a faith school might also be problematic.

'I think it's sort of a double-edged sword. I think it is very good to have other people here, but then I think from another perspective, and when you grow up in school and everyone is Christian, and until year 13 it's practically either White Europeans or Black African kids, and then when you get to the sixth form you start to get people from Pakistan and other places . . . a lot of people start saying "Why are they here? It is a Christian school".' (GORDON: male, Christian, religion quite important)

This participant went on to say how this reasoning had led one pupil, who believed only in Christianity, to rip down symbols of other religions put up alongside the cross in the sixth form common room. Even if he was exercising agency he was certainly not displaying liberal individualism.

On the whole there were few reports of serious tensions at mixed-faith schools, although there was mention of bullying and name-calling, and occasional fights. Sometimes pupils call each other 'Muslim' or 'Jew', even when they are not, just to be offensive, or say things like 'You're Muslim, you're a terrorist, go back to your country'. Clashes occurred between Goths and Muslims, or between homosexuals and Christians. It was fully apparent that disputes were not always about religion even if religious terms were used as a form of abuse.

> 'I've not received it myself, but I've seen a few other people just walking down the school through the corridor and someone's being nasty to some person. They'd shout out "Oh shut up you Muslim" or "Shut up you Jew" and obviously that person may not be a Jew or a Muslim but it's just like call them that because they think it's offensive.' (BOBBIE: female, no religion, religion not very important)

Despite appearances, however, the reality may not always have been quite as rosy as it seemed. In Goffman's terms, young people appeared to want to ally themselves with a positive discourse towards diversity, respect and tolerance, but it might sometimes be a case of impression management rather than exactly how they might be feeling at a particular moment in time.

> 'I am sure there are other people in the school that are silently saying in their head that they don't want to learn about something that doesn't affect them and things like that. So yeah, it goes on everywhere, on the street, at school, at work, anywhere you go.' (GORDON: male, Christian, religion quite important)

Many reported advantages of multi-faith schools were in essence disadvantages of faith schools. It was suggested a narrow focus can mean 'brainwashing' and learning about only a single religion in any depth, and leads to an unbalanced perspective: 'You can have a joke and a laugh about other religions' because there is not anybody there to be offended or challenge you, as one pupil said. According to another:

> 'I think a mix of religions is good because I think we're a bit like, especially in this school, we're a bit too comfortable with one another . . . Because like we've all got the same moral and religious views, well most of us, and like because we're all Indian, there's no like difference in our views and we need that contrast.' (SIMRAN: female, Sikh, religion quite important)

Sikhs in Hillingdon were nonetheless especially likely to extol the virtues of single-faith schools. Although receptive to the benefits of multi-faith education, they did also see the positive side of their faith school. One pupil remarked that 'if we wanted to go to a different school we got the option to go in our sixth form. But we decided to stay, so there's obviously got to be good points to it'. The advantage of their school, as they saw it, was that it brought together pupils from a similar background and culture who were able to get on well and it could provide in-depth teaching on Sikhism.

'Before I came here I literally knew nothing about the religion, and I didn't know how to write Punjabi – I probably could speak it, but that was about it. I didn't know about the gurus or anything . . . I was just really oblivious to everything. So when I actually came here, it's kind of like a big transformation because I've learned so much. I've had Punjabi lessons, Sikh studies lessons, and I've learned so much about my religion already.' (RAJ: female, Sikh, religion important in some ways but not others)

Knowing about one's own religion was important to counter fears that 'we'd lose our own background and stuff' and that Sikhism is becoming too Westernised. A young female Muslim added that faith schools might be more effective in getting messages across like 'don't be discriminating towards others', hence discouraging racism and promoting harmony. None-theless a balance was important, and many of the Sikhs in the faith school in Hillingdon indicated that they were not well integrated in the community and had not had the opportunity to develop good understandings of other ethnic and religious groups.

It was, however, also acknowledged that people might choose schools for educational (good examination grades) rather than religious reasons, and that not all pupils at a faith school would be devoutly religious. This suggestion is directly supported by recent research carried out in East Lon-don with middle-class parents from a range of ethnic backgrounds (Butler and Hamnett, 2012). In the YOR study, a pupil attending a Christian faith school described how, in a clear demonstration of impression management, many parents join churches for a required period of time so they can enrol their child in the school – with the inevitable outcome that only a minor-ity of pupils are actively engaged in practising religion. This exemplified another student's comparison between religion as 'something that can be easily swapped and changed and that is not valued' and religion that is 'something for life, something that needs to be stuck by'.

YOR survey participants overall suggested that school was one of the least important influences on their religious beliefs (see Chapter 4). This may relate to criticisms of Religious Education (RE) discussed later in this chapter, and particularly the likelihood that many pupils are taught by teachers who are not experts in their own particular religion. Face-to-face discussion with young people revealed additional possibilities. First there were several pupils, mostly Bystanders, who suggested that going to a religious school or being exposed to different religions is not sufficient to convert a non-religious person to religion. According to one, it 'never really rubbed off on me'. This view was countered by others, mainly Flexible Adherents, who suggested that faith schools might reinforce religious identity and make it difficult for pupils to question religion as much as they might like to. Occasionally they speculated that they might have been more or less religious themselves if they had been to a different school. A third view was that school could get pupils thinking about religion and have an impact in either direction.

> 'I would say lessons in school are what triggered the thought of whether there is a God or not. Before that I never really questioned it because I was so young. It didn't occur to me that there could not be a God. But then as we started to talk about it in class, and I did my own research out of interest, I saw things that gave evidence to there not being a God. And that gained weight and this is where I am now.' (SYDNEY: male, no religion, religion not at all important)

> 'I think in this school I've become more religious actually . . . Like before I wasn't at all. But I think over time this school's made me more aware of . . . religious stories and stuff like that really. So I think I've grown a bit.' (SIMRAN: female, Sikh, religion quite important)

> 'Mine (my beliefs) has sort of fluctuated a bit.... So obviously being brought up in a Catholic school, Catholic family, Catholic church every Sunday, that's just what I assumed to be proper and real . . . But once, like I went to a multi-faith school and I started not going to church every week, I sort of saw a different picture. So then I sort of didn't believe for a while, and now I'm sort of in the middle.' (LEON B: male, Christian, religion important in some ways but not others)

Practising religion at school

Practising religion at school was not always easy. A particular difficulty that affected Muslims more than any other group was finding the space and time to pray. Observing religious traditions and expectations could also be problematic.

From what participants said, schools and teachers were generally accommodating of pupils' religious needs, providing prayer rooms or allowing pupils to pray in the classroom or other spaces. The Sikh school in the study had a gurdwara attached to it for pupils to use: several young Sikhs said this meant they go to a place of worship more when at school than at home. Prayer rooms in other schools were often 'packed' and 'like a community within the college' and, although technically multi-faith, largely occupied by Muslims.

Despite a favourable school ethos and the availability of prayer spaces, many pupils said they still found it difficult to manage to pray as often as they should. The requirement for Muslims to cleanse themselves before-hand, and the competing pressures of doing well at school and observing their religion, were among the obstacles.

> 'It (praying) doesn't take long. I think it's just like the fact that you have to, obviously you have to cleanse yourself before and everything. So it's just a bit of a hassle five times a day.' (NAIHLA: female, Muslim, religion very important)

> 'When we're at school we don't get a chance, like we've got facilities to pray, but it's because it's so busy. We've got so much work to do, we won't find time to go to the prayer room and pray. So what we do is as soon as we get home we try to make up for them prayers.' (ALIA: female, Muslim, religion very important)

Several Muslims pointed to difficulties associated with Ramadan, and exemplified how trying to transport religious traditions between conditions of mechanical and organic solidarity (Durkheim, 1893) could produce con-flict of interests. Fortunately, in the year of the survey, this festival had occurred during the school holidays and had not competed with educational pressures. When it falls within term time, however, fasting means young people have little energy for additional activities such as physical education.

> 'You have to do the bleep test. You have to meet each line, and you're fasting. And you're just like, the energy you've got left, they just take it out of you. And you just go home and you collapse.' (MUNISA: female, Muslim, religion very important)

> 'At school, oh it's horrible. They do, they make you run and you can't have no water . . . Yes it was easier having Ramadan in the summer holidays. You'd wake up in the morning, close your eyes fast and then go to sleep for like ages. And then you didn't have to do anything all day apart from reading namaz.' (SAFUN: female, Muslim, religion very important)

One girl said she broke her fast to give her enough strength to perform in the school show, even though she felt bad at the time. As she put it, 'it's like a clash of culture and religion and life and sometimes you have to sacrifice one thing for another. That's when it gets a bit hard.' A young male partici-pant contrasted the perspectives of Flexible Adherents (modern Muslims) and Strict Adherents (true Muslims) on this matter.

'The modern Muslim . . . For us, I think, education is like the most important thing in our life right now. But, for the true Muslim, it would be Islam and then everything else . . . You can mix education with Islam and you'll still be a religious Muslim, a devout Muslim and get good grades. But it's about finding the balance, and it's really hard to do that for some people.' (WAZIR: male, Islam, religion very important)

Although Muslims and Sikhs were most likely to point to a certain clash between education and religion, there were similar comments from people with other religions too. A Christian female, for instance, commented how she felt bad doing homework on a Sunday as that should be a day to dedicate to God.

Learning about religion at school

The focus of RE in British schools has changed significantly over past decades with a shift from teaching about scriptures and religious beliefs to lessons on different religions and religious traditions (Copley, 1997). At the same time there has been a move from an almost exclusive focus on Christianity to a locally determined curriculum tailored to meet local needs. Although all schools are required to teach some form of RE, provision is highly variable across the UK in terms of what is taught, how it is taught, and the positive and negative outcomes (Barnes, 2011; Conroy et al., 2013).

Whatever its content and quality, and whether its purpose is to encourage personal belief and spirituality or promote social cohesion, most commentators suggest that school is among the most significant places for young people to learn about religion (Baumann, 1996; Ipgrave and McKenna, 2008). It may influence attitudes to religion and personal religiosity (Kay and Francis, 1996; Barrett et al., 2007; Mason et al., 2007) and it may contribute to knowledge and understanding of different faith positions. In Chapter 4 it was shown that YOR participants do not place teachers among the most significant influences on their beliefs, but Figure 8.5 suggests that over three-quarters of the sample as a whole said RE lessons are a key source of information on different religions, and about 46 and 35% respectively said school/college assemblies and festivals are also helpful.

The knowledge and understanding of different religions and beliefs reported by participants is shown in Figure 8.6. Overall it seems that young people with a specified faith position think themselves more knowledgeable than those with no religion. Ethnicity and number of books at home also make a difference once everything else is taken into account. These may reflect, first, the strong links between ethnicity and faith group and, second, the likelihood that more books at home is associated with higher

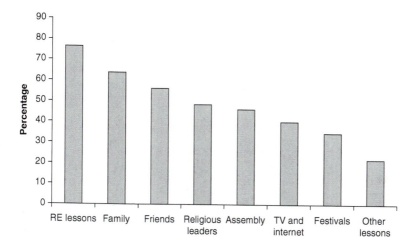

Figure 8.5 Sources of information for learning about and understanding different religions and beliefs (*N* = 8955)

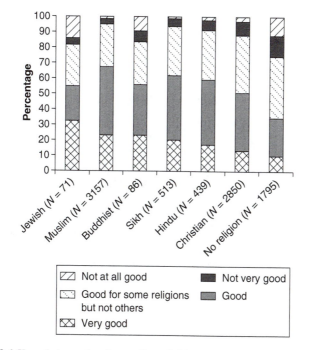

Figure 8.6 Knowledge and understanding of different religions and beliefs by faith group

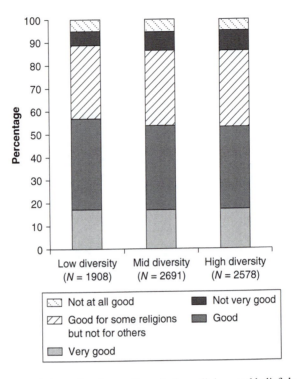

Figure 8.7 Knowledge and understanding of other religions and beliefs by school/
college ethnic diversity

levels of reading and education. Contrary to expectation, ethnic diversity at
school does not seem to make a difference (see Figure 8.7). Further analysis
confirmed that the range of ethnic backgrounds of pupils within a school or
college has no independent effect on perceived knowledge and understanding of different religions and beliefs.

Face-to-face discussions with YOR participants revealed considerable
appreciation of religious education lessons in principle, despite some criticism in practice. Although pupils might be 'silently saying in their head that
they don't want to learn about something that doesn't affect them', most
young people said it was important to learn about both their own and different faiths. Religious events, and experiences of different religious traditions, were particularly appreciated. However, they wanted to be taught in
an informed, balanced and experiential manner.

The issue of partiality in teachers was mentioned by a number of participants. Several said teachers can be biased if they over-generalise or put

forward their own beliefs. One pupil objected to a teacher saying that bombing drills have to be carried out 'because there is a chance that these specific people may do this again'. Another talked of the need to ensure teachers are well informed and do not need to be corrected by students. In his view, they need to 'get rid of misconceptions about terrorism first of all', and then give correct information and not just 'stuff that's going to cause fear'. It was pointed out that schools do not have all the answers, and that different teachers can give different answers. An example from the previous day was given when two teachers provided quite different interpretations of mukti.[1] There was a call for more focus on the similarities between religions rather than the differences, and for balanced accounts of religion.

> 'But like when you go to a Catholic school it's hard because when they teach you about God, it's all the really good things he does. And I mean as you get older, I suppose you become more aware of all the bad things that happen. And so it doesn't really tally with what you have been taught and it just kind of confuses you.' (MOZART: male, Catholic, religion very important)

Many participants believed you could only learn about a specific religion from somebody who knows about it at first hand and can answer questions. This meant, at the very least, that pupils representing the faith were present.

> 'I think Religious Education is only useful if there's people in the class of the religion so they're able to give first hand insight into it. If there's just a teacher teaching what a book says about it, because that might not always be right, there might be lots of different variants on a religion.' (STUART: male, no religion, importance of religion not specified)

But it did not necessarily matter what the teacher's background was.

> 'I'm a Muslim and I like, for example, Ms Brown. She's a . . . really strong Christian, she's from the RE department, and the only advice she gave me was "just pray. I don't care whichever God you pray to, but pray". And it helped me . . . She believes in something totally opposite, well not totally opposite but a bit different to what I believe in . . . but at the end of the day we're both aiming for the same thing. We're praying to God and we both want the same thing.' (IRAM: female, Muslim, importance of religion not specified)

There was a common view that RE taught only about certain religions and left others out. Participants pointed to a strong focus on Islam and

Christianity with other faiths, such as Buddhism and Hinduism, relatively ignored. This bias was reflected in public examinations and the requirement to study Christianity and one other faith. A Jehovah's Witness felt that her religion was not sufficiently addressed, leaving people thinking 'we are crazy people who got children dead because we cannot exchange our blood'. It was also suggested that atheism should be better taught, perhaps in philosophy classes.

> 'I always remember in primary school, like they say when you do kind of religious things, they say "Talk about what you do in your religion". And I'd just kind of sit there and say, "I don't do anything". So you just, well I think, I don't think primary schools kind of go over that.' (EDWARD: male, atheist, religion not at all important)

Participants also said that teaching often seemed too 'fact' based and did not properly convey the wider meaning of particular religions. It was suggested there should be more discussion of morals, laws and behaviours such as vegetarianism, as well as more teaching about why Muslim women wear the hijab and Sikhs wear the kara, and the meaning of events and occasions such as processions, fasting, or giving presents at Christmas.

Several young people talked about the benefits of experiential learning. Instead of relying on textbooks, what they have seen on the news, and 'teachers just standing there in front of the classroom', they said they would prefer to learn more actively about different religions. As the interpretive social scientists imply, learning about self and others works only through direct contact with people and sources of information. Fulfilling this requirement meant in part letting students talk more about their own religions and insights, and in part more 'fun stuff actually engaging with the subject' or multi-faith events. Participants recalled visits to different places of worship while at primary school but lamented the limited activities of this kind at secondary school.

> 'I remember when I went, my first trip was to a church and I was like wow, this is big. And like the whole stained glass window thing. And we came back and we had to write it up and research it all. And we kind of found out what it means and what it's for. But like, for me, I'd never been so to know about other religions is good.' (KIKI: female, Sikh, religion very important)

While some recollections of RE teaching at primary school were positive, others were not. Positive memories of going to different places of worship and meeting people from different religious backgrounds could be contrasted with the comments of a Catholic pupil who had no idea what Muslim meant when he came to secondary school, and had certainly not heard of Buddhists. Other pupils too felt their primary education had been very limited. A general feeling was that primary schools might now be making greater efforts to teach about different religions, which was good as the sooner you learn the less likely you are to be prejudiced. Nonetheless it was appreciated that younger children may not be very aware of differences between people and groups.

> 'I think it helps you to understand things more. Like when you're little and you see a Muslim woman with the full head thing on, you find it quite funny. Why's she all covered up?' (JOANNA: female, no religion, religion not very important)

O'Grady (2003) reported more positive reactions from pupils involved in setting their own RE agenda and it is evident that YOR participants had many ideas on what they wanted to learn and how they wanted to be taught. Questioning religion and each other's views in a positive and supportive way frequently emerged as important in promoting tolerance and understanding between different religious and non-religious groups. Other studies too have identified pupils' views on this issue. Knauth et al. (2008) carried out a European qualitative survey of 13–16-year-olds and asked participants for three wishes of things students should learn if religion is taught at school. More in-depth learning about actual beliefs, rather than a focus on food, festivals and traditions, and the inclusion of non-religious perspectives emerged as important among the English pupils (Ipgrave and McKenna, 2008). Most respondents supported the role of religion in school and all faiths being taught, and thought everyone should be taught together. It did not matter if a teacher was religious so long as this did not affect the way the subject was taught.

Besides formal education on religion, young people learn about other faith groups through experiences and discussions with friends. G. Smith (2005) found from primary school research that religious difference was reinforced at lunchtimes (because of different food requirements) and during assemblies (where children were withdrawn or offered different provision for worship), even in the context of school policies valuing diversity. Generally speaking, much learning about religion at school is informal rather than formal through everyday practices and discourses, including celebrating festivals and highlighting the food, dress and prayer needs of different groups (Hemming, 2011).

Summary

Young people's friendship groups depended on their age, faith group, where they lived, the school/college they attended, and family sociability and networks. A continuum of peer group relationships emerged that showed a range from 'Hi Bye' acquaintances to close intimate friends. While many suggested that religion was not important in choosing friends, it seemed in practice that probably the majority of friendships (particularly enduring friendships) were between those with faith position and cultural understanding in common. Even in schools or colleges with mid or high ethnic diversity, over four in ten pupils said they shared religious beliefs with the majority of their friends. Friendships across faith boundaries were nonetheless regarded as positive in providing first-hand information on different lifestyles and traditions, even if there might be activities (such as going to pubs or certain restaurants) such friends could not do together. Generally young people respected difference, but sometimes the multiple realities of religious tradition and Western culture could lead to pressures and tensions.

Influenced by the discourse of liberal individualism, the predominant view among those from all backgrounds and in all research areas was that multicultural schools are the ideal. The importance of contact with other faith groups was repeatedly stressed, both in dispelling stereotypes and in preparing young people for later life. Whether or not they attended multicultural schools, some but not all young people reported open discussion and debate about religion at school, sometimes with participant teachers. All the same, and despite the rhetoric about the value of mixing, there was evidence of tensions as well as segregation by religion and ethnicity within multi-faith schools. Strikingly, it was also the case that young people in highly diverse schools or colleges felt no more knowledgeable about other religions and beliefs than those in less diverse schools.

RE was generally welcomed as providing a context for learning more about one's own and other religions. Nonetheless, it was criticised in some schools for focusing disproportionately on particular religions and for being uninformed. Pupils stressed that experiential learning is best and that RE works only if teaching is accompanied by first-hand experience (some contrasts between primary and secondary schools were drawn in this context). Philosophy classes were also mentioned as a setting for debate on religion. More generally, schools can influence young people's attitudes to religion, whether through the broader curriculum or the social environment, leading either to more adherence or more questioning. Schools varied in opportunities provided for pupils to pray and in the take-up of these opportunities.

Contacts, tensions and feeling safe within the broader community are considered in the next chapter. Young people also provide their own suggestions for encouraging social cohesion between people from different faith backgrounds in their neighbourhoods.

Note

1 According to Sikhi Wiki, MUKTI and its synonym mokh (Sanskrit moksa, Pali mo(k)kha) are derived from the root much (to let go, release) and seem to be identical in primary meaning with the English words deliverance, liberation, release, freedom and emancipation.

9   Religion and the community

Earlier chapters have identified the concept of *locality ethos* to account for contrasts in patterns and meaning of religiosity among Youth On Religion (YOR) participants in the three multi-faith research areas. These are partly due to the populations in the localities but seem also to reflect some additional contextual effect. Newham, for instance, consistently shows the highest levels of religiosity, and young people confirm that most people are religious in some way and respectful and tolerant towards diversity: generally and explicitly they endorse the values of liberal individualism. This London borough is also characterised by recent and rapid population change and is now the first in Britain to record White members of the population as the minority. Bradford, by comparison, has a much more settled population but also a much higher degree of residential and school segregation by ethnicity and religion. Liberal individualism also flourishes in spirit even if opportunities to put principle into practice are more limited. Hillingdon shows the lowest levels of religiosity overall but is also an area of contrasts: it has a more advantaged and largely White population in the north of the borough but a more disadvantaged and diverse population in the south. Liberal individualism is also displayed despite geographical concentrations of members from specific cultures and faith groups.

This chapter looks in more detail at young people's descriptions of the locations they live in and the group dynamics they encounter. The main focus is on narratives of change, relationships and tensions between those from diverse backgrounds, locality and safety, and young people's suggestions for improving relationships between diverse groups in their localities.

Narratives of change

Constructions of the changing meaning and impact of religion were reflected in young people's descriptions of their own areas and communities, even though some appeared to be living 'on the periphery' and were relatively untouched by change. These narratives of change recognised how, as outlined in Chapter 2, an influx of new minorities, particularly in Newham and Hillingdon, was associated with a decline in the use of Christian churches and a proliferation of mosques, temples, gurdwaras and places of worship for other faith communities, as well as the growing diversity and multicultural character of the areas in which they lived. One male participant from Newham said he passes mosques, churches, chapels and a Jewish cemetery on the way to school while another said he passes seven mosques. Young people in Hillingdon talked about new population groups from Poland, other parts of Eastern Europe and India moving in. Even those who professed not to notice 'religious stuff' were aware of the massive changes taking place.

> 'Maybe because I'm not religious, but I don't seem to notice much religious stuff in my area. Well I've noticed a lot more people wandering around in them cloak things, that only show your eyes, and I've noticed a lot more temples etc. open up, but that's about it. I haven't noticed any religious crimes or anything out of the ordinary. But I know religion in my area has definitely changed. There's four or five churches within a mile of my house, but I never seem to notice people going in them, they look all derelict and abandoned. I can imagine probably not even like 100 years ago, maybe even like 20 years ago, people used to visit them churches all the time, but not anymore. No one seems to visit churches any more. But when it comes to these other religions, such as Muslims or Sikhs, you get people queuing up all around the block to go in. So it shows how religion in my area has changed.' (BOBBIE: female, no religion, religion not very important)

YOR participants in Hillingdon talked about living in either very diverse areas or largely White areas populated by Christians and the non-religious. Much depended on where they lived and went to school: the north of the borough is much more White than the more diverse south of the borough. Southall, outside Hillingdon but where a number of Hillingdon participants lived, was frequently given as an example of diversity where different religions are 'all crammed up into one'. Participants in Newham reported on a more uniform borough, in terms of both social class and the spread of diversity. This location has seen a rapid growth in minority groups in recent years accompanied by a large exodus of White families.

There are also signs of change in Bradford even though the population has been much more stable in recent years. Many new mosques have sprung up, whether converted from churches, pubs or purpose-built: young people said there could be four or five within walking distance. This increase in mosques was accompanied by a decline in the number of Christian churches, some of which have been decommissioned and left empty while others are now used as mosques or cafés. The transformation of three Catholic parishes into one further reflected the recent decline in Catholics in the location. The area is also home to a significant number of Hindus and houses the largest Hindu temple in northern England. As in London, young people told of a new influx of Eastern Europeans into the area, mainly from Poland, as well as some outward movement of the Jewish population to Leeds.

Young people further told how change in Bradford included increased social and geographical segregation, even within faith groups. They talked about areas, which they could demarcate on maps, where either Asians or White people were dominant. They also suggested that different castes and sects of Muslims might live in different parts of the city and remain separated. There were, however, different views on this question. While some participants said that an increased number of mosques meant that Muslims nowadays were more likely to pray locally, had different ways of praying, and were not so well networked across the city, others disagreed. These thought Muslims are 'more relaxed' on this issue than in the past, and that younger people, and new converts to Islam, are less influenced by tradition, caste and other traditional forms of cultural differentiation within Islam. 'They're Muslims, that's it' was how one participant put it.

These observations on population change were not always made dispassionately. Some young Muslims clearly saw the arrival of people from Poland as a perceived threat to local Muslim culture, while members of the White population discussed the possibility that the British National Party would soon win seats because of the high Muslim population. Young people referred back to times beyond their memory and talked about 'Paki bashing' and riots in Bradford, and Skinheads treating Indians badly in Southall, a diverse town just outside Hillingdon. On the whole, however, there was an impression that things were better than in the past.

> 'But now that everyone's used to it, like we're not the new thing that's come into the country now, I think it's alright for our generation.'
> (MAYA: female, Sikh, religion quite important)

Relations within the community

The overwhelming impression from the young people taking part in YOR interviews and discussion groups is that ethnic and religious diversity was (almost) fully accepted in the research areas. This was certainly the prevailing discourse that most young people subscribed to. Newham stood out among the three locations as embracing diversity: whatever their faith position, most young people in interviews and discussion groups gave the impression of both feeling accepted and accepting others. Numerous participants indicated that the highly multi-cultural nature of the borough, and the absence of a distinct and large majority group, made mutual acceptance easier and discrimination harder. As one participant said, even if people are from different religions they all believe in God, have a holy book and a place of worship. Young people did not deny the existence of prejudice, but held the view that 'generally you can believe what you want and people will accept that'. Several suggested it was probably harder not to have a religion than to have one. Most felt they could freely voice their opinions, even if they did have to be careful to avoid upsetting anybody. On the whole they stressed the advantages of a diverse community that taught young people to get on with different religions.

'Well I believe that because I've grown up in a place that's so diverse which consists of different types of races, ethnicity and religion, I believe that everyone is really used to it. So I feel okay and comfortable.' (CHARDANAY: female, Protestant, religion very important)

A young Sikh in Hillingdon also felt lucky to live in a multicultural setting.

'I think it's really good in a sense. I have never been to the Caribbean Islands at all, but walking down the aisle in Tesco, it's exciting. You just load the trolley up with Caribbean juices and all of these cultural things you would never see in life because you can't go on a trip there, you don't know anyone there . . . So I think it's actually really cool in a sense because even like if you look at Cineworld in Feltham they have . . . Bollywood movies that they play there, but if you look in a Cineworld in Aberdeen there are no Bollywood movies. So you can kind of, without being there, relate and understand what kind of segregations are there because they wouldn't play that kind of movie where it wouldn't sell tickets.' (ISHAN: male, Sikh, religion fairly important)

The advantages of living in multi-religion communities were widely stressed in all research areas. Apart from awareness and understanding of a range of religions, it gave people from different faith groups the opportunity to show others that 'you aren't a stereotype, you are just a normal person like everyone else but with different beliefs'. Sikhs in Hillingdon were particularly likely to stress how key commonalities between religious interpretations and traditions – such as an emphasis on living a good life and treating others well – could bring people together. As well as opportunities for sustained and more formal mixing between cultural and religious groups in the community, there was also mixing of a more transitory and informal kind. Many participants took advantage of events, such as carnivals and community events celebrating different religions and cultures, to learn about other faiths and traditions. Although these were sometimes tied to one particular religion, everyone was welcome and nobody was 'preached at or forced in any way'.

Whether through school, mixing in the community or attending multi-cultural events, YOR participants in effect endorsed the position of interpretivist theorists in stressing the need for awareness contexts where face-to-face interaction could take place if mutual understanding of identity was to develop (Glaser and Strauss, 1964). They were in overwhelming agreement that 'you can understand people only if you have talked to them and mixed with them'. A young Christian explained that people inevitably 'push aside the stereotypes' and learn about other religions in Newham where 'you get Pentecostal Christians, you get atheists, you get Catholics, you get Anglicans, you get Christians, you get Muslims and different sects of Muslims, you get agnostics and so many people from so many different cultures and from so many different backgrounds'. Some, mainly Sikhs in Hillingdon, nonetheless felt that those with very strong beliefs in their own religion find it harder to accept what another religion might stand for.

It has been pointed out that diversity and co-existence across cultures and religious traditions do not, however, necessarily equate with integration and social cohesion (Lewis, 2007; Mondal, 2008), and this was apparent in the research areas. Alongside the largely positive discourse on inter-ethnic and inter-religious acceptance in the research areas, there were varying accounts of how people from different ethnic, cultural and religious backgrounds got along together in practice. Not all mixing is positive, and superficial contact without understanding other people's religious beliefs and practices can be counter-productive. A pertinent example was given by a young Muslim who told of her White neighbours taking photographs of her family 'in case she sees us on the news'.

A very practical issue concerned opportunities to mix and really get to know people from different cultures and faith groups. Geographical segregation was a key factor for social segregation and particularly evident in Bradford where, despite a multi-faith population overall, the geographical area was divided according to ethnicity and religion. Young people gave the impression that the most segregated areas tended to be either council estates or affluent housing areas. The implications were clear for young people, as the comments from the following pupils living in a 'White area' demonstrate.

'Although we live in Bradford, and it's quite multicultural and stuff, it's strange because we are this side of Bradford rather than right in the centre where there is the most diversity. It is like . . . not being given the full opportunity to explore other religions. Obviously I know all about them, but although we live in Bradford I haven't had a great mixture, being with people of one culture all the time rather than at a school that is very diverse.' (JANE: female, no religion, religion important in some ways but not others)

'I was going to say one of the big problems with Bradford is there isn't many schools that are actually mixed as far as I am aware. It's either purely Asian or purely White or it's literally split straight down the middle. And the same with the communities. You have certain areas that are renowned for Asians and other communities where there is a lot of White people. And it's just split straight down the middle.' (JON: male, no religion, religion not at all important)

Residential segregation was also reported in Newham despite the more uniform multicultural nature of the area, and in Hillingdon where there are both residentially diverse and relatively segregated areas. Even living in the more diverse locations did not necessarily mean social integration. This was shown by several young Sikhs who appeared to mix almost entirely with others from the same cultural background. These young people vividly illustrated the very real possibility of social segregation amidst geographical integration. Southall (just outside Hillingdon) was given as another example, exemplified by the lifestyle of Somali people who had their own community centre and shops.

As young people pointed out, where you live affects where you go to school. Figure 2.7 (see Chapter 2) confirms the impression young people gave of much greater segregation by ethnicity in Bradford than in either Hillingdon or Newham. It shows how all survey participants in Bradford attended schools or colleges with low or mid ethnic diversity whereas around a half of those in Hillingdon and Newham experienced high ethnic diversity. No doubt related to these patterns, a tendency to select friends according to their beliefs was most marked in Bradford and least marked in Hillingdon (Figure 9.1).

Residential patterns reflect historical trends as well as socio-economic status but also involve an element of choice. Young people in Bradford, who tended to hold similar views whatever their faith position, talked about how religion assumed an importance when families thought about moving house.

'Well I know some people, like when they're moving house, they would cross off particular areas because they wouldn't want to live in that area because it's majority Muslim or whatever. Like areas that have bad reputations, sometimes linked to religion. And I think that like I know people that would like to live in places because it's strongly one religion.' (ROSE: female, no religion, religion not at all important)

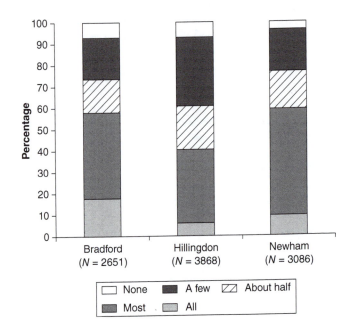

Figure 9.1 Friends with similar religious beliefs by study area

'I think the majority of the time it's not a conscious decision you know. I think it's a more subtle sort of subconscious segregation that happens. People of the same culture tend to live in the same areas and they tend to share the same religion, and I think that's something that's inevitably built over time. And so now, even if people want to break the culture barriers and, say, if there was a certain area where there was a certain group of people and an outsider wanted to join, even if those people were the nicest people in the world, the outsider still wouldn't feel that they were fully accepted. I think religion only really becomes a factor when you make conscious decisions like moving house. And that's when you kind of notice everybody's religious and you really start to take it into account.' (NAIHLA: female, Muslim, religion very important)

Those in other areas raised somewhat different issues concerning geographical mobility and 'White flight'. One Sikh girl in Hillingdon said that her English neighbours had left the locality because they felt like a minority amidst Indians. Others talked about people from minority groups gravitating to areas like Southall because they feel more comfortable there, even though another participant, again a Sikh, told how her family had moved from Southall as everyone there was Indian and they preferred a more mixed population. On the whole, however, the prevailing discourse was positive, perhaps reflecting the possibility that people unhappy with diversity had moved away or not settled in these locations in the first place.

The degree of mixing between different ethnic and religious groups living in the research areas was nonetheless very variable and depended considerably on the local population and the opportunities it provided. Ethnicity and culture often seemed more influential than religion, and examples of Asian groups sticking together were common. In Bradford, for instance, young people talked of a park where Asians from 'all over' hang out. Individual differences were, however, important, and sociable parents could also make a considerable difference.

> 'There's lots of different cultures and ethnicities on my street, and there's a lady from the bottom of the street who knocked on everyone's door and said there's going to be a little street party because there's lots of new people on our street so . . . everyone can get to know each other. There's White people, there's Indian people, there's Muslim people . . . So everyone's going to get together. So my community's kind of good like that. They don't discriminate about how you look.' (MIRIAM: female, Islam, religion very important)

Community tensions

Despite positive expression of liberal individualism, it was evident that tensions linked to ethnicity, culture and religion were also present in the research areas. According to Lewis (2007) problems arising in multi-faith communities can stem from 'the dislocation wrought by migration or learning to live as a religious minority in an environment perceived as either indifferent or hostile', and there was evidence that this was the case. Accounts of prejudice arose even in Newham where this positive discourse was most widespread. Reports of overt and covert conflict and mistrust, discrimination and abusive behaviour, restrictions on feeling safe, and reactions to religious activities such as evangelism and the siting of new mosques, were found in all areas. Although these underlying tensions might reflect religion, they were also linked to race and ethnicity. Young people said that conflict arose between Blacks and Asians, between Whites and Asians, or between Blacks and Whites, and it also emerged within groups, such as between different Muslim castes and sects. In Bradford they talked about particularly high levels of racism in White areas, particularly when these were located next to Asian areas. It was also suggested there is more conflict in working class areas where people are less educated and have less understanding. 'Really Conservative British people' were seen by some to have less understanding while others suggested racism is generally less pronounced among younger than older generations.

> 'My Dad's a bit racist, but my sisters have both got different views ... My Dad was brought up that way. He has always been like the kind of terrorist type ... Me and my sister, because we were brought up in this age are more accepting, so we don't focus on their ethnicity more than anything. It's just the actions. So it depends on whether they have done something wrong ... If that particular person or group of people hasn't done anything wrong, then we won't think anything of it. So it just depends.' (LEANNE: female, agnostic, religion not very important)

Young people speculated on reasons for conflict, often suggesting that hatred thrived among groups not used to interacting with each other, and that tolerance levels were higher among those growing up in diverse rather than single culture communities. They said there are always some people who do not understand another's religion and are not willing to learn, and that conflict and prejudice are inevitable when many different groups live alongside one another. The possibility that conflict is more likely where one religion is dominant is borne out by its more frequent mention in Bradford than Newham.

Other reasons for conflict included threatened identities, intense passion for religious beliefs, misinterpretation of religions, and power and politics dressed up as religion. One participant suggested 'it's not the religion causing the conflict, it's the people behind it'. Others pointed to historical conflicts between Asian religions such as Islam and Sikhism, or inter-religious conflicts between Jews and Muslims that ran counter to the usual narrative of the Western Christian world versus the Eastern Islamic world.

Tensions in all three research areas made young people feel uncomfortable, especially if they experienced abusive behaviour directly or indirectly. Typical scenarios were 'flippant comments', name-calling and verbal racial abuse, either called out in the street or from cars. Some White girls in Bradford mentioned feeling abused by young Pakistani men who seemed to assume they were prostitutes. The impression gained from YOR interviews was that these forms of discriminatory behaviour were particularly common in Bradford between Asian and White people. Name-calling because of skin colour was also mentioned in Hillingdon although in the main this was experienced vicariously. Participants in Newham reported fewest problems, although a young Muslim reported two incidents of prejudice and discrimination due to her religion. In the first she was taunted by comments that Muslims deserve to be tortured: she retorted that nobody says all Christians or atheists deserve to be tortured just because one person does something bad. In the second, which she ignored, young White men threw snowballs at her. On the whole, however, Muslims in Newham were most likely to report problems outside their local communities.

Most discriminatory behaviour, from what young people said, was targeted at Muslims. Fear of terrorism and stereotypical views of Muslims were generally held responsible. Segregation and discrimination in Bradford have become more marked since 9/11 and 7/7 and now 'there's a White community and a Brown community' in Bradford with frequent assumptions that Brown people are Muslims and hence terrorists. It seemed that Muslims faced a considerable amount of stigma in practice, probably in part attributable to the segregated nature of Bradford and the limited opportunities for individuals to have widespread contact and enhance their status within the wider setting (Berger and Luckmann, 1966). In particular contexts Muslims appeared to have achieved the status of a suspect community (Pantazis and Pemberton, 2009).

> 'No, like before the 9/11, life was just perfect . . . You used to get the few racist comments, but it wasn't to do with your religion, it was just to do with your culture. I mean straightaway after 9/11, I think everything went downhill for the Muslims.' (ABDA: female, Islam, religion very important)

> 'A few of (our friends) are quite racist, and they are just typically racist towards Asian people and Muslims, saying that they are terrorists. . . . And you hear jokes that go round that are based on them and terrorist activities and whatever.' (KATHLEEN: female, no religion, religion not at all important)

Many participants commented on how media-fuelled attitudes towards Muslims had led to suspicion at airports, and funny looks on trains and buses. There were accusations that young Muslims were being offensive when they moved away from White people to give them more space. One Muslim reported an incident on a bus when a woman yelled at her and said 'Don't sit next to me' and accused her of killing 'all them innocent people'. She had been about 12 at the time and scared and shocked. Another participant told a similar story.

> 'There was another day . . . I was going to church and I was reading my prayer book (on the bus) and there was another person that came and sat next to me. He thought I was a Muslim (I'm actually a Christian) and he started saying offensive things to Muslims . . . And I didn't actually think he was speaking to me, so I just carried on reading my

book, my prayer book. And he just kept saying things. And I realised, and I turned round and said, "excuse me, I'm not a Muslim. I don't think you should actually say those things to Muslims". And he said, "okay, I'm glad that you're not a Muslim".' (PRINCE: male, Christian (Ethiopian Orthodox), religion very important)

Against the backcloth of the stigmatisation of Muslims as a suspect community, otherwise innocent objects like rucksacks can acquire a potentially sinister and fear evoking symbolic significance. Carrying any bags was a problem, particularly for males, even at school. According to one young person, 'Britain is really paranoid'.

'If you have a rucksack, yeah you go to school to study, people like watch you . . . If I'm with a guy and he's got a bag . . . and if you're in the library people will watch you, where's that bag going?' (TAHIRA: female, Muslim, importance of religion not specified)

'This guy like in my year group he was saying, 'cos he's like a Muslim and he's got a beard, he was on the bus with a backpack and he was like "everyone was looking at me and moving away and stuff". And I was like, it shouldn't have to be like that in Bradford.' (ANGELA: female, agnostic, religion important in some ways but not others)

Religious dress could make matters worse, probably because it reinforced associations between Islamic dress and terrorism, and there were many reports of offensive comments that related to wearing the hijab or full veil for women, or the thobe for men. These were most commonly mentioned in Bradford. Sikhs also suffered discrimination and verbal comments if they had a turban. Interestingly, some of the female Sikhs said they received abusive comments, even from other Sikhs, when in school uniform but not when they put on Western clothes. The potential advantages of impression management (Goffman, 1959) are evident, and one participant suggested a double standard could be at work.

'It's like a double standard in society, with, let's say, like for example, a nun. They cover exactly the same things we cover, but then when people see them, they're like "Wow, don't do that, there's a nun over there for goodness sake, have some respect". It's like people think . . . she's so like committed to her religion and then she covers up and she does this. And then with us it's like we're oppressed.' (SUMAYA: female, Muslim, religion very important)

A few young females suggested that wearing the hijab could make you feel safer if it identified you as sharing the religious identity of potential assailants. Another side of the picture, however, was that young Muslims not wearing the hijab could be approached by other Muslims and asked why they were not. This was also considered intrusive and offensive.

Tensions within communities could also be within rather than between faith groups. Muslim participants, for instance, mentioned conflict between Shia and Sunni Muslims, while others talked about Christian denominational differences. Finally, it was acknowledged that tensions might sometimes reflect hypersensitivity rather than discrimination per se.

> 'I think they feel a bit paranoid. I feel a bit paranoid walking around sometimes. . . . I walked into McDonalds the other day in Leeds . . . and everyone was looking at us in a weird way. . . . It doesn't make you feel very comfortable and maybe we were just being paranoid. But then again I don't know.' (MIRIAM: female, Islam, religion very important)

Locality and safety

Most YOR survey participants said they felt safe in their local neighbourhoods. Those who did not, however, were more likely to be female and from Black and White backgrounds than male and Asian. Further differences emerged according to faith group. Young people with no religion, and living in Newham, were least likely to feel safe, followed closely by White Christians and Sikhs also in Newham. Although differences were small, Muslims were least likely to feel safe in Hillingdon (Figure 9.2).

The qualitative data confirmed that young people felt distinctly safer in some places than others. This was true not only between but also within research areas, and notably so in Bradford. Fears for security were often not related to race, culture or religion, but simply to a dislike of being out alone in unpopulated areas or places notorious for activities such as drug-dealing, violence, gang fights or prostitution. Sometimes young people, especially females, did not relish going out at night partly as they feared rape or because they saw late night buses as dangerous. Several participants made the point that there were areas they would be scared to go to regardless of whether they were populated by people of the same or a different religion to them.

As a generalisation, and all else being equal, young people felt safest when they were in more familiar territory, and when they felt part of the local population (Webster, 1996; Watt and Stenson, 1998). They also felt safe in areas comprising other religions and ethnicities if they knew people living there, but did not feel comfortable in places on the margin (Shields,

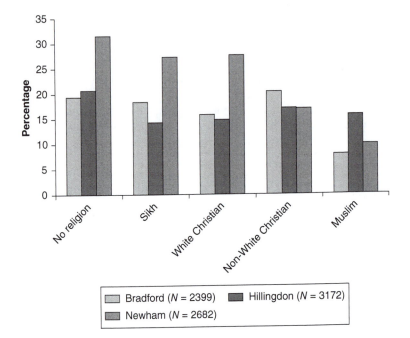

Figure 9.2 Never or mostly not feeling safe in the study areas by faith group

1991). To some degree it seemed that members of minority ethnic groups felt safer in multicultural than monocultural (White) areas, whereas White young people felt safer in predominantly White areas. Generally speaking, young people felt least comfortable where they were not known and local populations were 'different' from them. They seemed to have good knowledge of their own areas and almost always knew exactly which areas they were and were not happy in. Young people in Hillingdon suggested they usually know whether people they meet are from their area or not.

Nonetheless, changing times had led to changing populations and increased complexity. Young Muslims in Bradford stressed how it was not safe to 'play out and go to the corner shop after dark' as it had been in the past. Although members of the National Front and 'Paki Bashers' no longer came into the area to harass the Asians and Muslims, a recent influx of people from different backgrounds (which were not specified) meant, for one female, a dislike of leaving her house. Since the family had recently moved, both her brothers had got into fights. Things, however, might be improving as more Asians were moving into the area. As she said, 'you feel more safe having people of your own'. Another participant from Bradford agreed that being surrounded by people of the same culture makes life less stressful. As he said, 'You can walk past somebody's house and they'll come out holding a tray and say 'Oh, do you want some samosas?' The complex relationship between feeling safe, ethnicity and religion was reflected in other comments by young people: in Bradford a Muslim girl wearing the hijab with Western clothes was allegedly beaten up by a mixed group of Black and White girls, and there were tales of White people and Asians getting on 'nicely' during the day but in conflict at night.

Despite some apprehension, young people sometimes found it necessary to go to or through places where they felt less safe. This might be 'to go to the doctor's or go to the optician's or whatever' or because the route to school involved crossing a neighbourhood. As other studies have found (Seabrook and Green, 2004), young people adopt strategies in these instances to minimise risk. These included taking safe routes, even if longer, remaining respectful at all times, and taking precautions against muggers. Another suggested it was best to be with 'guys who can defend themselves' rather than girls. He also talked about 'playing the Muslim card', saying 'hey Muslim brother' to avert any possible threat. One female in Hillingdon had an additional strategy.

> 'I don't think there's anywhere that I particularly wouldn't go because I believe that God's with me wherever I go. And if I'm afraid of going somewhere for whatever reason, then I'd just be praying like in my head as I walked along. And I believe that God would protect me from any dangers of various places.' (CHARLOTTE: female, Protestant: Baptist, religion very important)

A high crime rate was specifically mentioned in Newham by participants who said they did not feel safe and suggested it was inadvisable to go around at night in groups smaller than ten – although this was contested by another participant who thought large groups could give out the wrong message and look intimidating themselves.

> 'It's the guys with the low trousers up to their underwear and the guys with vests that you have to be careful of. It doesn't really matter what faith you have. If they want something they'll get it from you some way.' (ADAM: male, Muslim, religion important in some ways but not others)

The threat from gangs was mentioned to a limited extent in the research areas, although particularly in Hillingdon where participants spoke of territorial 'postcode' gangs. While these could be Black, White or Asian, the view was that they were less based on religion or ethnicity than power and territory. Sometimes, however, rival groups were more directly based on religion. Young people talked about fights in Southall where different groups 'fight for their religion or they'll just fight'.

Another cause of tension in research areas arose when members of one religious group appeared to impose themselves on others. Participants told of tensions and battles in Newham when people were actively voicing their religion on the streets and trying to convince others to convert: a preacher who yells 'Repent', and is avoided only by crossing the road, was mentioned in this context. A young male atheist told of his fear that 'I'd probably be stabbed' before the police moved a group of Muslims from outside where he lived in Hillingdon.

> 'As I say, I come from a block of flats. A couple of weeks ago there was a white tent put up in our community green where all of the Muslims took off their shoes, went and prayed, put up a Qur'an and everything, and that was really intimidating . . . I mean I'm like an atheist so I don't believe anything, and these people who are deeply religious and everything went and set up their own like praying area in my area . . . in public space where they shouldn't be allowed.' (JACOB BLACK: male, atheist, religion not very important)

Most commonly, young people talked about tensions arising from the growing number of mosques in their areas, and disputes about their location. This issue arose in all three research areas, as has been found elsewhere (Eade, 1996), and was discussed by participants from all faith positions. Arguments seemed to centre on where money was coming from to pay for the new mosques, as well as fears about what was being taught in them, the spread of fundamentalist ideas, people losing their identity as British people, and the encouragement of more Muslims to the area. Many young people nonetheless saw both sides and asked if there would be similar complaints if somebody wanted to build a temple, Jewish synagogue or chapel.

Social cohesion

The concept of social cohesion has attracted considerable attention in recent years in response to population change, increased diversity in many city areas, and evidence of poor or absent relationships between groups from disparate cultural, racial, ethnic and religious backgrounds. Putnam (2000) developed the concept of 'bowling alone' and the idea that communities can be cohesive only if there is 'bonding' within societal groups, 'bridging' between them, and 'linking' between all these groups and those in power. Fears for reductions in these forms of social capital have heightened since the events of 9/11 and 7/7 amid concerns that violent extremism 'may begin with a search for answers to questions about identity, faith and belonging' (DCSF, 2008). Putnam's recent US research on religious affiliation and practice indicates that, despite the national political polarisation between conservative protestants and secular liberals, there is also growing tolerance of religious pluralism. This is linked to a shift among younger Americans from family inheritance to individual choice of faith, considerable inter-faith marriage and dense overlapping personal relationships. Hence, social cohesion is enhanced by 'creating a web of interlocking personal relationships among people of many faiths. That is America's grace' (Putnam and Campbell, 2010: 550). However, US patterns are not necessarily closely echoed in Europe. Baumann's (1996) study in Southall (adjoining Hillingdon, one of the research areas) found that two-thirds of the 12 to 18-year-olds in his study, half of whom were from Sikh backgrounds while the rest were from Hindu, Muslim, Christian or mixed or other backgrounds, cited religion as being a more divisive factor in the area than culture, race, class, money, racism, fear, politics, competition, media or school.

Many initiatives have been established in response to these concerns in the quest to make neighbourhoods pleasant places to live in where people can feel safe. The Commission on Integration and Cohesion (2007) report on *Our Shared Future* draws on the work of Forrest and Kearns (2001) in pointing to the benefit of shared religious values for encouraging integration and cohesion. It calls for more constructive conversations between those who are religious and those who are not, and highlights the contextual nature of cohesion issues and the need for local solutions. The British Government responded to this call with a ten-year strategy for positive activities entitled *Aiming High for Young People* (HM Treasury, 2007), a ten-point plan to build cohesion and tackle community tensions. This included the specific commitment to develop an interfaith strategy. The *Face to Face and Side by Side* report (DCLG, 2008) preceded the introduction of the widely criticised Prevent Strategy (HM Government, 2011) with an agenda to deter Muslim radicalisation.

A range of local initiatives accompany national strategy in this area. Holden (2009), for example, reports a project in Burnley in the North of England, which involved 15-year-old students at three schools (mainly White, mainly Asian and mixed), and aimed to 'build bridges' between Muslim and Christian groups. For the mainly White and mixed school, the street was cited as the most important place to mix with other young people, compared with sports centres, playing fields and parks for the mostly Asian school. The most worrying statistics were related to racial superiority, with 30% of respondents in the mainly White school believing that one race was superior to others and only 29% agreeing that faith communities should work together, compared with 76% in the mostly Asian school. This reflected the strong influence of the British National Party and family membership in the mainly White school. While the majority of students from all schools supported individualistic and liberal democratic values and the importance of showing loyalty to the UK, most of the students in the mainly White school did not think it was important to respect and tolerate others, cultivate mixed faith friendships or apply limits to free speech to avoid offending other groups. A project in Oldham and Rochdale (Thomas, 2011) mentioned in Chapter 1 is another example.

The YOR study sought young people's views on tackling community tensions. Participants have related their experiences in making friends, learning about different cultures and religions, and living in their neighbourhoods throughout this book, displaying a generally positive outlook on diversity and inter-group relations despite some evidence of segregation and conflict. To gain their specific ideas on how social cohesion could be improved in their communities, the YOR survey provided space at the end of the questionnaire for participants to write whatever they liked in response to the question 'What can young people, schools/colleges and the Government do to make sure that people from different religions get on well together?'

Just over half (52.6%) the survey participants provided classifiable comments (this excludes those who said things such as 'no', 'no comment' or who wrote something nonsensical) and comparable response rates were found in all three areas. Comments ranged from the fairly brief to the long and considered and were coded into eight main themes of: no changes need to be made; nothing can be done; more integration; better education; increased equality and respect; religions should be kept apart; religion should be less visible; and government activities are needed. The vast majority (83%) of those with viable comments were included in one of these categories, far fewer (15%) in two categories, and very few (2%) in three categories. Figure 9.3 shows the distribution of responses into these categories for the sample overall.

Most suggestions to increase social cohesion in the research areas reflected an ethos of liberal individualism and fell into the broad categories of more integration, better education, and improving equality and respect. Much smaller numbers indicated that keeping religions apart, and making religion less visible, was the best strategy, while only a few said that there was really nothing that could be done. Most young people therefore fell within the first and third of Holden's (2009) four categories of religious engagement: *'religious inclusivists'* (religious people willing to engage with other faiths; moderate in religious behaviour; respect for other religions);

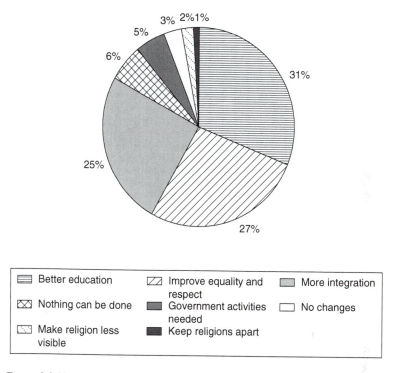

Figure 9.3 Young people's suggestions for encouraging people from different religions to get on well (total responses = 6671)

'religious exclusivists' (inter-faith dialogue seen as theologically risky; minimum contact with other religions); *'secular integrationists'* (respect right of others to religious beliefs so long as don't evangelise or indoctrinate; willing to work with faith groups for social justice); and *'secular aversionists'* (no religious beliefs and reject the idea that faith communities can promote the common good or that inter-faith partnerships are valuable).

Among ways of encouraging integration, young people mentioned a range of activities for multi-faith groups such as youth clubs, sports events, after-school clubs, mixed places of worship and multi-religious meetings in the community. At school they suggested mixed schools and mixed classes within schools, more diversity days, and multi-religious assemblies. Proposals for better education were targeted at school, in the community, and through the media. At school a focus was placed on more and better Religious Education (RE) classes, educating a wider age range of young people on religion, teaching on all faith positions (including atheism), bringing in experts and religious people to help with lessons, and providing experience of more religious materials. In the community, opportunities for everyone to experience different religions, and the food, places and festivals associated with them, at first hand were seen as important. Young people emphasised that, in both these contexts, engendering greater understanding of the effects of bullying and conflict, encouraging people to be non-judgemental, providing opportunities for positive communication between different groups, and focusing on both similarities and differences between religions, were very important. For the part of the media, they were encouraged to talk about religion in a balanced but honest way, improve their reporting, play a role in public education, provide educational programmes on television for all age groups, and use celebrities to convey positive messages. Some of their comments and suggestions were:

> It's really all up to the people to decide whether they are willing to put their differences aside. The government or whatever cannot really influence people's beliefs.

> You could probably sit all religions down and teach them about what they ALL have in common, that might help.

> Ideas to improve equality and respect include the creation of a public holiday for all to share, putting equal emphasis on all holidays and not just those that have a Christian basis, ensuring that everyone is respected and treated the same. Accept the differences between people, and put an end to stereotyping.

> The government could hold national days dedicated to bring religions and cultures together in a celebration of one another.

> We should have the same amount of holidays, for every festival, as then no-one will feel left out.

> The government could organize for more TV shows to include stuff about religion and they could put it in children's TV shows so they could learn about it from a young age.

> Make sure the government/media do not portray certain religious groups as hostile or to be feared of because that is one of the main reasons as to why there is diversity within groups.

A small number of survey participants urged keeping religions apart, or making religion less visible, to improve social cohesion. Among their suggestions were different schools for different faiths, banning people of certain religions from the country, abolishing RE, encouraging people to hide their religion and outlawing religious clothing, preventing the media from focusing on religion, and generally talking about religion less. Some urged government activities such as improving safety, punishing the disrespectful, reducing poverty, electing a more multi-faith and religion-aware government, and taking measures to stop wars, fights, abuse and bullying. Finally, several participants said that no changes are necessary and there is nothing extra that can be done. In their view either everything is fine, or the essential problem has more to do with ethnicity or individual people than religion.

> Organised religion has no place in the modern world, its existence is only hindering progression for the human relation. Outlaw it completely.

> Remove it from all policy, decision-making and rhetoric. Religious beliefs are by definition not related to reason or logic and therefore must not be discussed in a way that they might hinder either. People should be allowed to believe what they want, but in order to ensure we do not ostracise others, we should remove our religious or spiritual beliefs from the public realm.

> Unfortunately there is not much we can do . . . TIME IS THE ONLY SOLUTION.

Patterns of responses were not markedly different by age, gender, faith group, the importance of religion or research areas, although there were some differences. Table 9.1 illustrates the distribution of responses in Bradford, Hillingdon and Newham. Respondents in Hillingdon were least likely to call for change, while those in Bradford were marginally most likely to emphasise the need for greater integration and those in Newham called for more and better education. Generally speaking, however, there seemed agreement across the study sample on how social cohesion could best be promoted.

Table 9.1 Young people's suggestions for encouraging people from different religions to get on well by research area (%)

	Bradford (N = 1941)	*Hillingdon (N = 2641)*	*Newham (N = 2068)*
Better education	29	31	33
Improve equality and respect	27	27	27
More integration	29	21	27
Nothing can be done	5	7	5
Government activities needed	6	5	4
No changes	2	4	2
Make religion less visible	1	4	2
Keep religions apart	2	2	1

Summary

Young people's constructions of the changing meaning and impact of religion were reflected in their descriptions of their own areas and communities (although it was also noteworthy that some young people, particularly in Bradford or the North of Hillingdon, appeared to be living 'on the periphery' and were relatively untouched by change). Their narratives of change recognised how an influx of new minorities was associated with a decline in the use of Christian churches and a proliferation of mosques, temples, gurdwaras and places of worship for other faith communities. These symbolic locations demonstrated the growing diversity and multi-faith character of the areas in which they lived.

A largely comfortable blend of tolerance and tension characterised the research areas. Young people were keen to stress the advantages of living in multi-faith communities but yet were not oblivious to the disadvantages it could bring. In Bradford there was a definite sense that inter-group relations were better than in the past, but that ethnic and religious conflict and suspicion had not disappeared. Some pointed to the tension between lessons on different faiths and cultures in school and what is learned experientially in the community. Asked if there is religious conflict or if religious difference is celebrated, one participant said 'I wouldn't say it's celebrated or there's any religious problems either'.

Most young people talked positively about diversity and stressed how it was much harder for discrimination to arise in settings, such as Newham where White Christians are now in a minority, where everyone is different. Nonetheless rhetoric may sometimes be stronger than reality. Thus in Bradford there was much rhetorical reference to diversity on the one hand, but emphasis of segregated schools and neighbourhoods, particularly differentiating White Christian and secular populations from Muslim-dominated schools and neighbourhoods, on the other. Opportunities to celebrate religious/community festivals in local areas were nonetheless everywhere seen positively as providing the chance for different groups to mix and learn more about each other.

Despite a discourse of liberal individualism, and an appreciation of diversity, accounts of tensions emerged. Not everyone was seen as tolerant and accepting of other cultural groups, and prejudice seemed particularly likely to arise amongst those not used to inter-ethnic contact and mixing. Tensions might also arise if particular groups attempted to redefine the character of an area, such as by building a new mosque. Segregation, whether mainly in racial, ethnic or religious terms, was also apparent. This occurred not only between ethnic and religious groups but also (particularly in Bradford and Newham) between some caste groupings and religious sects within Islam. Segregation could also occur within culturally mixed areas.

Few young people had personal experiences of discriminatory behaviour although most had stories to tell. Name-calling seemed to occur in all areas, and Muslims with bags or headscarves, or Sikhs with beards, seemed particularly targeted. While most communities appeared harmonious, young people reported how there could be underlying tensions and oversensitivity towards different religious groups. Most young people nonetheless felt generally safe and did not venture far afield, especially at night. All areas could be dangerous, but they did not usually feel at risk on account of their religion.

Suggestions for encouraging people from different religious backgrounds to get on well together were provided. Most responses focused on more integration of different groups, better education at school, in the community and by the media, and increased equality and respect within the population as a whole.

10 The overall picture

The young people whose voices take prominence throughout this book live in unprecedented times of change, contrasts and complexity. Growing up in multicultural Britain, whether or not their heritage lies in this country, they are witnessing the evolution of population, institutional structure and accompanying systems of beliefs and morality within their communities, and making personal and shared adjustments to their religious identities, faith and practice. There are echoes between the experiences of these young people and their counterparts in other European countries, in North America, Australasia and other advanced societies (Scheffer, 2011) and, in investigating modern-day stories, the classic themes of early social science in the late 19th and early 20th centuries have been revisited. It was argued in the first chapter that despite great differences between then and now, both periods have experienced enormous demographic movement and the transformation of city life.

The Youth On Religion (YOR) study sought to determine how young people negotiate their identities within these changing settings and amidst the commonalities and differences they display. With a focus on three specific religiously diverse geographical locations, and participants across the adolescent years, it asked about the development of religious identity and practice, the influences in young people's lives on these patterns, the ways in which religion affects everyday behaviours, and how members of diverse groups interact and get on. The findings are brought together in this chapter to feed into key contemporary debates in social science and help improve the knowledge base for policy-makers concerned with issues of identity, social cohesion and multiculturalism in uncertain times. They reflect the perspectives of young people themselves who are actively making sense of their lives and negotiating shared experiences with others who may differ in history, culture and beliefs. Their voices are significant as what they say and suggest is not necessarily in accordance with the favoured interpretations and solutions of policy-makers.

The picture that emerges is one of a generation in transition, with much evidence of recent change and optimism about the future. At present religion is very important in many young lives in these locations even though its expression increasingly involves choice rather than simple obligation to traditional values and practices (Davie, 2005). This is particularly evident for young Muslim participants, influenced by both their culture of origin and modern-day Western life, who are divided into Strict and Flexible Adherents: whereas some continue to observe religious traditions as closely as possible, others have negotiated ways of accommodating their religiosity within Western lifestyles. All young people have been exposed to the influences of modernity, including the rise in supremacy of science and technology and contact with others from a range of cultural and ethnic backgrounds. There may be some movement away from religion under these conditions, particularly among White British young people without a strong family faith position, but the influence of religion nonetheless remains strong. However there is some evidence to suggest that processes of social mixing may, over the longer term, lead to reduced levels of religiosity and shifting forms of religious expression. It would seem that processes in the UK are likely to parallel those found in the US (Putnam and Campbell, 2010).

Durkheim (1912) proclaimed the enduring nature of religion, whatever its form, and its significance for community cohesion. He believed, to use a modern term, that some sort of 'glue' is necessary to provide a value base for social solidarity and hold diverse societies together in contexts of increasing economic interdependence and rapid population movement. Given the diversity of faith groups in the YOR study research areas, it did not seem likely that a specific religious tradition alone could serve this function. Indeed what emerged as a central theme running throughout the findings is how young people in these locations espouse an ethos of liberal individualism embracing personal agency and morality. It is suggested that these common values, instilled through faith communities, families, schools and other institutions, may be part of the 'glue' that Durkheim was referring to. In other words, a common ideology of respect, tolerance and a concern to do right unto others may be a major factor, combined with other elements, contributing to healthy cohesive communities. The findings overall do not, however, provide a completely rosy picture and it is evident that both rhetoric and reality come into play. There are constraints alongside the choices in young people's lives, there are sensitivities and tensions that accompany the positive interactions they are keen to report, and there are examples of segregation and separation amidst a backcloth of diversity and commonality.

The rest of this chapter outlines these findings in greater depth. It considers patterns of identity development within the study sample, the operation of personal agency and choice in the process, the realities and limitations of cohesion within diverse communities, and the future of religion. Three key messages inform the final conclusion: first it is important to listen to young people's own accounts of the meaning and role of religion in their lives, second to take heed of their suggestions for greater social cohesion in their communities, and third to ensure that their mutual respect for one other, and optimism for the future, is fostered and not ignored.

Developing religious identities

All young participants in the YOR study had some kind of personal and/ or group religious identity, whether this was all-encompassing or largely insignificant in their lives. YOR findings suggest that religious identity is formed through a complex interaction between young people's biological, physical and cognitive development, the cultural values and prevailing discourses they are exposed to, and the material and spatial settings in which they live and are growing up.

The importance of developmental stage in identity formation was highlighted by young people's qualitative accounts of their religious journeys. They told a single story, in line with the interpretive school of thought (Berger and Luckmann, 1966), about the starting point for their faith position and the significant early influence of their parents. Almost all reported how their first notions of religion were strongly linked to family tradition and religiosity, and how these provided the initial basis for their subsequent faith position. As they grew older, and expanded their cognitive powers of understanding and reasoning, they either confirmed their allegiance to the family faith position or determined a separate course for themselves. Identity transformations affected by status passages and key life events (Glaser and Strauss, 1971), notably the death of a relative or friend, were significant turning points (Lindesmith et al., 1999) in many young lives.

By their teenage years (when the YOR study was carried out), young people displayed a wide variety of faith positions and ways of expressing their religiosity, both across and within faith groups. Religious identity embodies elements of labelling and affiliation, belief, belonging, and public and private practice, and there is enormous individuality in how these elements are reflected. For instance, some identify with a particular faith even if they have no strong beliefs and do not practise, some have strong beliefs but do not practise publicly, some go to a place of worship but do not have strong beliefs, some believe but do not belong, and some belong but do not believe. Many denied that outer religion meant stronger faith, and considerable emphasis was placed on private religion. A four-category typology was developed to help describe these variations. This identified young people as Strict Adherents, devout in their religion and the following of tradition, Flexible Adherents, also devout but willing to adapt their religious expression in accordance with other priorities in their lives, Pragmatists, who saw religion as important but had no strong and consistent faith position, and Bystanders, for whom religion was not very important. Young people had reached these positions over the course of their lives so far and already determined whether to retain or discard their faith position of origin, and whether to express religiosity in traditional or modified ways. They had made these choices in the contexts of family cultural identities and the prevailing Western culture (which might be similar or dissimilar) as well as a wide range of other influences. This typology was applicable across both the quantitative and qualitative study datasets.

There was a wide range of influences on religious journeys. Adherence to family attitudes and values was important in most cases, and by the time of the YOR study almost six in ten survey participants still report close similarity in religious beliefs to their mothers. Patterns are strongest for those who say religion is very important in their lives. These findings clearly indicate that YOR participants have not become detached from their families and wider collective groupings even if some have become individuated. This raises questions about widely accepted theoretical claims within social science that the impact of globalisation has disembedded people from local attachments to kin, place and faith, even in highly diverse areas (Giddens, 1991; Beck, 1992). It is apparent that modernity is not entirely liquid (Bauman, 2000).

Many influences other than the family were also important. No striking differences were found for either age or gender. Faith group was particularly significant, with Muslims in particular showing the highest levels of religious belief and adherence, as was the relationship between faith group and ethnicity: there was a marked distinction between Christians from White and non-White backgrounds. The number of books in the house, used as a proxy for socioeconomic status, was associated with greater importance of religion, while attendance at a school or college with a high level of eligibility for free school meals was linked with a tendency to share religious beliefs with all or most friends. These findings are suggestive of some impact of social class, although their implications require further investigation.

In terms of YOR survey rankings, the influence of scriptures and religious leaders on religious beliefs were reported as particularly important for Christians, Muslims and Sikhs while, relatively speaking, friends, teachers, science and the media had a lesser impact. This did not mean these aspects were unimportant, but rather that they were perceived as less significant. Indeed it is clear that friends have a strong influence on each other in many and varied ways (see Chapter 8) and that teachers and schools are likely to play an important role in encouraging the widespread liberal views characterising young people in the YOR study. Furthermore, even though science seemed to have a relatively unimportant effect on beliefs for religious groups (who found a wide range of influences important), but was most important for those with no religious faith (who cited few important influences), similar proportions of those from no religion, Christian, Muslim and Sikh groups said their beliefs had been influenced by science. This suggestion that young people could be influenced by both religion and science does not provide clear evidence for either Weber's (1948) thesis that the rise of science will lead to an erosion of religion or Dawkins' (2006) claim that religion and science are largely incompatible. Findings on the role of the internet, which were not contradicted by the interviews and discussion groups, do not generally support the growing influence of the digital age on young people's identities including attitudes to religion and popular culture (Beaudoin, 1998; Foresight Future Identities, 2013). Nonetheless virtual realities were not a central focus of our research and modern media may impinge more heavily on young people than the YOR study was able to ascertain.

The broader settings in which young people were growing up also had an impact on their religiosity, even if in sometimes intangible ways. It seemed that in addition to local differences explicable in terms of the religious and ethnic mix of research areas, there was some kind of overarching *locality ethos* that meant greater numbers found religion important in their lives, and more believed in God, in Newham than in either Hillingdon or Bradford. Setting was also important for inter-ethnic and inter-faith mixing: Bradford, where many young people lived and went to school in fairly ethnically segregated locations, stood out in this respect. A measure of school ethnic density confirmed the contrasting characteristics of schools and colleges in the three research areas and was in turn independently associated with perspectives on religion. Generally speaking, students attending schools with the greatest ethnic mix tended to be the least religious and have the least positive attitudes towards religion, but were more interested in the faith group of a new friend and had more friendships across religious boundaries. These patterns are hard to interpret. However, it is likely that both the school/college selection process and opportunities provided for social mixing in multi-faith settings contribute to these patterns.

The weakening of religious tradition in contexts of diversity was indeed a key finding. An inferential measure of the time families had spent in the UK was computed according to the number of family members (the participant in the YOR survey, and his/her mother and father) born in this country. Striking differences were found between those seemingly more and less settled in the UK. Even when factors such as faith group, ethnicity and research area were controlled for, participants with more family members born in the UK said religion was less important in their lives, had less strong beliefs about God, were less likely to be affected in their daily lives by their faith, were less likely to hold similar views on religion to their mothers, and were less likely to regard religion as positive. Many remained religious to a considerable degree, but were still far more likely to be Flexible Adherents than Strict Adherents. These findings reflect the multiple realities in their lives that many participants talked about in interviews and discussion groups, particularly the contradictions there might be between the traditions of their faith group and modern-day Western culture. The pressures and challenges faced by many young people from traditional religious backgrounds, such as Islam or Sikhism, living within contemporary Britain is a key theme running through this book.

Personal agency: choices and constraints

Whatever their faith position and strength of adherence, young people profess their own personal agency (James et al., 1998) in both their choice of religion and how it is practised. They strongly assert the right to lead their own lives, suggesting they are more likely to follow a faith position achieved on their own than one imposed on them, and are indignant when not able to take their own decisions. This is an unsurprising finding given the individualised nature of Western society, the prominence of the human rights agenda, and the current focus on children and young people's participation in the determination of their own lives. Greater freedom of choice is also predictable from the writings of Durkheim (1893) on population movement, particularly between conditions of mechanical and organic solidarity. In addition, this emphasis on personal determination reinforces Davie's (2005) emphasis on the shift from obligation to consumption in modern times.

The strong reliance on personal agency and choice underpinning young people's accounts appeared to be a useful tool permitting them to cope with contradictions and dilemmas, and negotiate difficult situations. Agency, which may have been exercised within tight constraints in their parents' generations, gave them the freedom to act as they thought best. It allowed them to question the tenets of their faith and pick and mix the aspects that suited them. For example, young Muslims might pray fervently but then go out to drink alcohol at a party, wear the hijab with family but not with friends, or behave differently at home and on holiday. While these behaviours could be seen as contradictory in some way (Jacobson, 1998; Hopkins, 2006), this was not necessarily the interpretation presented by young people themselves. Many YOR participants seemed happy with multiple identities and regarded this as a consequence of personal agency. In the view of many, taking a detour from the traditionally prescribed form of their religion did not mean they were any less devout, simply that they were being more circumspect about the aspects that mattered. It also gave them personal authority to confront multiple realities and to deal with each on its merits. Flexible Adherents illustrated this point well in acknowledging allegiance to both religious tradition and competing pressures and priorities in a modern Westernised society. It seemed they were adept at negotiating roles and identities, and that this was a normal part of their everyday lives. This was exemplified by those from mixed faith backgrounds who valued the extra opportunities they had to exercise choice.

Despite this assertion of the predominance of personal agency and choice in their lives, it was also apparent that young people are subject to pressures and constraints. Indeed a recurring theme is the competition between faith values and the absorbed ethos of personal agency and liberal individualism fostered by modern Western culture. In this area of enquiry, as in others, it seems that rhetoric is in some imbalance with reality and that there may be an illusion of choice. This seemed to apply particularly to Muslims from more traditional cultural backgrounds. There were reports of how young people from this faith group could feel under pressure, whether self-imposed or by family or friends, to conform to particular behaviour and dress codes, or to pray and read scriptures at 'inconvenient' times. Some participants mentioned spatial and temporal strategies to negotiate these expectations, such as the brother and sister who watched out for each other while they found food during Ramadan, the young males who talked about holding late extended prayer sessions to catch up with what had been missed earlier, or a young female saying namaz in a shop changing room while trying on the latest fashions. Several participants also relayed strong pressures in the sphere of dating and marriage, and told of family disruptions when somebody had married out of the fold. The issue of gender differences arose in this context, particularly for female Muslims who felt they were often treated more harshly than their male counterparts. Coping strategies were again apparent, as shown by the Sikh girl who met her white boyfriend in Central London to avoid being spotted by family and friends. Often it seemed that choice operated within certain constraints, as in the case of Muslim fashion. It could also lead to contradictions, such as when young people say both that they have freedom to choose how they lead their lives and also how they would feel a failure if they did not bring their children up in the religious tradition of their family.

Diversity, liberal individualism, sensitivities and tensions

As well as maintaining the right to decide on matters affecting their own lives, young people commonly stressed that it is only fair to let others do the same. Tolerance, mutual respect and enthusiasm for integration across ethnic, cultural and religious divides contributed to the headline discourse of almost all participants in the qualitative study. This discourse led to a resounding endorsement of the opportunities provided by multicultural life, multi-faith rather than single-faith schools, a focus on the similarities rather than the differences between religions, an openness to religious pluralism, and an underlying message that difficulties between groups either at school or in the community were minimal and generally not due to religious difference. It was also associated with a call for fair treatment at school such as the festivals celebrated, time allowed off for religious reasons, the choice of food, and rules on permitted dress and jewellery. These liberal views were associated with strong moral values that involved helping others and doing the 'right thing'. A similar rhetoric was reported by both religious and non-religious young people: while the former attribute their values to faith, the latter stress the influences of society, upbringing and family. The development of these common views exemplify the interpretive account of 'taking the role of the other' (Cooley, 1902; Mead, 1934) and, in this context, empathising with those beyond a personal reference group of other young people from similar ethnic and religious backgrounds. It also involves front and back stage performances (Goffman, 1959) and subtle strategies to avoid offence and disrespect towards others.

Is it possible that this widespread discourse and focus on equality and respect is part of the 'glue' that binds young people together, reinforced by religious communities, families and, even if not acknowledged by young people in the YOR survey, the ideological messages conveyed through schools? This seemingly universal emphasis on what are essentially principles of liberal individualism (Durkheim, 1893; Douglas, 1967) is intrinsically neither religious nor secular. It could, however, be an important performative tool or form of bridging capital facilitating interaction and communication across cultural and religious boundaries (Calhoun, 2011). In this sense, if not necessarily in others, these findings support Dawkins' (2006) thesis that religion in its traditional form is not necessary for social solidarity. An espousal of some form of liberal individualism does, nonetheless, provide a basis for a new moral order as Durkheim (1893) predicted would occur under conditions of social change.

While liberal individualism may command widespread acceptance and includes elements that would be familiar and, allied with human rights discourses, would probably meet with much approval internationally, it is unlikely to be sufficient on its own. Liberal values and discourses have always interacted in combination with other, particularistic, values and ideologies that are more tied to living in particular localities and regions, such as forms of nationalism (Smith, 1998). Liberal individualism may provide sufficient bridging capital (Putnam, 2000) to foster dialogue across religious and ethnic boundaries within school and college settings, but it is likely that other modes of collective identity are also needed to bind national populations over time (Goodhart, 2013). While beyond the scope of this book, there are necessary implications for informed public debate on how appropriate narratives of religion, ethnicity and the nation can be incorporated into the national curriculum as well as public education.

For liberal individualism as with personal agency, there was inevitably some discordance between the ideal and the real. First, some young people admitted they, or more commonly others, might be uninterested in or prejudiced against other groups. Second, despite living in highly diverse locations, and appearing willing (and wishing) to actively learn about each other's cultures, traditions and beliefs, many lack the opportunities to do so. The young Sikh reporting her first ever proper conversation with a white person, young people encountering new religious experiences through friends, or learning about another religion from a book, illustrate how isolation and segregation from members of other religious and ethnic groups can be a reality even in multi-faith communities. It was perfectly possible to endorse liberal individualism even if there were few opportunities for its practical application. Third, sensitivities and tensions emphasised the reality of social division. These reflected politically correct reactions, such as renaming Christmas holidays as Winter Holidays, or preventing a Lollipop Lady from wearing a Father Christmas hat, avoiding discussion of religion in case offence was caused, or local fears of a changing landscape such as the location of new mosques. Sometimes sensitivities and tensions might be presumed rather than proven, as when members of minority groups felt prominent, uncomfortable or unsafe in settings dominated by the white majority. It was not always clear how far these tensions stemmed from religion, and how far ethnicity or culture was more significant. Whatever the case, there was a clear impression that, in general, young people prefer to be in familiar places with people they know. Sometimes tensions had a firmer basis. There is little doubt that members of the Muslim faith, or others who by dint of ethnicity or dress were mistaken for Muslims, did experience genuine stigma and prejudice, particularly since events such as 9/11 and 7/7. These tensions changed over time and some young people referred to the threat to Islam from newcomers from Eastern European countries, or the growth in certain political parties.

Linked to the notion of liberal individualism are young people's assertions that different ethnic groups get on well and that religion does not matter in choosing friends. The examination of friendship patterns in the YOR survey shows, however, that friendship patterns are far from fully diverse and that there is a marked tendency for association between those from similar backgrounds, especially in Bradford. More than 70% of Muslims, and almost half of Christians and Sikhs, say that all or most of their friends are from similar faith backgrounds. For those with no specific religion the proportion was somewhat over a third. Survey respondents also indicated that young people from similar religious backgrounds are most likely to get on at school/college, and that many young people have limited knowledge and understanding of other religions. Reports that members of cultural and ethnic groups tend to cluster together at school provided additional support for a preponderance of same-faith friendships. Furthermore, even when young people report friends from a range of religious backgrounds, it is unclear how often they meet beyond the school or college gates. Previous research has, on the whole, tended to suggest that multi-faith friendships at school are not necessarily mirrored in the community (G. Smith, 2005; Mondal, 2008), and available evidence from the YOR study would tend to support this conclusion. One participant alluded to 'Hi Bye' friends to distinguish between acquaintances at school and closer intimates.

While young people themselves professed liberal individualism, they did not necessarily believe that everybody else did and provided many examples of how social cohesion could be improved in their communities. In short, they called for more integration, better education, and improved equality and respect. These challenges are addressed briefly in the final section.

The future of religion

There are many hypotheses and theories about the future of religion and secularity, but these are especially difficult to evaluate in multi-faith locations such as the YOR research areas. Such locations have shown enormous recent population change and are not typical of the country as a whole. They represent specific mixes of ethnic and faith groups and, as a result, show especially high levels of religious belief and practice.

Weber (1948) suggested that advances in science and technology, and greater freedom of thought, would urge a shift to secularity while Berger (1999) suggested that pluralism would lead to secularisation. The YOR data provide a level of support for these theses. There is some evidence of a trend towards secularity among White young people without strong religious beliefs, as well as an indication of a movement away from strict to more flexible adherence to religious tradition among minority faith groups such as Islam and Sikhism among longer-established families in the UK. Moreover, it seems that mixing across faith groups, as measured by school ethnic density in the present study, is associated with a lesser reliance on religious belief. These findings give some endorsement for the role of interculturalism (Cantle, 2012) and Putnam and Campbell's (2010) findings in the US that national polarisation between conservative protestants and liberal secularists is offset by the effects of social mixing across religious and cultural boundaries.

It is likely, nonetheless, that patterns of change will affect faith groups in different ways, and Muslims stand out as particularly embedded in religion. Never before have so many settled in broadly Christian societies, and the future of Islam in the modern West is a key question. As mentioned, evidence from the YOR study suggests that successive generations are likely to show decreasing compliance with the traditional forms of their religion. Modern Muslims, or Flexible Adherents in the YOR study terminology, are already discernible and well able to balance the fundamental tenets of religion with the pressures of peers and contemporary Western society more generally. The direction of travel is suggested by the direct relationship between an increasing number of family members born in the UK and a tendency to be a Flexible rather than a Strict Adherent. Other research too has indicated changing patterns of practice among Muslims who while remaining strongly attached to their religion are reconciling its demands with those of Western society (Sahin, 2005), including the freedom to make their own choices in life (Mondal, 2008). Davie (2007a) claims that it is perfectly possible for a person to be both fully religious and fully modern, and the YOR data support her supposition.

These findings are in some contradiction to a reported resurgence of orthodox and literal interpretations of doctrine in most of the main religious faiths, downplaying and leaving little room for pragmatic, individual interpretations (Armstrong, 2001). Some young people are attracted to fundamentalist, even Jihadist, interpretations of Islam (House of Commons Home Affairs Committee, 2012), and it would be naïve to underestimate the impact of this. However, the numbers are likely to be small and this form of extremism was not picked up in the research. YOR study data did not provide support for the view that the generality of young Muslims in urban, multicultural Britain are radically apart from mainstream culture, a threat to the dominant liberal culture, or likely to parallel the development of sections of the population in, for example, the Middle East (Caldwell, 2009).

A tendency towards greater flexibility in religious expression applies to all young people, whatever their faith position, and it is likely that this trend will continue. The current generation of young people's endorsement of personal agency to reason about the individual meaning of religion will secure similar opportunities for the next. As in the US, there are shifting attitudes towards religion and its role in everyday life. Although based on predominantly Christian populations, findings from several studies (Smith and Denton, 2005; Flory and Miller, 2010) generally support the emphasis on agency, liberal individualism, respect for diversity, personal expression of religion, hybrid and multiple religious identities, and a strong moral code reported from the YOR study. Nonetheless, young people say they may become more religious themselves as they get older, particularly as they do not want their faith to die out and often want to be in a position to pass religious culture onto their own children. The implications for intergenerational continuities are that, while considerable concordance in religious adherence is likely in some form between parents and their children for the foreseeable future, patterns will be more complex than in the past with less direct replication.

In conclusion

The preceding discussion relates to a snapshot in time of young people negotiating and displaying their religious identity in three multi-faith areas. It relies on subjective accounts of their lives and has not heard (formally) from the families, schools and religious communities they report on, nor has it taken account of the views of other young people living in less diverse neighbourhoods (which is a next urgent priority). Moreover, and in keeping with an interpretive stance, it must be borne in mind that young people may to some degree manage the impressions they convey in the research process just as they might use similar techniques in their everyday lives (Trinitapoli, 2007).

The story told has, however, been consistent in its messages. It has been about a generation in transition whose members remain rooted in their families and communities but are developing their attitudes towards their own and others' religiosity: they are negotiating their own personal religious identities within a prevailing ideology of liberal individualism. Members of this generation share notions of personal agency, respect and tolerance for others, and a common sense of what is right and wrong, and generally celebrate diversity of belief and practice even if in reality they are leading somewhat parallel lives. While the picture has not been identical in the three research areas, the message everywhere is broadly positive albeit not without some display of sensitivities, tensions and hostilities. The situation today was not predictable a generation or two ago, and the future too is largely unknown. Much depends on future patterns of population stability and change, future world events, changing societal norms and values, and patterns of integration and interaction more locally.

Despite some encouraging findings on multicultural integration (Heath and Demireva, 2013), there is no room for complacency and three messages from this study warrant particular attention. The first is the need to discard long-held assumptions about what religion means to young people in contemporary multi-faith locations and listen to what they themselves say. The second is to take their views on ways to promote social solidarity and cohesion seriously. And the third is to capitalise on the widespread optimism, liberalism and respect for diversity that seems so apparent amongst most of them.

Young people have clearly and in detail described their personal perceptions and meanings of religion throughout this book. They have reported their individual perspectives and personal adaptations to traditional faith positions, and highlighted how religion is fluid and flexible, and intertwined with ethnic, cultural and other values in complex ways. These accounts reinforce the variable meaning of religion, even among young people who choose to label themselves in similar ways. They provide an up-to-date picture of religion in contemporary multi-faith locations that is likely to challenge the proclamations of religious leaders, policy makers, outdated textbooks and members of the population at large. Equitable and effective national governance relies on fully understanding the identities and values of its citizens and this includes young people growing up in religiously diverse communities.

For governance and nation building, it is also important to take heed of the interventions young people suggest would help to promote a socially cohesive society. Better education, for themselves and for the population more broadly, was called for, underlining the significance of accurate portrayal of contemporary religiosity in the community, in the media, and in the school curriculum. Within the school setting, knowledgeable teachers, experiential learning and an up-to-date Religious Education curriculum, that take account of the reality of young lives, are crucial if young people are able both to convey their own religious identities and to understand those of others.

Better integration is another priority for young people and reflects growing evidence in the US and UK (Putnam and Campbell, 2010; Cantle, 2012) on inter-culturalism and the role of positive contact and interaction in encouraging mutual and meaningful understanding within diverse communities. Young people value opportunities to learn directly from each other, and findings from this study suggest that greater mixing is associated with friendships across a wider range of faith groups. Nonetheless, and contrary to expectation, ethnic diversity at school or college did not make a difference to the knowledge and understanding of different religions and beliefs reported by YOR survey participants. Moreover, while it did have some link with friendship patterns, the effect was not marked. These findings suggest that integration involves more than just proximity. The challenge is to find the most effective ways of developing bridging capital between groups and linking capital between all groups and public institutions (Putnam, 2000).

Increased mutual respect is the third main concern for young people, reflecting the prevailing discourse of liberal individualism. This study has provided convincing evidence that young people in general subscribe to a value system embracing equality, respect and freedom and the right for everyone to determine the life they wish to lead. While proclaiming this ideal, however, they are aware that conflict and tensions remain prevalent within their communities. It would seem that the need to develop and encourage means of bridging the gaps between population groups are again highlighted.

While this form of liberal individualism shown by young people provides optimism for the future, it is at once precarious. First, their ideals are not always matched by the realities they face in their daily lives, and social solidarity is undoubtedly easier to forge and sustain during times of economic growth than in periods of relative austerity, scarcity, sharpening inequalities and competition (Wilkinson and Pickett, 2009; MacDonald et al., 2010). There is a danger that young people may retreat to individual and collective identity based on religion and ethnicity should future society and markets appear unfair and discriminatory. Second, while liberal individualism may contribute to the 'glue' Durkheim considered essential for cohesive communities, it is unlikely to be enough. Nation building in some sense is almost certainly another part of the equation. Maintaining a spirit of liberalism and optimism among both present and future generations of young people as they become adults and parents to their own children, through both societal equity and a developing national identity, is no doubt the biggest challenge of all.

References

Allport, G.W. (1954) *The Nature of Prejudice,* Perseus Books, Cambridge, MA.

Armstrong, K. (2001) *The Battle for God: A history of fundamentalism,* New York, Random House Publishing Group.

Arnett, J.J. (1999) 'Adolescent storm and stress, reconsidered', *American Psychologist,* vol. 54, pp. 317–326.

Arweck, E. and Nesbitt, E. (2010) 'Young people's identity formation in mixed faith families: continuity or discontinuity of religious traditions?', *Journal of Contemporary Religion,* vol. 25, pp. 67–87.

Barker, E. (ed.) (2010a) *The Centrality of Religion in Social Life,* Ashgate, Farnham.

Barker, E. (2010b) 'The Church without and the God within' in *The Centrality of Religion in Social Life,* ed. E. Barker, Ashgate, Farnham.

Barnes, L.P. (ed.) (2011) *Debates in Religious Education,* Routledge, London.

Barrett, J.B., Pearson, J., Muller, C. and Frank, K.A. (2007) 'Adolescent religiosity and school contexts', *Social Science Quarterly,* vol. 88, no. 4, pp. 1024–1037.

Barry, C.M. and Nelson, L.J. (2005) 'The role of religion in the transition to adulthood for young emerging adults', *Journal of Youth and Adolescence,* vol. 34, no. 2, pp. 245–255.

Barth, F. (1969) *Ethnic Groups and Boundaries: The social organisation of culture difference,* Universitetsforlaget, Oslo.

Bates, S. (2006) 'Devout Poles show Britain how to keep the faith', *The Guardian,* 23 December.

Bauman, Z. (2000) *Liquid Modernity,* Polity Press, Cambridge.

Baumann, G. (1996) *Contesting Culture: Discourses of identity in multi-ethnic London,* Cambridge University Press, Cambridge.

Beaudoin, T. (1998) *Virtual Faith: The irreverent spiritual quest of Generation X,* Jossey-Bass, San Francisco, CA.

Beck, U. (1992) *Risk Society: Towards a new modernity,* Sage, London.

Berger, P.L. (ed.) (1999) *The Desecularization of the World: Resurgent religion and world politics,* Wm. B. Eerdmans Publishing Company, Grand Rapids, MI.

Berger, P.L. and Luckmann, T. (1966) *The Social Construction of Reality,* Doubleday & Co., Garden City, NY.

Bicknell, C. (2003) 'Performativity or performance? Clarifications in the sociology of gender', *New Zealand Sociology,* vol. 18, no. 2, pp. 158–178.

Bisin, A., Patacchini, E., Verdier, T. and Zenou, Y. (2008) 'Are Muslim immigrants different in terms of cultural integration?', *Journal of the European Economic Association,* vol. 6, no. 2–3, pp. 445–456.

Bourn, D. (2008) 'Young people, identity and living in a global society', *Policy & Practice: A Development Education Review,* vol. 7, pp. 48–61.

Bowlby, J. (1969) *Attachment and Loss,* Volume 1, Hogarth Press, London.

Bradley, H. (1996) *Fractured Identities: Changing patterns of inequality,* Polity Press, Cambridge.

Braun, V. and Clarke, V. (2006) 'Using thematic analysis in psychology', *Qualitative Research in Psychology,* vol. 3, pp. 77–101.

Brill, L., Athwal, B. and others (2011) *Recession, Poverty and Sustainable Livelihoods in Bradford,* Joseph Rowntree Foundation, York.

Brown, C.G. (2009) *The Death of Christian Britain: Understanding secularisation 1800–2000,* 2nd edn, Routledge, London.

Bruce, S. and Voas, D. (2010) 'Vicarious religion: an examination and critique', *Journal of Contemporary Religion,* vol. 25, no. 2, pp. 243–259.

Butler, T. and Hamnett, C. (2012) 'Praying for success? Faith schools and school choice in East London', *Geoforum,* vol. 43, no. 6, pp. 1242–1253.

Caballero, C., Edwards, R. and Puthussery, S. (2008) *Parenting 'mixed' children: difference and belonging in mixed race and faith families,* Joseph Rowntree Foundation, York.

Caldwell, C. (2009) *Reflections on the Revolution in Europe: Can Europe be the Same with Different People in it?* Penguin Books, London.

Calhoun, C. (2011) 'Secularism, citizenship and the public sphere' in *Rethinking Secularism,* eds C. Calhoun, M. Juergensmeyer and J. Van Antwerpen, Oxford University Press, Oxford.

Cantle, T. (2001) *Community Cohesion: A Report of the Independent Review Team,* Home Office, London.

Cantle, T. (2008) *Community Cohesion: A new framework for race and diversity,* Palgrave Macmillan, Basingstoke.

Cantle, T. (2012) *Interculturalism: The new era of cohesion and diversity,* Palgrave, Basingstoke.

Castells, M. (2000) *Rise of the Network Society, The Information Age: Economy, society and culture,* Volume I, 2nd edn, Blackwell, Oxford.

Castells, M. (2004) *The Power of Identity, The Information Age: Economy, society and culture,* Volume II, 2nd edn, Blackwell, Oxford.

Clydesdale, T. (2007) *The First Year Out: Understanding American teens after high school,* University of Chicago Press, Chicago.

Coles, R. (1990) *The Spiritual Life of Children,* Houghton Mifflin, Boston, MA.

Commission on Integration and Cohesion (2007) *Our Shared Future,* Department for Communities and Local Government, London.

Conroy, J.C., Lundie, D., Davis, R.A. and others (2013) *Does Religious Education Work? A multi-dimensional investigation,* Bloomsbury, London.

Cooley, C. (1902) *Human Nature and the Social Order,* Scribner's, New York.

Copley, T. (1997) *Teaching Religion: Fifty years of religious education in England and Wales,* University of Exeter Press, Exeter.

Crockett, A. and Voas, D. (2006) 'Generations of decline: Religious change in twentieth-century Britain', *Journal for the Scientific Study of Religion,* vol. 45, no. 4, pp. 567–584.

Crossley, M. (2000) *Introducing Narrative Psychology,* Open University Press, Buckingham.

Davie, G. (1994) *Religion in Britain since 1945: Believing without belonging,* Blackwell, Oxford.

Davie, G. (2005) 'From obligation to consumption: A framework for reflection in northern Europe', *Political Theology,* vol. 6, no. 3, pp. 281–301.

Davie, G. (2007a) *The Sociology of Religion,* Sage, London.

Davie, G. (2007b) 'Vicarious religion: a methodological challenge' in *Everyday Religion: Observing modern religious lives,* ed. N. Ammerman, Oxford University Press, Oxford.

Davie, G. (2010) 'Vicarious religion: a response', *Journal of Contemporary Religion,* vol. 25, no. 2, pp. 261–266.

Davies, T. (1997) *Humanism,* The new critical idiom series, Routledge, London.

Dawkins, R. (2006) *The God Delusion,* Bantam Books, London.

Day, A. (2009) 'Believing in belonging: an ethnography of young people's constructions of belief', *Culture and Religion,* vol. 10, no. 3, pp. 263–278.

Day, A. (2011) *Believing in Belonging: Belief and social identity in the modern world,* Oxford University Press, Oxford.

DCLG (2008) *'Face To Face and Side By Side': A framework for interfaith dialogue and social action.* Consultation, Department for Communities and Local Government.

DCSF (2008) *Learning Together to be Safe: A toolkit to help schools contribute to the prevention of violent extremism,* DCSF Publications, Nottingham.

Denzin, N.K. (2009) *The Research Act: A theoretical introduction to sociological methods,* Transaction Publishers, New Brunswick, NJ.

Din, I. (2006) *The New British: The impact of culture and community on young Pakistanis,* Ashgate, Aldershot.

Douglas, J. (1967) *The Social Meanings of Suicide,* Princeton University Press, Princeton, NJ.

Durkheim, E. (1893) *The Division of Labour,* Dissertation, 1997 edition, The Free Press, New York.

Durkheim, E. (1912) *Elementary Forms of Religious Life,* 1995 translation by K.E. Fields, The Free Press, New York.

Durkheim, E. (1953) *Sociology and Philosophy,* Cohen and West, London.

Durkheim, E. (1961) *Moral Education: A study in the theory and application of education,* The Free Press, Collier Macmillan, London.

Eade, J. (1996) 'Nationalism, community and the Islamization of space in London' in *Making Muslim Space in North America and Europe,* ed. B.D. Metcalf, University of California Press, Berkeley, CA.

Elkind, D. (1964) 'Piaget semi-clinical interview and the study of spontaneous religion', *Journal for the Scientific Study of Religion,* vol. 4, no. 1, pp. 40–47.

Erricker, C., Erricker, J., Ota, C., Sullivan, D. and Fletcher, M. (1997) *The Education of the Whole Child,* Cassell, London.

Etzioni, A. (1993) *The Spirit of Community: Rights, responsibilities and the communitarian agenda,* Crown Publishers, New York.

Finney, N. and Simpson, L. (2009) *'Sleepwalking to Segregation?': Challenging myths about race and migration,* Policy Press, Bristol.

Flory, R. and Miller, D.E. (2010) 'The expressive communalism of post-boomer religion in the USA' in *Religion and Youth,* eds S. Collins-Mayo and P. Dandelion, Ashgate, Farnham.

Foresight Future Identities (2013) *Final Project Report,* The Government Office for Science, London.

Forrest, R. and Kearns, A. (2001) 'Social cohesion, social capital and the neighbourhood', *Urban Studies,* vol. 38, no. 12, pp. 2125–2143.

Francis, L.J. (2001) *The Values Debate: A voice from the pupils,* Woburn Press, London.

Francis, L.J. (2008) 'Family, denomination and the adolescent worldview: an empirical enquiry among 13–15-year-old females in England and Wales', *Marriage and Family Review,* vol. 43, pp. 185–204.

Francis, L.J. and Katz, Y.J. (2007) 'Measuring attitude toward Judaism: the internal consistency reliability of the Katz–Francis scale of attitude towards Judaism', *Mental Health, Religion and Culture,* vol. 10, no. 4, pp. 309–324.

Francis, L.J. and Kay, W.K. (1995) *Teenage Religion and Values,* Gracewing, Leominster.

Freathy, R.J.K. (2006) 'Gender, age, attendance at a place of worship and young people's attitudes towards the Bible', *Journal of Beliefs and Values,* vol. 27, no. 3, pp. 327–339.

Fussey, P., Coaffee, J., Armstrong, G. and Hobbs, D. (2011) *Securing and Sustaining the Olympic City: Reconfiguring London for 2012 and beyond,* Ashgate, Aldershot.

Gallaher, S. (2007) 'Children as religious resources: the role of children in the social re-formation of class, culture and religious identity', *Journal for the Scientific Study of Religion,* vol. 46, pp. 169–183.

Gallup and the Coexist Foundation (2009) *A Global Study of Interfaith Relations. With an in-depth analysis of Muslim integration in France, Germany and the United Kingdom,* Gallup Inc.

Garfinkel, H. (1984) *Studies in Ethnomethodology,* Polity Press, London.

Gergen, K. (1999) *An Invitation to Social Construction,* Sage, Thousand Oaks, CA.

Giddens, A. (1984) *The Constitution of Society,* University of California Press, Los Angeles.

Giddens, A. (1991) *Modernity and Self Identity,* Polity Press, Cambridge.

Gilroy, P. (2005) 'Multiculture, double consciousness and the "War on Terror"', *Patterns of Prejudice,* vol. 39, no. 4, pp. 431–443.

Gilroy, P. (2006) *Postcolonial Melancholia,* Columbia University Press, New York.

Glaser, B.G. and Strauss, A.L. (1964) 'Awareness contexts and social interaction', *American Sociological Review,* vol. 29, pp. 669–679.

Glaser, B.G. and Strauss, A.L. (1967) *The Discovery of Grounded Theory: Strategies for qualitative research,* Aldine Publishing Company, Chicago.

Glaser, B.G. and Strauss, A.L. (1971) *Status Passage: A formal theory,* Aldine-Atherton, Chicago.

Glock, C.Y. and Stark, R. (1965) *Religion and Society in Tension,* Rand McNally, San Francisco.

Goffman, A. (1959) *The Presentation of Self in Everyday Life,* University of Edinburgh Social Sciences Research Centre, Anchor Books, Garden City, NY.

Goffman, E. (1961) *Asylums: Essays on the social situation of mental patients and other inmates,* Doubleday, New York.

Goffman, E. (1963) *Stigma: Notes on the management of spoiled identity,* Simon and Schuster, New York.

Goldman, R. (1964) *Religious Thinking from Childhood to Adolescence,* Routledge & Kegan Paul, London.

Goodhart, D. (2013) *The British Dream: Successes and failures of post-war immigration,* Atlantic Books, London.

Gregson, N. and Rose, G. (2000) 'Taking Butler elsewhere: performativities, spatialities and subjectivities', *Environment and Planning D: Society and Space,* vol. 18, pp. 433–452.

Guest, M., Olson, E. and Wolffe, J. (2012) 'Christianity: loss of monopoly' in *Religion and Change in Modern Britain,* eds L. Woodhead and R. Catto, Routledge, London.

Gunnoe, M.L. and Moore, K.A. (2002) 'Predictors of religiosity among youth aged 17–22: a longitudinal study of the National Survey of Children', *Journal for the Scientific Study of Religion,* vol. 41, no. 4, pp. 613–622.

Gunter, A. (2010) *Growing Up Bad,* Tufnell Press, London.

Halpern, D. and Nazroo, J. (2000) 'The Ethnic Density Effect: Results from a national community survey of England and Wales', *International Journal of Social Psychiatry,* vol. 46, no. 1, pp. 34–46.

Hargreaves, D. (1979) 'Durkheim, deviance and education' in *Schools, Pupils and Deviance,* eds L. Barton and R. Meighan, Studies in Education, Nafferton, Driffield.

Heath, A. and Demireva, N. (2013) 'Has multiculturalism failed in Britain?', *Ethnic and Racial Studies,* http://www.tandfonline.com/eprint/pxmwc78xtBEz5kxZM-EHs/full#.UhN0s9KHvTp (e-pub ahead of publication).

Heelas, P., Woodhead, L., Seel, B., Szerszynski, B. and Tusting, K. (2005) *The Spiritual Revolution: Why religion is giving way to spirituality,* Blackwell, Oxford.

Hemming, P.J. (2011) 'The place of religion in public life: school ethos as a lens on society', *Sociology,* vol. 45, no. 6, pp. 1061–1077.

Hemming, P.J. and Madge, N. (2011) 'Researching children, youth and religion: identity, complexity and agency', *Childhood,* vol. 19, no. 1, pp. 38–51.

Hervieu-Léger, D. (2000) *Religion as a Chain of Memory,* Polity Press, Cambridge.

Himmelfarb, G. (2004) *The Roads to Modernity: The British, French and American Enlightenments,* Alfred A. Knopf, Westminster, MD.

HM Government (2011) *Prevent Strategy,* HM Government, London.

HM Treasury (2007) *Aiming High for Young People: A ten year strategy for positive activities,* HM Treasury/Department for Children, Schools and Families, London.

Holden, A. (2009) *Religious Cohesion in Times of Conflict: Christian–Muslim relations in segregated towns,* Continuum, London.

Hopkins, P., Olson, E., Pain, R. and Vincett, G. (2011) 'Mapping intergenerationalities: the formation of youthful religiosities', *Transactions of the Institute of British Geographers,* vol. 36, no. 2, pp. 314–327.

Hopkins, P.E. (2004) 'Young Muslim men in Scotland: inclusions and exclusions', *Children's Geographies,* vol. 2, no. 2, pp. 257–272.

Hopkins, P.E. (2006) 'Youthful Muslim masculinities: gender and generational relations', *Transactions of the Institute of British Geographers,* vol. 31, no. 3, pp. 337–352.

House of Commons Home Affairs Committee (2012) *Roots of Violent Radicalisation. Nineteenth Report of Session 2010–12,* The Stationery Office Ltd, London.

Hunter, I. (1998) 'Uncivil society: liberal government and the deconfessionalisation of politics' in *Governing Australia: Studies in contemporary rationalities of government,* eds M. Dean and B. Hindess, Cambridge University Press, Cambridge.

Hyde, K.E. (1990) *Religion in Childhood and Adolescence: A comprehensive review of the research,* Religious Education Press, Birmingham, AL.

Ipgrave, J. and McKenna, U. (2008) 'Diverse experiences and common vision: English students' perspectives on religion and religious education' in *Encountering Religious Pluralism in School and Society: A qualitative study of teenage perspectives in Europe,* eds T. Knauth, D. Jozsa, G. Bertram-Troost and J. Ipgrave, Waxmann, Munster, pp. 113–147.

Jackson, R. (1997) *Religious Education: An interpretive approach,* Hodder & Stoughton, London.

Jackson, R. (2004) *Rethinking Religious Education and Plurality: Issues in diversity and pedagogy,* RoutledgeFalmer, London.

Jacobson, J. (1998) *Islam in Transition: Religion and identity among British Pakistani youth,* Routledge, London.

James, A. and James, A.L. (2008) *Key Concepts in Childhood Studies,* Sage, London.

James, A., Jenks, C. and Prout, A. (1998) *Theorizing Childhood,* Polity, Cambridge.

Kant, I. (1788) *Critique of Practical Reason,* 2004 translation by T.K. Abbott, Dover Publications, Mineola, NY.

Kaufmann, E. (2010) *Shall the Religious Inherit the Earth: Religion, demography and politics in the 21st century,* Profile Books, London.

Kaufmann, E., Goujon, A. and Skirbekk, V. (2012) 'The end of secularization in Europe? A socio-demographic perspective', *Sociology of Religion,* vol. 73, no. 1, pp. 69–91.

Kay, W.K. and Francis, L.J. (1996) *Drift from the Churches: Attitude toward Christianity during childhood and adolescence,* University of Wales Press, Cardiff.

Keating, A., Kerr, D., Lopes, J. and others (2009) *Embedding citizenship education in secondary schools in England (2002–08): Citizenship Education Longitudinal Study seventh annual report,* NFER, Slough.

King, K. and Hemming, P.J. (2012) 'Exploring multiple religious identities through mixed qualitative methods', *Fieldwork in Religion,* vol. 7, no. 1, pp. 29–47.

Knauth, T., Jozsa, D., Bertram-Troost, G. and Ipgrave, J. (eds) (2008) *Encountering Religious Pluralism in School and Society: A qualitative study of teenage perspectives in Europe,* Waxmann, Munster.

Knott, K., Poole, E. and Taira, T. (2013) *Media Portrayals of Religion and the Secular Sacred: Representation and change,* Ashgate, Farnham.

Kohlberg, L. (1976) 'Moral stages and moralization: the cognitive-developmental approach' in *Moral Development and Behavior: Theory, research and social issues,* ed. T. Lickona, Rinehart and Winston, Holt, New York.

Levey, G.B. and Modood, T. (2009) *Secularism, Religion and Multicultural Citizenship,* Cambridge University Press, Cambridge.

Lévi-Strauss, C. (1966) *The Savage Mind,* University of Chicago Press, Chicago.

Levitt, M. (2003) 'Where are the men and boys? The gender imbalance in the church of England', *Journal of Contemporary Religion,* vol. 18, no. 1, pp. 61–75.

Lewis, P. (2007) *Young, British and Muslim,* Continuum, London.

Lewis, R. (ed.) (2013) *Modest Fashion. Styling bodies, mediating faith,* I.B. Tauris, London.

Lindesmith, A.R., Strauss, A.L. and Denzin, N.K. (1999) *Social Psychology,* 8th edn, Sage Publications, London.

Local Government Association (2006) *Leading Cohesive Communities: A guide for local authority leaders and chief executives.* LGA, London.

Lynch, G. (2010) '"Generation X" religion: a critical evaluation' in *Religion and Youth,* eds S. Collins-Mayo and P. Dandelion, Ashgate, Farnham.

MacDonald, R.T., Shildrick, T. and Blackman, S. (2010) *Young People, Class and Place,* Routledge, London.

Madge, N. and Hemming, P.J. (2013) 'Using a survey to investigate the role of religion in young people's lives' in *Innovative Methods in The Study of Religion: Research in practice,* ed. L. Woodhead, Open University Press, Maidenhead.

Madge, N., Hemming, P.J., Goodman, A., Goodman, S., Stenson, K. and Webster, C. (2012) 'Conducting large-scale surveys in schools: The case of the Youth On Religion (YOR) Project', *Children & Society,* vol. 26, no. 6, pp. 417–429.

Malik, Z. (2010) *We are a Muslim, Please,* Heinemann, London.

Marcia, J.E. (1980) 'Identity in adolescence' in *Handbook of Adolescent Psychology,* ed. J. Adelson, Wiley, New York.

Marcuse, H. (1958) *Soviet Marxism: a critical analysis*, Columbia University Press, New York.

Martin, D. (2002) *Pentecostalism: The world their parish,* Blackwell, Oxford.

Martin, D. (2010) 'The religious and the political' in *The Centrality of Religion in Social Life,* ed. E. Barker, Ashgate, Farnham.

Martin, D. with Catto, R. (2012) The religious and the secular. In *Religion and Change in Modern Britain,* eds. L. Woodhead and R. Catto, Routledge, London.

Marx, K. and Engels, F. (1846) *The German Ideology,* Lawrence and Wishart, London, 1970 edition with introduction by C.J. Arthur.

Mason, M., Singleton, A. and Webber, R. (2007) *The Spirit of Generation Y: Young people's spirituality in a changing Australia,* John Garratt, Melbourne.

Massey, D. (2007) *World City,* Polity, London.

McCutcheon, A.L. (1987) *Latent Class Analysis,* Sage Publications, Beverley Hills, CA.

McIntyre, A. (1981) *After Virtue: A study in moral theory,* Gerald Duckworth, London.

Mead, G.H. (1934) *Mind, Self and Society,* University of Chicago Press, Chicago.

Merton, R.K. (1957) 'Continuities in the theory of reference groups and social structure' in *Social Theory and Social Structure,* ed. R.K. Merton, Free Press, Glencoe, IL.

Mondal, A.A. (2008) *Young British Muslim Voices,* Greenwood World Publishing, Oxford.

Morgan, P. and Lawton, C.A. (eds) (2007) *Ethical Issues in Six Religious Traditions,* 2nd edn, Edinburgh University Press, Edinburgh.

Musolf, G.R. (1996) 'Interactionism and the child: Cahill, Corsaro and Denzin on childhood socialization', *Symbolic Interactionism,* vol. 19, no. 4, pp. 303–321.

Myers, S.M. (1966) 'An interactive model of religiosity inheritance: the importance of family context'', *American Sociological Review,* vol. 61, no. 5, pp. 858–866.

Nesbitt, E. (2004) *Intercultural Education: Ethnographic and religious approaches,* Sussex Academic Press, Brighton.

Ofsted (2006) *Towards Consensus? Citizenship in secondary schools,* Ofsted, Manchester.

Ofsted (2010) *Citizenship Established? Citizenship in schools 2006/2009,* Ofsted, Manchester.

O'Grady, K. (2003) 'Motivation in religious education: a collaborative investigation with year eight students', *British Journal of Religious Education,* vol. 25, no. 3, pp. 214–225.

Ong, W.J. (1982) *Orality and Literacy: The technologizing of the word,* Methuen, London.

Pantazis, C. and Pemberton, S. (2009) 'From the "old" to the "new" suspect community: examining the impacts of recent UK counter-terrorist legislation', *British Journal of Criminology,* vol. 49, pp. 646–666.

Parekh, B. (2000) *The Future of Multi-Ethnic Britain: The Parekh Report,* Profile Books, London.

Parsons, T. (1951) *The Social System,* Free Press, Glencoe, IL.

Peach, C. and Gale, R. (2003) 'Muslims, Hindus, and Sikhs in the new religious landscape of England', *The Geographical Review,* vol. 93, no. 4, pp. 469–490.

Perfect, D. (2011) *Religion or Belief. EHRC Briefing Paper No. 1,* Equality and Human Rights Commission, Manchester.

Phillips, T. (2005) 'After 7/7: Sleepwalking to segregation', Speech given to Manchester Council for Community Relations, 22 September.

Piaget, J. (1936) *The Origin of Intelligence in the Child,* Routledge and Kegan Paul, London.

Pickering, M. (1993) *Auguste Comte: An intellectual biography,* Cambridge University Press, Cambridge.

Pries, L. (ed) (1999) *Migration and Transnational Social Spaces*, Ashgate, Aldershot.

Putnam, R.D. (2000) *Bowling Alone: The collapse and revival of American community*, Simon and Schuster, London.

Putnam, R.D. (2007) 'E Pluribus Unum: Diversity and community in the twenty-first century. The 2006 Johan Skytte Prize Lecture', *Scandinavian Political Studies*, vol. 30, no. 2, pp. 137–174.

Putnam, R.D. and Campbell, D.E. (2010) *American Grace: How religion divides and unites us*, Simon & Schuster, New York.

QSR International Pty Ltd (2012) *NVivo qualitative data analysis software. Version 9*, QSR International Pty Ltd.

Regenus, M.D., Smith, C. and Smith, B. (2004) 'Social context in the development of adolescent religiosity', *Applied Developmental Science*, vol. 8, no. 1, pp. 27–38.

Robbins, M. and Francis, L. (2010) 'The Teenage Religion and Values Survey in England and Wales' in *Religion and Youth*, eds. S. Collins-Mayo and P. Dandelion, Ashgate, Farnham.

Rock, P. (1979) *The Making of Symbolic Interactionism*, Rowman & Littlefield, Totawa, NJ.

Ryan, K.W. (2012) 'The new wave of childhood studies: breaking the grip of biosocial dualism?', *Childhood*, vol. 19, pp. 439–452.

Rymarz, R. and Graham, J. (2005) 'Going to church: attitudes to church attendance amongst Australian core catholic youth', *Journal of Beliefs and Values*, vol. 26, no. 1, pp. 55–64.

Sahin, A. (2005) 'Exploring the religious life-world and attitude toward Islam among British Muslim adolescents' in *Religion, Education and Adolescence: International empirical perspectives*, eds L.J. Francis, M. Robbins and J. Astley, University of Wales Press, Cardiff, pp. 164–184.

Said, E. (1978) *Orientalism: Western conceptions of the Orient*, Harmondsworth, Penguin.

Sampson, R. (2012) *Great American City: Chicago and the enduring neighborhood effect*, University of Chicago Press, Chicago.

Sardar, Z. (2008) *Balti: A journey through the British Asian experience*, Granta Books, London.

Saunders, D. (2009) 'France on the knife edge of religion: commemorating the centenary of the law of 9 December 1905 on the separation of church and state' in *Secularism, Religion and Multicultural Citizenship*, eds B.G. Levey and T. Modood, Cambridge University Press, Cambridge, pp. 56–81.

Savage, M. and Savage, M. (2010) *Identities and Social Change in Britain since 1940: The politics of method*, Oxford University Press, Oxford.

Savage, S., Collins-Mayo, S., Mayo, B. and Cray, G. (2006) *Making Sense of Generation Y: The world view of 15–25-year-olds*, Church House Publishing, London.

Scheffer, P. (2011) *Immigrant Nations*, Polity Press, Cambridge.

Seabrook, T. and Green, E. (2004) 'Streetwise or safe? Girls negotiating time and space' in *Young People, Risk and Leisure: Constructing identities in everyday life*, eds W. Mitchell, R. Bunton and E. Green, Palgrave Macmillan, Basingstoke.

Shaw, R.J., Atkin, K., Becares, L., Albor, C.B., Stafford, M., Kiernan, K.E., Nazroo, J.Y., Wilkinson, R.G. and Pickett, K.E. (2012) 'Impact of ethnic density on adult mental disorders: narrative review', *British Journal of Psychiatry*, vol. 201, pp. 11–19.

Shibutani, T. (1955) 'Reference groups as perspectives', *American Journal of Sociology*, vol. 60, no. 6, pp. 562–569.

Shields, R. (1991) *Places on the Margin: Alternative geographies of modernity*, Routledge, London.

Silverman, D. (2005) *Doing Qualitative Research: A practical handbook*, 2nd edn, Sage, London.

Simmel, G. (1903) *The Metropolis and Mental Life*, Petermann, Dresden. (Reproduced in G. Bridge and S. Watson (eds) (2002) *The Blackwell City Reader*, Oxford and Malden, MA, Wiley-Blackwell.)

Singh, G. (2010) 'Head first: young British Sikhs, hair, and the turban', *Journal of Contemporary Religion*, vol. 25, no. 2, pp. 203–220.

Singh, J. (2012) 'Keeping the faith: reflections on religious nurture among young British Sikhs', *Journal of Beliefs and Values*, vol. 33, no. 3, pp. 369–383.

Smith, A.D. (1998) *The Sociology of Religion*, Routledge, New York & London.

Smith, C. (2010) 'On "moralistic therapeutic deism" as US teenagers' actual, tacit *de facto* religious faith' in *Religion and Youth*, eds. S. Collins-Mayo and P. Dandelion, Ashgate, Farnham.

Smith, C. and Denton, M.L. (2005) *Soul Searching: The religious and spiritual lives of American teenagers*, Oxford University Press, Oxford.

Smith, C. and Sikkink, D. (2003) 'Social predictors of retention in and switching from the religious faith of family origin: another look using religious tradition self-identification', *Review of Religious Research*, vol. 45, no. 2, pp. 188–206.

Smith, C., Faris, R., Denton, M.L. and Regenerus, M. (2003) 'Mapping American adolescent subjective religiosity and attitudes of alienation toward religion: a research report', *Sociology of Religion*, vol. 64, no. 1, pp. 111–133.

Smith, D.J. (2005) 'Ethnic differences in intergenerational crime patterns', *Crime and Justice*, vol. 32, pp. 55–129.

Smith, G. (2005) *Children's Perspectives on Believing and Belonging*, National Children's Bureau for Joseph Rowntree Foundation, London.

Snow, J. (2007) 'Foreword' in *Young, British and Muslim*, in P. Lewis (ed.), Continuum, London.

Somers, M.R. (1994) 'The narrative constitution of identity: a relational and network approach', *Theory and Society*, vol. 23, no. 5, pp. 605–649.

SPSS Inc. (2009) *PASW Statistics for Windows. Version 18.0*, SPSS Inc., Chicago.

Stafford, M.L., Becares, L. and Nazroo, J. (2009) 'Objective and perceived ethnic density and health: findings from a United Kingdom general population survey', *American Journal of Epidemiology*, vol. 170, no. 4, pp. 484–493.

Stark, R. and Glock, C.Y. (1968) *American piety: The nature of religious commitment*. University of California Press, Berkeley, CA.

Stenson, K. (2012) 'The state, sovereignty and advanced marginality in the city' in *Criminalisation and Advanced Marginality: Critically exploring the work of Loic Wacquant*, eds P. Squires and J. Lea, Policy Press, Bristol.

Stenson, K. and Brearley, N. (1991) 'Left realism in criminology and the return to consensus theory' in *Beyond Law and Order: Criminal Justice Policy and Politics into the 1990s*, eds R. Reiner and M. Cross, Macmillan, Basingstoke.

Stoker, G. (ed) (2006) *Why Politics Matters: Making democracy work*, Palgrave, Basingstoke.

Stone, G. (1984) 'Conceptual problems in small group research', *Symbolic Interactionism*, vol. 5, pp. 3–21.

Sullivan, H.S. (1953) *The Interpersonal Theory of Psychiatry*, W.W. Norton, New York.

Suttles, G.D. (1972) *The Social Construction of Communities*, University of Chicago Press, Chicago.

Tarlo, E. (2010) *Visibly Muslim*, Berg, Oxford.

Taylor, C. (1989) *Sources of the Self: The making of modern identity*, Cambridge University Press, Cambridge.

Taylor, C. (2007) *A Secular Age*, Harvard University Press, Cambridge, MA.

Thomas, P. (2011) *Youth, Multiculturalism and Community Cohesion*, Palgrave, Basingstoke.

Thomas, W.I. and Znaniecki, E. (1918) *The Polish Peasant in Europe and America: Monograph of an immigrant group*. University of Chicago Press, Chicago.

Torstenson, T. (ed.) (2006) 'Children and God in the multicultural society', *British Journal of Religious Education*, vol. 28, no. 1, pp. 33–49.

Trinitapoli, J. (2007) '"I know this isn't PC but ..." Religious exclusivism among U.S. adolescents', *The Sociological Quarterly*, vol. 48, no. 3, pp. 451–483.

Trzebiatowska, M. (2010) 'The advent of the 'EasyJet priest': dilemmas of Polish Catholic integration in the UK', *Sociology*, vol. 44, no. 6, pp. 1055–1072.

Turner, J.C. (1991) *Social Influence*, Brooks/Cole Publishing Company.

Turner, R., Hewstone, M. and Voci, A. (2007) 'Reducing explicit and implicit outgroup prejudice via direct and extended contact: The mediating role of self-disclosure and intergroup anxiety', *Journal of Personality and Social Psychology*, vol. 93, pp. 369–388.

Valentine, G. (1999) 'Being seen and heard? The ethical complexities of working with children and young people at home and at school', *Ethics, Place and Environment*, vol. 2, pp. 141–155.

Valentine, G. (2008) 'Living with difference: reflections on geographies of encounter (Progress in Human Geography lecture)', *Progress in Human Geography*, vol. 32, no. 3, pp. 363–381.

Valentine, G. and Sporton, D. (2009) '"How other people see you, it's like nothing that's inside": the impact of processes of disidentification and disavowal on young people's subjectivities', *Sociology*, vol. 43, no. 4, pp. 735–751.

Vernon, M. (2011) *How to be an Agnostic*, Palgrave Macmillan, Basingstoke.

Voas, D. (2010) 'Explaining change over time in religious involvement' in *Religion and Youth*, eds S. Collins-Mayo and P. Dandelion, Ashgate, Farnham.

Voas, D. and Crockett, A. (2004) 'Spiritual, Religious or Secular: Evidence from National Surveys', paper presented at the conference of the British Sociological Association Sociology of Religion Study Group, Bristol, March.

Voas, D. and Day, A. (2009) *Recognizing Secular Christians: Toward an unexcluded middle in the study of religion*, Association of Religion Data Archives.

Vygotsky, L. (1962) *Thought and Language*, MIT Press, Cambridge, MA.

Wallace, J.M.J., Forman, T.A., Caldwell, C.H. and Willis, D.S. (2003) 'Religion and U.S. secondary school students: current patterns, recent trends, and sociodemographic correlates', *Youth and Society*, vol. 35, no. 1, pp. 98–125.

Watt, P. (2007) 'From the dirty city to the spoiled suburb' in *Dirt: New Geographies of Cleanliness and Contamination*, eds B. Campkin and R. Cox, I.B. Tauris, London.

Watt, P. (2008) 'Moving to a better place? Geographies of aspiration and anxiety in the Thames Gateway' in *London's Turning: The making of Thames Gateway*, eds P. Cohen and M. Rustin, Ashgate, Aldershot.

Watt, P. and Stenson, K. (1998) 'The street: "it's a bit dodgy around there": safety, danger, ethnicity and young people's use of public space' in *Cool Places: Geographies of youth cultures*, eds. T. Skelton and G. Valentine, Routledge, London, pp. 249–265.

Weber, M. (1965) *The Sociology of Religion*, Methuen, London (first published in German in 1920).

Weber, M. (1948) 'Science as a vocation', in *From Max Weber: Essays in sociology*, eds. H.H. Gerth and C. Wright Mills. Routledge and Kegan Paul, London.

Weber, M. (1949) *Methodology of the Social Sciences*, translation by E. Shils and H.A. Finch, Transaction Publishers, South Piscataway, NJ, 2010.

Webster, C. (1996) 'Local heroes: violent racism, localism and spacism among Asian and white young people', *Youth and Policy*, vol. 53, pp. 15–27.

Wetherell, M. (2009) 'Introduction: Negotiating liveable lives – identity in contemporary Britain' in *Identity in the 21st Century: New trends in changing times*, ed. M. Wetherell, Palgrave Macmillan, Basingstoke.

Wilkinson, R.G. and Pickett, K. (2009) *The Spirit Level: Why more equal societies almost always do better*, Allen Lane, London.

Woodhead, L. (2010) 'Epilogue' in *Religion and Youth*, eds S. Collins-Mayo and P. Dandelion, Ashgate, Farnham.

Woodhead, L. (2012) 'Introduction' in *Religion and Change in Modern Britain*, eds L. Woodhead and R. Catto, Routledge, London.

Yip, A.K., Keenan, M. and Page, S. (2011) *Religion, Youth and Sexuality: Selected key findings from a multi-faith exploration*, University of Nottingham, Nottingham.

Zimdars, A., Sullivan, A., and Heath, A. (2009) Elite higher education admissions in the arts and sciences: Is cultural capital the key? *Sociology*, vol. 43, pp. 648–666.

Index

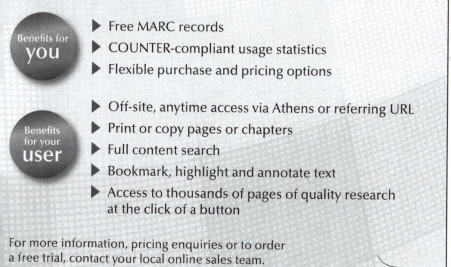